PASTE-UP
FOR GRAPHIC ARTS
PRODUCTION

PASTE-UP

FOR GRAPHIC ARTS PRODUCTION

Kenneth F. Hird

Department of Industrial Studies
California State University, Los Angeles

PRENTICE-HALL, INC., Englewood Cliffs, New Jersey 07632

Library of Congress Cataloging in Publication Data

Hird, Kenneth F. (date)
  Paste-up for graphic arts production.

  Includes index.
  1. Printing, Practical—Paste-up
techniques. I. Title.
Z253.5.H57   686.2′24   81–10524
ISBN 0-13-652875-9   AACR2

Editorial/production supervision and
    interior design by *Rosalie Herion*
Cover design by *Mark Binn*
Manufacturing buyer: *Ed O'Dougherty*

Printed in the United States of America

10 9 8 7

PRENTICE-HALL INTERNATIONAL, INC., *London*
PRENTICE-HALL OF AUSTRALIA PTY. LIMITED, *Sydney*
PRENTICE-HALL OF CANADA, LTD., *Toronto*
PRENTICE-HALL OF INDIA PRIVATE LIMITED, *New Delhi*
PRENTICE-HALL OF JAPAN, INC., *Tokyo*
PRENTICE-HALL OF SOUTHEAST ASIA PTE. LTD., *Singapore*
WHITEHALL BOOKS LIMITED, *Wellington, New Zealand*

CONTENTS

PREFACE   *ix*

chapter 1

GRAPHIC ARTS INDUSTRY   *1*
Layout Artist   *3*
Phototypesetting Operator   *4*
Paste-Up Artist   *4*
Process Camera Operator   *5*
Stripper   *6*
Platemaker   *8*
Press Operator   *9*
Bindery Worker   *11*

chapter 2

TYPESETTING AND TYPOGRAPHY   *12*
Typesetting   *12*
Typography   *13*
Type   *14*
Horizontal Spacing   *19*
Vertical Spacing   *20*
Arranging Type Lines   *21*
Unit System   *23*

chapter 3

HOT-TYPE COMPOSITION   *24*
Hand Set   *24*
Machine Set   *28*

chapter 4 COLD-TYPE COMPOSITION   *32*
Strike-On   *32*
Photocomposition   *36*

chapter 5 TYPE CLASSIFICATIONS   *58*
Roman Oldstyle   *58*
Sans Serif   *60*
Square Serif   *60*
Textletter   *61*
Script   *61*
Decorative   *61*
Typographic Specimens   *62*

chapter 6 ART AND COPY PREPARATION   *63*
Copy Preparation   *63*
Art Preparation   *70*

chapter 7 PASTE-UP FOR PROCESS PHOTOGRAPHY   *93*
Tools for Paste-Up   *94*
Beginning the Paste-Up   *95*
Attaching Copy Elements   *106*
Checking Paste-Up Alignment   *108*
Paste-Up Cleanliness   *110*
Final Assembly   *110*
Flat Color Paste-Up   *112*
Kinds of Register   *113*
Use of Solids   *115*
Orientation to Paste-Up   *117*

chapter 8 CAMERA AND DARKROOM OPERATIONS   *122*
Horizontal Process Camera   *122*
Vertical Process Camera   *123*
Parts of a Process Camera   *124*
Darkroom Operations   *128*
Continuous Tone Copy   *130*
The Darkroom   *135*
Photographic Film   *135*
Film Processors   *137*

chapter 9 PRINTING PROCESSES   *138*
Letterpress   *138*
Offset Lithography   *142*
Gravure   *150*
Screen Process   *152*

chapter  **PRINTING IMPOSITIONS** *155*

Two-Page Imposition *158*
Four-Page Imposition *158*
Eight-Page Imposition *158*
Sixteen-Page Imposition *159*
Determining Imposition *159*

chapter 11 PRINTING PAPERS *161*

Paper Manufacture *161*
Paper Characteristics *166*
Watermarks *167*
The Two Sides of Paper *167*
Paper Grain *167*
Deckled Edges *167*
Basis Weight *167*
Opacity *168*
Paper Grades *168*
Envelopes *171*
Paper Estimating *172*
Spoilage Allowance *173*
Paper Cutting *174*

chapter 12 BINDING AND FINISHING *177*

Binding Operations *177*
Finishing Operations *180*

chapter 13 PRINTING INKS *190*

Ingredients *190*
Manufacture of Ink *192*

GLOSSARY OF TERMS *196*

PASTE-UP ASSIGNMENTS FOR GRAPHIC ARTS PRODUCTION *201*

assignment 1 Point System *203*
assignment 2 Letterhead, Envelope, and Business Card *207*
assignment 3 Poster *219*
assignment 4 Business Reply Mail Card *229*
assignment 5 Display Advertisement *237*
assignment 6 Bus Schedule *247*
assignment 7 Direct Mail Advertisement *263*
assignment 8 Airline Flight Schedule *273*
assignment 9 Pacific Telephone Brochure *281*

assignment 10   Newsletter Make-Up   *291*
assignment 11   Simple Newspaper Display Advertisement   *299*
assignment 12   Complex Newspaper Display Advertisement   *307*
assignment 13   Supermarket Display Advertisement   *321*
assignment 14   Daily Tab-Size Newspaper Page   *333*
assignment 15   Silhouette Halftone   *343*
assignment 16   Catalog Page With Overlay   *349*
assignment 17   Ruled Business Form   *357*
assignment 18   Die-Cut Folder   *363*
assignment 19   Combining Process Color Inks   *377*
assignment 20   Record Album Jacket   *389*

INDEX   *399*

PREFACE

This text is intended for students interested in the preparation of paste-up copy for graphic arts photography. It provides a complete overview of the various printing processes as they relate to paste-up planning and production.

Producing quality paste-ups is a challenge. This text can assist you in making production decisions to meet this challenge. There are paste-up activities included to help you gain practical experience in producing a variety of commercial jobs.

This text is organized into chapters. Each chapter contains an overview of a particular graphic arts process. The processes are then explained in greater detail and descriptions given on how to do specific tasks. This text includes 20 paste-up assignments that provide a practical basis for compiling a portfolio of your work.

The technology of graphic arts is undergoing dramatic changes. Specialization is almost universal. The day of the "all-around" printer is gone. This phenomenon poses a special challenge to the student. It is no longer possible to know every skill in the graphic arts. Instead, you should be concerned with learning the principles and the whys of each job skill. This requires patience and dedication to the practice of these skills.

ACKNOWLEDGMENTS

The author is grateful to the following organizations for allowing use of their materials in the preparation of the paste-up section of this book. It has been possible to make the paste-up assignments more realistic due to their efforts and cooperation in this matter.

Albertsons Food Stores, Los Angeles, California
Brown Camera, Inc., Woodstock, Illinois
Bullocks Department Stores, Los Angeles, California

General Binding Corp., Northbrook, Illinois
Hammermill Papers Group, Erie, Pennsylvania
High Fidelity Records, Inc., Hollywood, California
J.C. Penney Department Stores, Los Angeles, California
North County Transit District, San Diego, California
Pacific Telephone, Los Angeles, California
Peace Corps/VISTA, U.S. Government, Washington, D.C.
Pepco Litho, Cedar Rapids, Iowa
Rileys Clothing Store, Los Angeles, California
The Christian Science Monitor, Boston, Massachusetts
Trans World Airlines, Los Angeles, California

KENNETH F. HIRD

PASTE-UP
FOR GRAPHIC ARTS
PRODUCTION

chapter 1

GRAPHIC ARTS INDUSTRY

Graphic arts starts with an idea and the need to communicate that idea to someone. To do this, the idea must be turned into an image. In the graphic arts industry, many people work to turn ideas into images. The process requires people who have varied talents and abilities. This chapter describes some of the key occupations in offset lithography, which is the predominant printing process within the graphic arts industry.

What is this more than ten-billion-dollar industry that employs over one million people? You come face to face with some form of the industry called *graphic arts* every day of your life.

To some people graphic arts means printing. It's much more than that. All the jobs needed to produce multiple copies of our written and pictorial language—news, photos, music, advertising, and works of art—make up the industry called graphic arts.

Newspapers, magazines, books, wrist watch dials, business forms, greeting cards, letterheads, labels, and cartons make up just a fraction of the graphic arts. All the people engaged in this industry do not operate printing presses. Some are managers, secretaries, clerks, accountants, sales people, advertising specialists, shippers, quality controllers, estimators, and, of course, paste-up artists.

Many other organizations and agencies employ graphic arts specialists. These include government, armed forces, banks, corporations, manufacturers, retailers and wholesalers, art studios, advertising agencies, and suppliers to the graphic arts industry.

There are few businesses that could operate without the services of people in graphic arts. Whether it's a simple, one-page price list or a large catalog for some giant in the mail-order field, a newspaper advertisement, or a billboard, printed material is vital to a company's

PRODUCTION STEPS IN PHOTO-LITHOGRAPHY

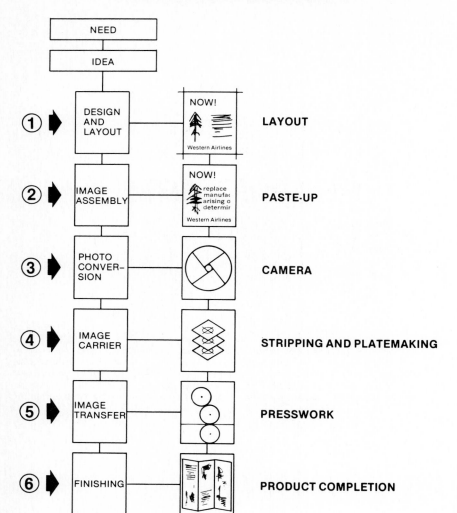

FIG. 1-1 Most printed materials start with an idea and then follow a sequential pattern. This diagram shows the usual steps followed in photo-offset lithography.

survival. Because of this most companies use products of the graphic arts. Many companies have their own "in-plant" printing departments to handle the routine visual communications necessary to daily operations.

Regardless of whether or not the printing is done by a commercial printer or in an in-plant department of a company, certain specialized jobs are necessary. So let's take a closer look at some of these jobs.

Whatever the printing process used, the flow of work follows a sequential pattern (Fig. 1-1). Most printed material, whether a newspaper advertisement, a new product bulletin, or a sales letter, starts the same way—with an *idea*. Ideas can originate anywhere. Dedicated men and women put their resources behind these ideas to produce millions of valuable goods and services needed by our society.

An idea doesn't mean much until it is put into words. Putting ideas in written form so that others will get the message is essential. Most people can put their ideas in written form. However, those who specialize in it and make it their work are known in the graphic arts industry as copywriters, authors, reporters, and editors.

Expressing ideas in pictorial form (drawings and photos) helps get ideas across to others. One of the early stages of planning a printed piece is sketching the pictures that are to be used to illustrate the idea.

LAYOUT ARTIST

The *layout artist* is specially trained to prepare the printing layout (Fig. 1-2). The artist sketches several layouts based on the client's ideas and requirements (Fig. 1-3). The sketches show the most effective arrangement of illustrations and text matter. A working knowledge of type styles and the ability to estimate the amount of space that the words will need are basic requirements for this position. Design ability is the most important qualification (Fig. 1-4).

FIG. 1-2 Layout artists must have a good background in design and color theory. (Courtesy Times-Mirror Press, Los Angeles.)

FIG. 1-3 Layouts begin with ideas based on the client's product requirements.

FIG. 1-4 Layout artists play a key role in the initial steps of designing a printed product. (Courtesy Dynamic Graphics, Inc.)

FIG. 1-5   Phototypesetting operators work at typewriter-like keyboards, where they set the required type for a job. (Courtesy Multigraphics Division of AM International.)

FIG. 1-6   Phototypesetting operators must enjoy sitting for long periods of time and be able to type at a rapid rate.

PHOTOTYPESETTING OPERATOR

A *phototypesetting operator* (Fig. 1-5) sets copy on computerlike machines that produce photographic type images on paper or film. To do this, the operator types the client's copy on a keyboard similar to that of a typewriter (Fig. 1-6). In addition to knowing how to run the phototypesetting machine, the person should know the basics of photography. Mechanical ability is important. Since a phototypesetting operator should also be able to make minor repairs on the machine, a knowledge of electronics is helpful.

PASTE-UP ARTIST

The *paste-up artist* (Fig. 1-7) prepares a paste-up or mechanical following the layout artist's sketch. The paste-up artist measures and marks a paste-up board to determine the exact positions of the illustrations and words. The photographic and typeset material is cut apart to fit the spaces on the paste-up (Fig. 1-8). The material is carefully pasted on illustration board in the proper position. Paste-up artists are usually required to have a knowledge of drafting techniques. The ability to do precise work is also necessary. The quality of the finished printed product will only be as good as the assembled paste-up.

FIG. 1-7 The paste-up artist works at a drafting table doing the precise work of arranging all type and illustrations into camera-ready copy. (Courtesy Allan McMakin.)

FIG. 1-8 Photo-typeset material and illustrations are cut apart to fit the spaces on the paste-up. (Courtesy Dynamic Graphics, Inc.)

PROCESS CAMERA OPERATOR

The graphic arts *process camera operator* photographs the paste-up material (Fig. 1-9). This starts the process of making a photoreproduction printing plate of the job to be printed. This person is required to be familiar with the special films, chemistry, and lighting techniques used to photograph flat (two-dimensional) copy such as the paste-up. A camera operator may specialize in either black-and-white

FIG. 1-9 The process camera operator must have a good knowledge of optics, photographic emulsions, and chemistry. (Courtesy Chemco Photoproducts Co.)

FIG. 1-10 Camera operators specialize in either black and white or color photography. (Courtesy Chemco Photoproducts Co.)

FIG. 1-11 Camera operators are accustomed to handling many different types of copy. (Courtesy Allan McMakin.)

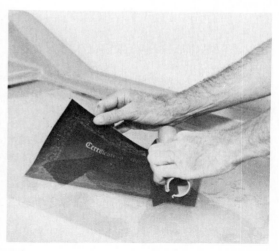

FIG. 1-12 Most camera operators are responsible for processing films and photographic papers. (Courtesy Stephen B. Simms, photographer.)

or color photography (Fig. 1-10). In either case, the camera operator must also be able to process graphic arts films and photographic papers (Figs. 1-11 and 1-12).

STRIPPER

After all the illustrations and word copy for a job have been photographed, the negatives and positives are sent to a *stripper* (Fig. 1-13).

FIG. 1-13 Strippers work in subdued light on a light table.

FIG. 1-14 The stripper cuts window openings from the golden-rod material to expose the images that will later be made into an offset printing plate. (Courtesy Stephen B. Simms, photographer.)

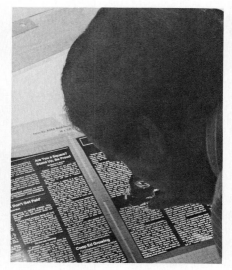

FIG. 1-15 The stripper must have the ability to do very precise work in a fast and efficient manner. (Courtesy Stephen B. Simms, photographer.)

FIG. 1-16 Strippers work with both negatives and positives as they prepare these materials for eventual offset platemaking. (Courtesy Stephen B. Simms, photographer.)

The stripper tapes the films into final position on sheets of goldenrod paper or plastic. When all the pieces are in position, the stripper cuts window openings from the goldenrod material (Fig. 1-14). This allows light to pass through the illustrations and words to expose a printing plate. The stripper must have a knowledge of drafting techniques. The ability to do precise work is essential (Fig. 1-15). The stripper works in a room over a light table. The room lighting is usually subdued for optimum visibility of the film material on the light table (Fig. 1-16).

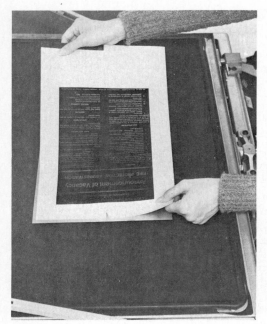

FIG. 1-17 The platemaker exposes the film materials previously prepared by the stripper to make an offset printing plate. (Courtesy Stephen B. Simms, photographer.)

PLATEMAKER

The goldenrod sheet containing film negatives and positives is passed along to the *platemaker*. The platemaker exposes the film material to a printing plate by using a vacuum frame and high-intensity light source (Fig. 1-17). When more than one page of the same image is run on a single plate, an automatic plate exposure unit is used (Fig. 1-18). The platemaker must know how to use various kinds of

FIG. 1-17 The platemaker exposes the film materials previously prepared by the stripper to make an offset printing plate. (Courtesy Stephen B. Simms, photographer.)

FIG. 1-18 This unit, called a *step-and-repeat machine,* is used to automatically expose more than one page of the same image to a single offset printing plate. (Courtesy Enco Plates, Inc.)

FIG. 1-19 The platemaker must understand chemistry and know how to use various kinds of printing plates. (Courtesy Stephen B. Simms, photographer.)

FIG. 1-20 Offset printing plates are available in a variety of sizes and surface coatings. (Courtesy Stephen B. Simms, photographer.)

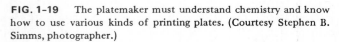

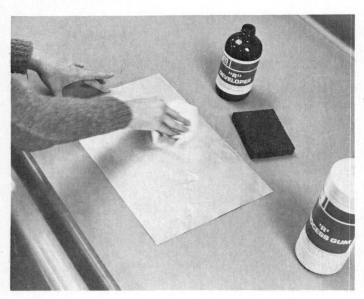

FIG. 1-21 The automatic offset plate processor is much faster than the manual method of processing a plate. (Courtesy S.D. Warren Co.)

printing plates and must also know the chemistry for each (Fig. 1-19). Some plates come with photosensitive chemicals already applied. Other plates are coated with photosensitive materials just prior to exposing (Fig. 1-20). Automatic platemaking equipment is also used to simplify and speed up the operation (Fig. 1-21).

PRESS OPERATOR

The *press operator* prepares and tends the printing press (Fig. 1-22). This work may vary greatly, depending upon the kind and sizes of presses used. The press operator must be able to install the printing

FIG. 1-22 Press operators work on small and large presses. (Courtesy *The Daily Report*, Ontario, California.)

FIG. 1-23   Press operators must have good mechanical ability. (Courtesy 3-M Co.)

plate, adjust roller pressures, care for and adjust water and ink rollers, mix inks, and operate the press (Figs. 1-23 and 1-24). Mechanical ability is important for this job. In large plants and on large presses, the press operator must be able to supervise crews of press feeders and helpers. Press operators must have excellent color perception.

FIG. 1-24   Installing an offset plate on the press plate cylinder. (Courtesy David Moise, photographer.)

BINDERY WORKER

Once the job is printed, it usually ends up in the bindery. The *bindery worker* (Fig. 1-25) performs a variety of operations, such as folding, trimming, punching, fastening, and wrapping (Figs. 1-26 and 1-27). A bindery worker must know how to operate and set up several kinds of machines. Bindery work closely resembles an assembly line and requires repetitive tasks. The work requires the ability to do precise work since a mistake can cost valuable time and materials.

FIG. 1-25 Bindery workers operate a variety of equipment either of the manual or automatic type.

FIG. 1-26 The bindery worker performs tasks such as folding, trimming, collating, and wrapping. (Courtesy Hammermill Paper Co.)

FIG. 1-27 Punching and fastening small booklets is one of many operations included under bindery work. (Courtesy GBC Corp.)

chapter 2

TYPESETTING AND TYPOGRAPHY

The method of typesetting to be used for any printed job is usually determined in the design stage. All methods of typesetting that use molten metal to create the image are considered "hot metal." This classification is further divided into hand-set and machine-set type. All other methods of typesetting that do not use molten metal are called "cold type."

This chapter discusses the various typesetting and typographic nomenclature required of the paste-up artist. An understanding of this nomenclature is necessary when conveying instructions and information to the printer.

This chapter will introduce you to the terminology and processes of typesetting and typography. Typesetting, referred to as a preparatory function in the graphic arts, is an important first step in producing printing.

TYPESETTING

The term typesetting refers to the process of setting and arranging type. There are basically only two classifications into which all type generation methods fall: (1) hot type; and (2) cold type. The names of these two classifications represent a broad generalization of how type images are created. Figure 2-1 illustrates the various image classifications of hot and cold type.

All methods of type generation that use molten metal to create the image are considered hot type. This classification can be subdivided into the type generation methods of hand-set type and machine-set type.

The cold-type classification of image generation includes all methods that do not use molten metal. Cold type includes a wide

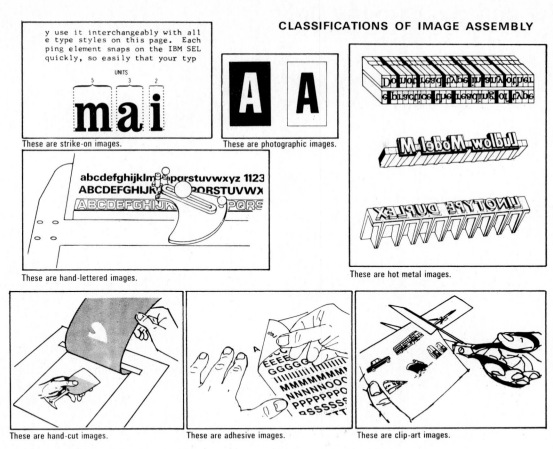

These are strike-on images.

These are photographic images.

These are hand-lettered images.

These are hot metal images.

These are hand-cut images.

These are adhesive images.

These are clip-art images.

FIG. 2-1 Hot type refers to all methods of image generation that use molten metal to create the image. Hot type is three-dimensional. (Courtesy A.B. Dick Co.)

variety of image generation methods. These methods usually include drawing, preprinted type and artwork, typewriters, photocomposition, and photographic prints.

TYPOGRAPHY

What is typography? Simply stated, typography is the arrangement of letters, figures, and punctuation marks in such a way that ideas are conveyed from one person to another. The assumption is that everybody knows what sounds the various letter forms represent. This definition of typography is very basic. Typography is that, but much more.

Typography involves the ease with which we recognize the letters of the alphabet. It includes their grouping into words and lines and masses. It involves the proper understanding of the message so that visual communication between writer and reader takes place. Typography involves the selection of the appropriate types for specific purposes in communicating. This includes such things as the kind of message, type of reader, printing process, and printing paper used. Most important, typography involves the pleasing arrangement of all these elements so that reader appeal is achieved.

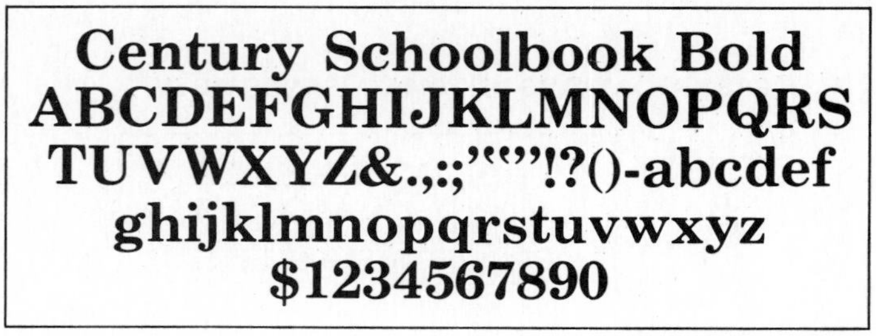

Century Schoolbook Bold
ABCDEFGHIJKLMNOPQRS
TUVWXYZ&.,:;'""!?()-abcdef
ghijklmnopqrstuvwxyz
$1234567890

FIG. 2-2   A font of type. (Courtesy Typographic Sales, Inc.)

TYPE

The individual letter, figure, or punctuation mark is called a *character*. Capital letters are called *uppercase* and small letters are called *lowercase*. A *font* contains a complete assortment of type. It includes uppercase, lowercase, figures, and punctuation marks for one size and style (Fig. 2-2). The entire range of sizes of one style of type is known as a *series* (Fig. 2-3). A group of all the type sizes and styles of a particular typeface (bold, light, extended, condensed, italic, etc.) is known as a *family* (Fig. 2-4).

Kinds of Type

There are two kinds of type used in graphic arts. These are referred to as *hot type* and *cold type*. Hot type means any kind of three-dimensional (metal or wood) characters used for direct printing by the letterpress process. Cold type means characters that are two-dimensional and are used to prepare camera-ready paste-ups for photo-offset lithography.

FIG. 2-3   A type series. (Courtesy Typographic Sales, Inc.)

TRADE GOTHIC EXT
Cat. No. 1240-30   30 Point   Caps, Numerals

TRade Gothic abc
Cat. No. 1240-36   36 Point   Caps, Lower Case, Numerals

TRADE GOTHIC E
Cat. No. 1240-36   36 Point   Caps & Numerals

TRAde Gothic
Cat. No. 1240-42   42 Point   Caps, Lower Case, Numerals

TRADE GOTHIC
Cat. No. 1240-42   42 Point   Caps, Numerals

TRAde Gothi
Cat. No. 1240-48   48 Point   Caps, Lower Case, Numerals

TRADE GOTH
Cat. No. 1240-48   48 Point   Caps & Numerals

TRAde Goth
Cat. No. 1240-54   54 Point   Caps, Lower Case, Numerals

TRADE GOT
Cat. No. 1240-54   54 Point   Caps & Numerals

TRAde Go
Cat. No. 1240-60   60 Point   Caps, Lower Case, Numerals

TRADE GO
Cat. No. 1240-60   60 Point   Caps & Numerals

TRAde G
Cat. No. 1240-72   72 Point   Caps, Lower Case, Numerals

LETRASET TYPEFACE FAMILIES

The major type families available on Instant Lettering sheets are shown here. (The complete range—over 330 styles—is shown in alphabetical order in the Letraset catalog). These families constitute both proven and currently popular styles. Letraset's range of weights allows you to work freely within a type family knowing that it can meet your most selective type requirements.
(*Letraset exclusive design).

American Typewriter LIGHT
American Typewriter MEDIUM
American Typewriter BOLD

Avant Garde GOTHIC EXTRA LIGHT
Avant Garde GOTHIC MEDIUM CONDENSED
Avant Garde GOTHIC MEDIUM
Avant Garde GOTHIC BOLD CONDENSED
Avant Garde GOTHIC BOLD

*Belwe LIGHT
*Belwe MEDIUM
*Belwe BOLD

Futura LIGHT
Futura MEDIUM
Futura MEDIUM ITALIC
Futura DEMI BOLD

Futura BOLD CONDENSED
Futura EXTRA BOLD CONDENSED
Futura DISPLAY
Futura BOLD
Futura BOLD ITALIC
Futura EXTRA BOLD
Futura BLACK

Franklin Gothic EXTRA CONDENSED
Franklin Gothic CONDENSED
Franklin Gothic
Franklin Gothic ITALIC
***Franklin Gothic** BOLD

Gill Sans LIGHT
Gill Sans
Gill Sans BOLD CONDENSED
Gill Sans BOLD
Gill EXTRA BOLD CONDENSED
Gill EXTRA BOLD
Gill EXTRA BOLD OUTLINE
Gill Kayo

Helvetica EXTRA LIGHT
Helvetica LIGHT CONDENSED
Helvetica LIGHT
Helvetica LIGHT ITALIC
Helvetica MEDIUM CONDENSED
Helvetica MEDIUM
Helvetica MEDIUM ITALIC
Helvetica COMPACT
Helvetica BOLD CONDENSED
Helvetica BOLD
Helvetica BOLD ITALIC
Helvetica OUTLINE

Horatio LIGHT
Horatio MEDIUM
Horatio BOLD

*Italia BOOK
*Italia MEDIUM
*Italia BOLD

Korinna
Korinna BOLD
Korinna EXTRA BOLD

Lubalin Graph EXTRA LIGHT
Lubalin Graph MEDIUM
Lubalin Graph BOLD

Peignot LIGHT
Peignot MEDIUM
Peignot BOLD

*Playboy
*Playboy INLINE
*PLAYBOY ULTRA

Pump LIGHT
Pump MEDIUM
Pump BOLD
*Pump TRILINE

Rockwell LIGHT 390
Rockwell 371
Rockwell BOLD 391

Serif Gothic
Serif Gothic BOLD
Serif Gothic HEAVY

Souvenir LIGHT
Souvenir MEDIUM
Souvenir DEMI BOLD
Souvenir BOLD

Tiffany LIGHT
Tiffany MEDIUM
Tiffany HEAVY

Times NEW ROMAN
Times BOLD
Times BOLD ITALIC
***Times** EXTRA BOLD

Univers 45
Univers 59
Univers 57
Univers 55
Univers 53
Univers 67
Univers 65
Univers 75

FIG. 2-4 Typeface families. (Courtesy Letraset USA, Inc.)

FIG. 2-5 Cold type being composed using a manual system of operation. (Courtesy Strip Printer, Inc.)

FIG. 2-6 Most cold-type composition is set on high-speed photographic composing equipment. (Courtesy Mergenthaler Linotype Co.)

Cold-type characters are prepared by hand lettering, art-type alphabet sheets, and photographically. Some cold type is set into lines manually (Fig. 2-5), but most type is set by photographic composing machines (Fig. 2-6). These machines vary from manually operated letter-by-letter transfer to the highly automated models.

Measuring Type

There are two basic units of measurement in graphic arts. These include *points* and *picas*. There are 12 points in a pica and 6 picas in an inch (Fig. 2-7). The sizes of type (whether hot type or cold type) are always expressed in points.

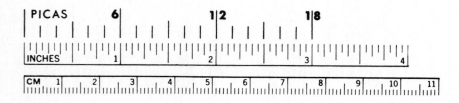

FIG. 2-7 Points and picas are the basic units of measure in graphic arts. There are 12 points in one pica. This illustration compares the point system to inches and metrics.

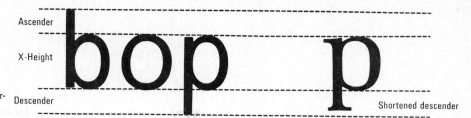

FIG. 2-8 Ascenders and descenders. (Courtesy A.B. Dick Co.)

In lowercase letters the upper stroke (as in the letter "d") is called the *ascender*. The downstroke (as in "q") is called the *descender* (Fig. 2-8). The short crossline at the end of the main stroke is called the *serif* (Fig. 2-9). The *body* makes up the greatest part of a piece of three-dimensional type (Fig. 2-10). The printing surface is called the *face* (Fig. 2-11). These elements are illustrated in Fig. 2-4.

Type is measured from the top of an ascending letter such as "d" to the bottom of a descending letter such as "q" (Fig. 2-12). It should be noted that in most instances metal type is used for this reference to measurement. The face of any single letter is not the full point size of the body. For example, the face of a 48-point letter may measure only 40 points. Correspondingly, letters in the same size type may vary in size.

The height of three-dimensional type is 0.918 inch and is referred to as *type high*. The width, which is called the *set width*, is

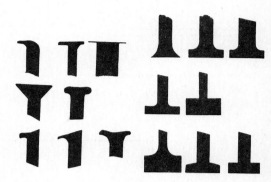

FIG. 2-9 Serifs are the fine, end strokes on some letter forms.

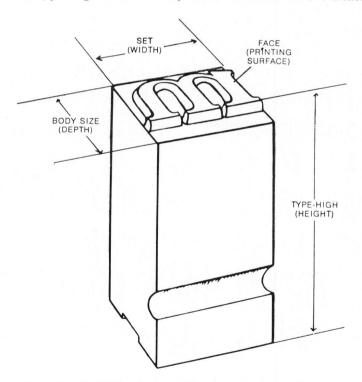

SET (WIDTH)

FACE (PRINTING SURFACE)

BODY SIZE (DEPTH)

TYPE-HIGH (HEIGHT)

FIG. 2-10 The body of a piece of three-dimensional type.

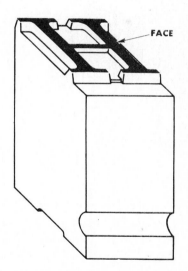

FACE

FIG. 2-11 The face of a piece of three-dimensional type.

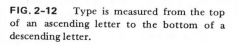

FIG. 2-12 Type is measured from the top of an ascending letter to the bottom of a descending letter.

BODY SIZE 60 POINTS

17

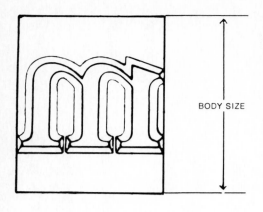

BODY SIZE

determined by the individual width of each letter. The capital "W" is the widest and the lowercase "l" is the narrowest. The depth, called the *body size,* is the dimension by which type is specified and measured (Fig. 2-13).

Type comes in a wide range of sizes. The smallest type in common use is 5 point and the largest is 72 point (Fig. 2-14). Type sizes 14 point and smaller are designated *text-size types.* Types larger than 14 point are designated *display-size.*

FIG. 2-13   Body size of type.

FIG. 2-14   Type sizes are available in a wide range of sizes. (Courtesy Typographic Sales, Inc.)

THIS IS 6 POINT OPTIMA LIGHTFACE. IT IS A SANS-SERIF TYPEFACE USED IN MODERN PRINTING LAYOUTS. THE DESIGN ARTIST MUS
This is 6 point Optima lightface. It is a sans-serif typeface used in modern printing layouts. The design artist must have experience in the t

THIS IS 8 POINT OPTIMA LIGHTFACE. IT IS A SANS-SERIF TYPEFACE USED IN MODERN PRINTING LAY
This is 8 point Optima lightface. It is a sans-serif typeface used in modern printing layouts. The design artis

THIS IS 10 POINT OPTIMA LIGHTFACE. IT IS A SANS-SERIF TYPEFACE USE
This is 10 point Optima lightface. It is a sans-serif typeface used in modern pri

THIS IS 12 POINT OPTIMA LIGHTFACE. IT IS A SANS-SERIF TYPEFAC
This is 12 point Optima lightface. It is a sans-serif typeface used in mo

THIS IS 18 POINT OPTIMA LIGHTFACE. IT IS
This is 18 POINT Optima lightface. It is a sa

THIS IS 24 POINT OPTIMA LIGH
This is 24 point Optima lightface. It is

THIS IS 36 POINT OPTIM
This is 36 point Optim

THIS IS 48 POIN
This is 48 point Opt

18

HORIZONTAL SPACING

Wordspacing

Spacing between words is called *wordspacing*. In three-dimensional typesetting, *quads* and *spaces* are pieces of metal cast less than type high to be used between words. These quads and spaces do not take ink and do not print when the type is put on the press.

The *em quad* is the square of a given point size. The *en quad* is one-half the square. The usual quads and spaces furnished with a font of type are the em quad, 2-em quad, 3-em quad, 3-em space, 4-em space, and 5-em space (Fig. 2-15). These spaces are all based on the em quad, which is the square of the body size. For example, if the body is 12 points, the em quad is 12 points square; in 8-point type, the em quad is 8 points square; and in 10-point type, the em quad is 10 points square; etc. A *3-em space* is generally used between words that are set in uppercase and lowercase.

Words composed with narrow spacing appear to run together and are difficult to read (Fig. 2-16). On the other hand, if the spacing is too wide, the line appears choppy and to lack unity (Fig. 2-17).

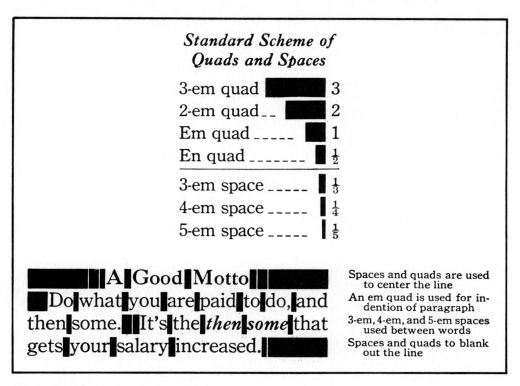

FIG. 2-15   The relationship of quads and spaces.

FIG. 2-16   Words set with narrow spacing are difficult to read.

> This line of type is set tight and results in poor legib

FIG. 2-17   Words set with too much space appear choppy and lack unity.

> This   line   of   type   is   set   loose   and

If the spacing between words is noticeably uneven, a displeasing effect is created. This interferes with the readability of the type.

It is important to remember that all of the principles and rules of three-dimensional hot-type wordspacing apply equally to two-dimensional cold type. This includes mechanical and photocomposition methods. Most photographic machines are built to allow for wordspacing either manually or automatically.

> Words which are l e t t e r s p a c e d result in poor

FIG. 2-18 Spacing placed between individual characters refers to letterspacing.

Letterspacing

Spacing placed between individual characters is called *letterspacing* (Fig. 2-18). When words are to be letterspaced, extra space must be allowed between the words so that they do not appear to run together when read. Letterspacing makes short words in titles or headings appear longer. The use of letterspacing usually improves the appearance of larger type sizes set in capitals. However, letterspacing reduces readability of words set in lowercase type. A general rule of typography is: Do not letterspace words set all in lowercase. Most letterspacing involves placing ½ to 1 point of space between letters. Finer spacing is available and is often used in quality typographic productions.

Because of some irregular capital letter combinations (such as VALLEY), it is necessary to *mortise* the characters to make them interlocking. This procedure equalizes the space between letters (Fig. 2-19). In three-dimensional type, mortises are cut by hand or machine. Two-dimensional cold type is cut apart with an X-acto knife and positioned to fit properly.

VATICAN
VATICAN
VATICAN
VATICAN

FIG. 2-19 Mortising refers to the equalizing of space between irregular capital letter combinations.

VERTICAL SPACING

Leading

The amount of space between lines of type is called *leading* (Fig. 2-20). Generally, the amount of leading should be increased as the line length is increased. Type set without leading between the lines is called *solid matter* (Fig. 2-21).

The spacing unit for leading is generally the *2-point lead*, which in three-dimensional type is a strip of metal 2 points thick. The

FIG. 2-20 Leading refers to the amount of space used between lines of type.

FIG. 2-21 Solid matter refers to type set with no extra spacing between lines.

> Since the printed word is intended primarily to be read, it is essential that the type should be of a size to produce maximum legibility. If the type is too small, it very quickly creates eye-strain and fatigue. If it is too large, it spreads out upon too great an area on the retina of the eye to be perceived quickly in as large groups as possible.

> Since the printed word is intended primarily to be read, it is essential that the type should be of a size to produce maximum legibility. If the type is too small, it very quickly creates eye-strain and fatigue. If it is too large, it spreads out upon too great an area on the retina of the eye to be perceived quickly in as large groups as possible.

most common sizes of leads are 1-, 2-, 3-, and 4-point. Spacing materials above 4 points in thickness are called *slugs*. These are available in 6-, 12-, 24-, and 36-point thicknesses. Both leads and slugs are less than type high and do not print.

If 8-point type is to be set with 2-point leading, it is set "8 on 10," which is shown as 8/10. The first figure indicates the type size. The second figure indicates the type size plus the leading desired. The type you are now reading is 11/12 Baskerville Medium. Specifically, it is 11-point type with 1 point of leading. All of the terms and procedures discussed here for three-dimensional hot type are identical for two-dimensional cold type.

ARRANGING TYPE LINES

Type can be arranged in any one of several different ways (Fig. 2-22). The arrangement to be used should be carefully selected with the purpose of the printed piece in mind.

The most common arrangement is referred to as *justified*. This calls for all lines of type to be the same length and to align both on the left and right margins of the column (Fig. 2-23).

The News North Plant

Designed to help The Detroit News serve its customers better, the new plant means faster and better production and improved delivery for subscribers both in the suburbs and in Detroit.

Now northern and eastern suburbs and a major part of Detroit get their papers from the North Plant. The remainder of Detroit and the western and southern suburbs receive their papers from the downtown Times Square Plant.

As a result, all subscribers get dependable on-time service of the latest News edition possible.

News Main Building in downtown Detroit

Times Square Plant
The downtown production facility
at Cass Avenue and Times Square

FIG. 2-22   Type arrangements vary to suit the purpose of the printed piece. (Courtesy *The Detroit News.*)

FIG. 2-23   Justified lines of type.

Since the printed word is intended primarily to be read, it is essential that the type should be of a size to produce maximum legibility. If the type is too small, it very quickly creates eye-strain and fatigue. If it is too large, it spreads out upon too great an area on the retina of the eye to be perceived quickly in as large groups as possible.

Since the printed word is intended primarily to be read, it is essential that the type should be of a size to produce maximum legibility. If the type is too small, it very quickly creates eye-strain and fatigue. If it is too large, it spreads out upon too great an area on the retina of the eye to be perceived quickly in as large groups as possible.

Since the printed word is intended primarily to be read, it is essential that the type should be of a size to produce maximum legibility. If the type is too small, it very quickly creates eye-strain and fatigue. If it is too large, it spreads out upon too great an area on the retina of the eye to be perceived quickly in as large groups as possible.

FIG. 2-24 Unjustified lines of type are referred to as ragged right or ragged left.

Since the printed word is intended primarily to be read, it is essential that the type should be of a size to produce maximum legibility. If the type is too small, it very quickly creates eye-strain and fatigue. If it is too large, it spreads out upon too great an area on the retina of the eye to be perceived quickly in as large groups as possible.

FIG. 2-25 Centered lines of type.

We shall not cease from exploration
    And the end of all our exploring
Will be to arrive where we started
    And know the place for the first time.
                                    —T. S. Eliot

"I am not poor, but I am proud
    Of one inalienable right,
Above the envy of the crowd,
    Thought's holy light."

FIG. 2-26 Poetic type arrangements are commonly used in the typesetting of poetry and similar verse.

Unjustified differs in that the lines are of various lengths and align on the left and are ragged on the right. In a similar arrangement, the type can be set to align on the right and appear ragged on the left. These methods are frequently referred to as either "ragged right" or "ragged left" (Fig. 2-24).

Centered type refers to lines that are of unequal lengths. Each line has equal space on either side (Fig. 2-25).

Poetic or *asymmetrical* arrangement is a style commonly used in the typesetting of poetry and similar verse. This method does not necessarily have a predictable pattern in the placement of space and lines (Fig. 2-26).

Once the arrangement of type lines for a job has been determined, consistency must be maintained throughout. This determination is called *style*. The style for any given printed job is generally different from that for all other printed jobs.

UNIT SYSTEM

All typesetting systems, whether hot or cold type, are based upon some counting system to specify type sizes and spacing. Cold type uses the point and pica system (12 points equal 1 pica; 6 picas equal 1 inch). However, a variety of specifications are used to determine character width (set width) and spacing. All specifications are based upon the *unit system* of measurement. Remember that the size of the em quad depends upon the size of type. A 10-point type uses em quads 10 points by 10 points square.

The unit system divides the em quad into 18 uniform elements (Fig. 2-27). Each element is called a unit and can be used to define individual character set widths. The smaller the unit size, the more accurate the word and letterspacing for most text composition.

On most phototypesetting machines, the units of space between characters can be adjusted. This means that the type can be set with regular, loose, or tight letterspacing. It is also possible to letterspace selectively. This is called *kerning*. In kerning it is possible to reduce space between certain letters and maintain normal spacing between the remaining letters (Fig. 2-28).

FIG. 2-27   The unit system divides the em quad into 18 equal parts.

FIG. 2-28   Kerning refers to the special spacing arrangement given between letters so that part of one extends over the body of the next. Kerned letters are common in italic, script, and swash type fonts.

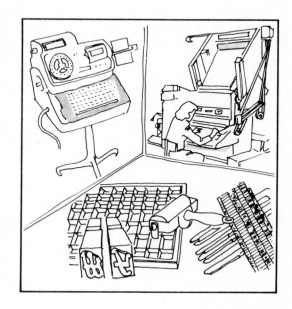

HOT-TYPE COMPOSITION

chapter **3**

Typesetting is divided into two categories: hot type and cold type. This chapter discusses hot-type composition. Hot type includes all of the several methods used to compose metal types into lines and pages. Some larger types are made of special hardwood. For practical purposes, wood types are classified as hot type. Hand and machine operations are involved in the hot-type category. The primary ingredient of hot-type composition is molten metal. The metal consists of an alloy of lead, antimony, tin, and copper. All hot-type composition is considered three-dimensional.

Hot-type composition, as previously stated, includes all methods of typesetting that make use of molten metal cast into relief printing characters. The two methods of typesetting in this category include: (1) hand set; and (2) machine set.

HAND SET

Hand-set type is composed with individual metal or wood characters assembled into single lines. The process has not changed since Johann Gutenberg's invention of movable types in 1450.

A *composing stick* (Fig. 3-1) is held in one hand while the individual type characters are selected from a *type case* (Fig. 3-2). The type case has a standard arrangement of small compartments for each character and a variety of spaces. The characters are assembled in the composing stick until a full line is set. Different size spaces are then used to *justify* the line. Justifying the line means filling it out to the desired length.

If spacing is required between lines, metal leads or slugs are inserted. This is referred to as *leading*. When the composing stick is full, the type is transferred to a shallow, three-sided tray called a

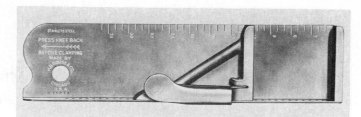

FIG. 3-1 Composing stick. (Courtesy Rouse & Co., H.B.)

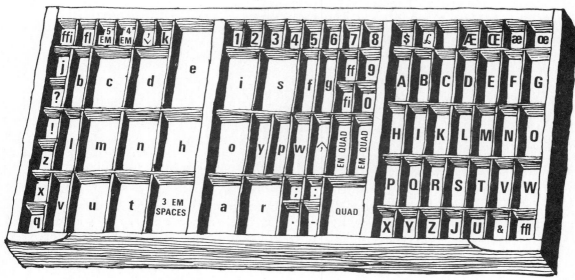

FIG. 3-2 Arrangement of a California type case. (Courtesy Mackenzie and Harris, San Francisco, California.)

galley. The compositor then continues to set type until the galley is full or the job is completed.

After all the type has been set, the compositor arranges or "makes-up" the job in the galley according to the layout specifications. This may include adding display lines, rules, decorative elements, or *photoengravings* (Fig. 3-3). A photoengraving is a metal plate that has the image in relief. These type-high illustrations and photographs are also called *cuts*.

FIG. 3-3 Type and photo engravings are assembled as a complete page in a galley. (Courtesy Times-Mirror Press, Los Angeles.)

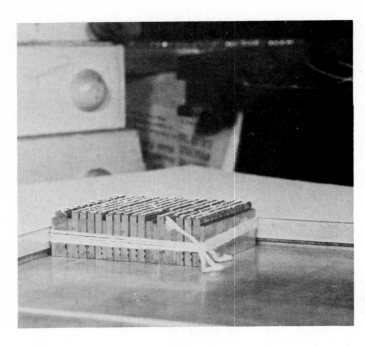

FIG. 3-4 Type is tied up with string to hold it firmly and securely in a galley. (Courtesy American Type Founders.)

When the type has been properly arranged in the galley, it is "tied up" with string (Fig. 3-4). A piece of string wound around the type several times holds it firmly and securely. Collectively, type and other related printing elements tied up and ready to be proofed or printed is called a *form*.

Proofing

After a type form is tied up, a *proof* is taken, and corrections, if necessary, are made. A proof is a print of the type prepared for the purpose of proofreading. The galley containing the type form is placed on the bed of a *proof press* (Fig. 3-5). The type is inked with a small rubber roller called a *brayer*. A sheet of paper is placed on the inked form, and a proof is made by turning a cylinder over the type form. Proofs made in this manner are generally called *galley proofs* (Fig. 3-6).

FIG. 3-5 Type in a galley is placed on the bed of a proof press ready for proofing. (Courtesy Times-Mirror Press, Los Angeles.)

The Story of the Lost Sheep

Now the taxgatherers and sinners were all approaching him to listen to him, but the Pharisees and and scribes complained, "He welcomes sinners and eats along with them! So he told them this parable, "Which of you with a hundred sheep, if he loses one does not leave the ninty-nine in the Desert and go after the lost one till he finds it? When he finds it he puts it on his shoulders with joy, and when he home he gathers his friends and neighbors; 'Rejoice with me,' he says to them, 'for I have found the sheep I lost.' So, I tell you, there will be joy in heaven over a single sinner who repents, more than over ninety-nine good people who do not need to repent. Or again, suppose a woman has ten shillings if she loses one of them, does she not light a lamp and scour the house and search carefully till she finds it? And when she finds it she gathers her woman-friends and neighbours, saying, 'Rejoice with me, for I have found the shilling I lost.' So, I tell you, there is joy in the presence of the angels of God over a single sinner who repents."

FIG. 3-6   A galley proof sheet.

FIG. 3-7 Proofreaders' marks are used to correct galley proofs.

PROOFREADING

ℒ	Delete	?/	Insert interrogation point
	Take out and close up	(!)	Insert exclamation mark
	Upside down, reverse	[/]	Insert brackets
⌒	Close up	(/)	Insert parentheses
#	Insert space		Insert superior letter or figure
¶	Make a paragraph	∧	Insert inferior letter or figure
no ¶	No paragraph	Qu?	Query to author
run in	Make no break in reading—no ¶	em	Em dash
		en	En dash
⊡	Indent one em	SP	Spell out
⊏	Move to left	Tr	Transpose
⊐	Move to right	wf	Wrong font
⊓	Raise to position	bf	Set in bold face type
⊔	Lower to position	rom	Set in roman
✗	Broken letter	ital	Set in italic
↓	Push down space	___	Under letter means italic
	Straighten line	S.C.	Set in small caps
∥	Align type	===	Under letter means S. C.
⋏	Insert comma	caps	Set in capitals
⋎	Insert apostrophe	≣	Under letter means caps
	Insert quotes	l.c.	Set in lower case
=/	Insert hyphen		Line drawn through caps means lower case
⋎	Insert semicolon		
⊙	Insert colon	stet	Let it stand
⊙	Insert period	out see copy	An omission—see copy

Proofreading

After a proof of the type form has been made, it is carefully *proofread* for errors. *Proofreaders' marks* (Fig. 3-7) are standard throughout the United States. It is important that these marks be used for both hot-type and cold-type proofreading. The person marking changes on the proof should use a colored **pencil or pen** to make the task easier. (All proofreaders' marks are written on a tissue overlay when working with cold-type paste-ups.)

Once the proofreader has marked the proof, it is sent back to the compositor, who then makes the necessary corrections. When these corrections have been made, a *revised proof* is prepared and checked against the original proof. Original proofs always accompany revised proofs when being submitted for approval.

Type Distribution

When the hand-set type form has been printed, or has served its purpose, the type is returned to the case. The leads and slugs are sorted and placed in the storage racks. The process of returning type to its proper compartments in the case is called *distribution* (Fig. 3–8). When a type form has been printed, or for any reason is not to be used further, it is called a *dead form*. All type that is ready for distribution is called *dead matter*. To *kill* a type form is to designate it for distribution.

FIG. 3-8 Returning type to the case is called *distribution*. (Courtesy Times-Mirror Press, Los Angeles.)

MACHINE SET

Machine-set type can be produced on any of three machines. The Linotype machine casts a single line of type called a *slug*. The Monotype machine casts single-type characters similar to hand-set type. The Ludlow machine casts a single line of type and is used mainly for large types.

Fig. 3–9 Linotype machine. (Courtesy Mergenthaler Linotype Co.)

Linotype

The Linotype (Fig. 3-9) casts single complete lines of type. The type lines consist of letters and spaces on a single body, rather than letters or characters on individual bodies (Fig. 3-10). The operator sits at a keyboard similar in appearance to that of a typewriter. At the touch of a key a *matrix* is released. Matrices are brass molds containing characters (Fig. 3-11). Once all the matrices for a line are assembled, the line is automatically spaced out by *spacebands* (Fig. 3-12). These are wedge-shaped spacers that spread the words to fill the line. Molten metal is forced into the lines of matrices forming a solid line or slug.

After the slug is cast, the matrices are automatically replaced in proper order within a storage compartment called a *magazine*. Each size of each type face has its own magazine. The slug is delivered to a tray called a galley in front of the machine near the operator. If the operator makes an error, the entire line is reset.

FIG. 3-10 The Linotype machine casts a single line of type called a *slug*. (Courtesy A.B. Dick Co.)

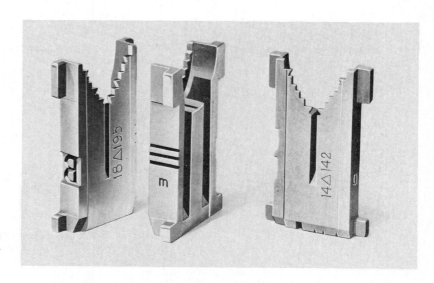

FIG. 3-11 Linotype brass type molds are called *matrices*. (Courtesy Mergenthaler Linotype Co.)

FIG. 3-12 Linotype spacebands automatically spread the words to fill the line ready for casting into a slug. (Courtesy Mergenthaler Linotype Co.)

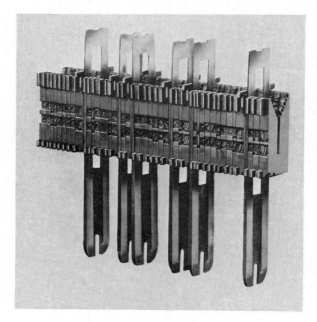

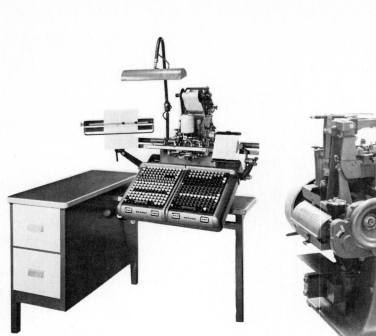

FIG. 3-13 Monotype keyboard machine. (Courtesy Monotype International.)

FIG. 3-14 Monotype caster machine. (Courtesy Monotype International.)

FIG. 3-15 Monotype machine font matrix. (Courtesy Monotype International.)

Monotype

The Monotype consists of two machines, a *keyboard* (Fig. 3-13) and a *caster* (Fig. 3-14). The keyboard machine perforates or punches a roll of paper type as the operator presses the keys. The tape is then run through the caster which casts single characters properly spaced in lines of preset length. A complete set or font of type in the form of a matrix (mold) is placed in the caster (Fig. 3-15). One complete matrix must be used for each size and style of type desired. Since the pieces of type are individual characters, single letters can easily be removed and corrected by hand. Monotype is well suited to setting complicated forms such as timetables and columns of financial figures. Monotype forms can be remelted and the metal used again for further casting.

Ludlow

The *Ludlow* (Fig. 3–16) is used to cast lines of type from matrices that are set by hand in a special composing stick (Fig. 3–17). The justified line is then inserted into the Ludlow machine and mechanically cast into a single slug. The slug formed by the Ludlow is "T"-shaped (Fig. 3–18) and has the face of the type on the wide end of the "T". To give the typeface added strength, slugs are used to support the overhanging portion.

This system is similar to hand-set type, but new lines of type can be cast at any time from the brass-type matrices. Any number of cast slugs may be produced from one assembly of matrices. The individual matrices are then distributed back into their proper storage compartments.

FIG. 3-16   Ludlow machine. (Courtesy Stephen B. Simms, photographer.)

FIG. 3-17   A special composing stick is used to assemble a line of brass matrices. (Courtesy Stephen B. Simms, photographer.)

FIG. 3-18   A Ludlow slug is "T"-shaped. The overhanging portions of the slug must be supported with other lower slugs to avoid breakage. (Courtesy Stephen B. Simms, photographer.)

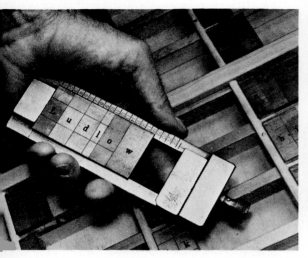

chapter 4

COLD-TYPE COMPOSITION

The most popular method used to compose type for printing today is by cold type. The term cold type developed in the language of the graphic arts industry in the 1950s. It was selected to fill the need for a term to cover the methods of typesetting that do not involve molten metal. All cold type is two-dimensional. These materials are generated by hand-mechanical and computerized methods. The majority of type composition produced is composed on high-speed computerized photocomposition equipment. The emphasis on cold-type methods practiced in industry is reflected in this chapter.

"Cold-type" composition was originally a term applied to a typewritten manuscript that was used as direct camera copy run by the offset process. Today, it is used to differentiate that kind of printing material from composition produced on "hot metal" typecasting machines. Some cold type is still produced by typewritten methods, called *strike-on*. However, the majority of composition is generated on phototypesetting equipment, giving quality text and display typography on paper or film bases. This material, in turn, is used in the preparation of camera-ready copy for offset lithography.

STRIKE-ON

Almost any typewriter can be used to set cold type. Typewriters are available in a variety of styles. Ordinary standard office typewriters are adequate for small quantities of unjustified type composition. Each of the characters and spaces on most standard typewriters has the same width. As a result, most type prepared on a standard typewriter does not have a flush right-hand margin. However, it is possible to manually justify type on a standard typewriter.

```
 Fix up those/      Fix/up those/       Fix  up those
flat tires, boys   flat tires, boys    flat tires, boys
and girls, and//   and√girls,√and//    and  girls,  and
load your camera   load your camera    load your camera
with films--it's   with films--it's    with films--it's
our annual bi-//   our√annual√bi-//    our  annual  bi-
cycle trip back/   cycle√trip back/    cycle  trip back
to nature come//   to√nature√come//    to nature  come
Saturday, May 17   Saturday, May 17    Saturday, May 17
```

FIG. 4-1 Setting justified type on a standard office typewriter requires two typings. (Courtesy A.B. Dick Co.)

FIG. 4-2 IBM Selectric Composer. (Courtesy IBM Corp.)

To manually justify the right-hand margin, the same copy must be typed twice. The first typing is marked at the end of each line with the number of units needed to justify to the desired line length. During the first typesetting, the type never exceeds the length of the desired line. A vertical line is drawn down the right-hand margin of the paper to indicate the maximum line length. During the second typing, the units necessary for justification are added between words in the form of spaces (Fig. 4-1). Several specialized typewriters have been developed to help make the job of justifying typed lines easier. In addition, these machines make typed copy look more attractive.

The copy that is being typed for reproduction is prepared on smooth, dull-white paper. In most cases, a one-time carbon ribbon is used to produce sharp, dense, black images. This is necessary because the typewritten composition becomes part of a paste-up, which in turn is photographed with a graphic arts process camera.

FIG. 4-3 IBM Selectric Composer type fonts. (Courtesy IBM Corp.)

IBM Selectric Composer

The IBM Selectric Composer (Fig. 4-2) features a stationary carriage and interchangeable type fonts called *elements* (Fig. 4-3). Typing elements are available in 6-, 7-, 8-, 9-, 10-, 11-, and 12-point sizes. Because it carries a single type ball font, it cannot set mixed composition in the same line without changing balls.

3	4	5	6	7	8	9
i ;	I (	J	P y	B	A Y	M
j '	f)	a	S *	C	D w	W
l '	r !	c	b †	E	G ¾	m
. -	s /	e	d $	F	H ½	
,	t	g	h +	L	K &	
	:	v	k =	T	N %	
		z	n]	Z	O @	
		?	o		Q ¼	
		[	p		R –	

FIG. 4-4 IBM Selectric Composer characters are divided into nine different unit widths. (Courtesy IBM Office Products Division.)

The Selectric Composer features proportional spacing. This means that the individual characters have varying widths or units (Fig. 4-4). It is unlike an ordinary typewriter that allows as much space for a narrow character like "i" as it does for a wide character like "W." The unit values range from 3 to 9. As an example, the lowercase "i" is 3 units wide, and the capital "W" is 9 units wide. All of the proportionally designed typefaces can produce justified composition. It is necessary to type each line of type twice. The first typing shows where space must be added or removed. The second typing is done to accurately justify the line (Fig. 4-5).

IBM Electronic "Selectric" Composer

A newer version of the direct-impression Selectric Composer featuring a built-in electronic memory is available. Called the IBM Electronic "Selectric" Composer (Fig. 4-6), its memory is capable of retaining up to 8000 characters of keyboarded text that the machine will play out automatically at a speed of 150 words per minute.

Another feature of the new composer is automatic justification of the right-hand margin with one typing. There are over 125 fonts available for the composer in 11 different type styles. These fonts are available in 13 languages.

FIG. 4-5 Justifying lines of type on the IBM Selectric Composer. (Courtesy Allan McMakin.)

FIG. 4-6 IBM Electric "Selectric" Composer. (Courtesy IBM Corp.)

IBM Magnetic Card System

The IBM Magnetic Card Selectric Composer (MC/SC) system is more sophisticated than the standard Selectric Composer (Fig. 4-7). It consists of one or more *recorders* that produce unjustified proofing copy and magnetic cards (Fig. 4-8). The proofing copy, similar to an ordinary typewritten page, is used to proofread the typeset copy. The Selectric Composer unit then sets the justified type composition in final form ready for paste-up. If there are corrections, these can be made on other magnetic cards, and the card reader merges the correction cards with the original cards to produce the final composition.

FIG. 4-7 IBM Magnetic Card Selectric Composer (MC/SC). (Courtesy IBM Corp.)

FIG. 4-8 IBM Magnetic Card Selectric Composer uses magnetic card system. (Courtesy IBM Corp.)

FIG. 4-9 VariTyper composer. (Courtesy VariTyper Division of AM International.)

VariTyper

The VariTyper (Fig. 4-9) is a specialized strike-on machine for producing typewritten composition. This machine features proportional spacing and uses a one-time carbon ribbon. Interchangeable type *fonts* (Fig. 4-10) contain all the necessary characters, figures, and punctuation marks. Two different fonts can be held and mixed at the same time in the same line. This makes it possible to use a bold and light typeface without replacing type fonts.

To justify the type composition, it must be typed twice. The rough draft copy is typed to the desired column length on the left side of the paper. A margin dial pointer and justification dial are used to guide the operator in starting and ending a line. A character unit counting system makes it possible for the operator to record individual line unit counts. The same typewritten composition is then typed again on the right-hand side of the paper, at which time the VariTyper automatically inserts the required spacing and produces finished type composition ready for paste-up.

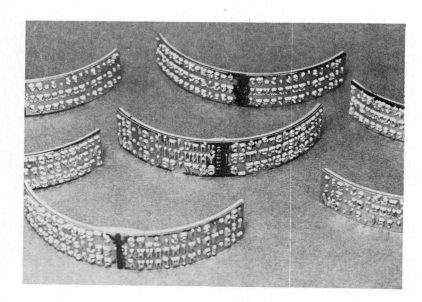

FIG. 4-10 VariTyper composer type fonts. (Courtesy Stephen B. Simms, photographer.)

PHOTOCOMPOSITION

Type composition produced by means of photography is called *photocomposition*. Characters are imaged by exposing photographic paper or film through a film negative that contains all the characters of a font. The principle of photocomposition is illustrated in Fig. 4-11.

After the photographic paper or film is exposed, it is chemically processed. The processing machine automatically develops, fixes, and washes the exposed material. The photographic paper, when dried, is then used in the paste-up process or goes directly to the process camera in finished form.

First-Generation Phototypesetters

First-generation phototypesetting devices were adaptations of two of the "hot-metal" typesetting machines and one impact machine. The Fotosetter (Fig. 4-12), marketed in 1950, was basically an Inter-

A typical phototypesetting system is made up of three units: the *keyboard* for input, the *computer* for making end-of-line decisions such as hyphenation and justification (H/J), and the *photounit* for output, or typesetting. Let's examine each more closely.

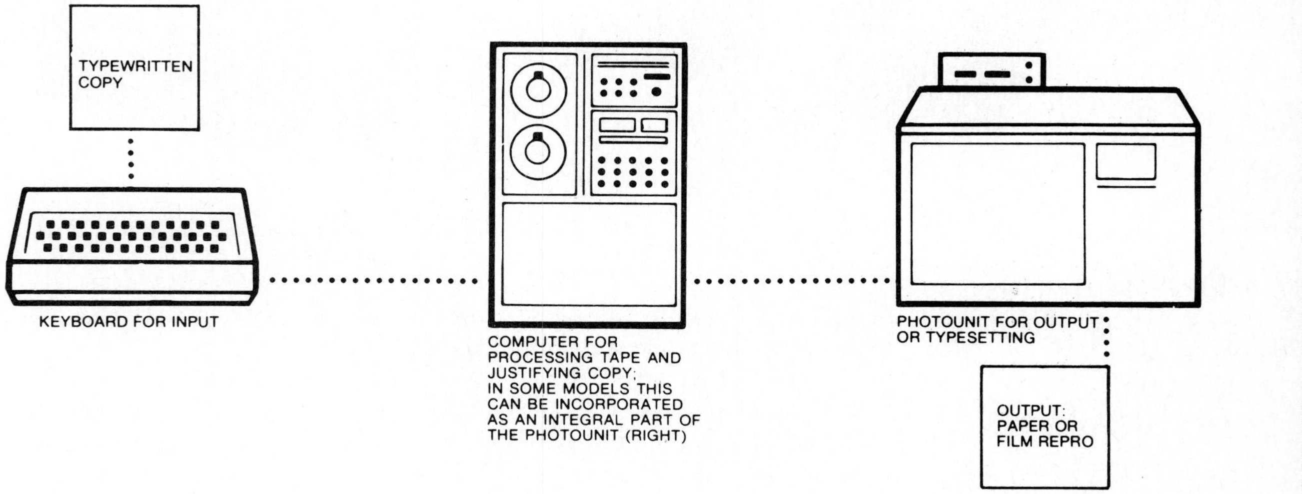

TYPEWRITTEN COPY

KEYBOARD FOR INPUT

COMPUTER FOR PROCESSING TAPE AND JUSTIFYING COPY; IN SOME MODELS THIS CAN BE INCORPORATED AS AN INTEGRAL PART OF THE PHOTOUNIT (RIGHT)

PHOTOUNIT FOR OUTPUT OR TYPESETTING

OUTPUT: PAPER OR FILM REPRO

FIG. 4-11 Schematic drawing illustrates the principle of photocomposition. (Courtesy Versatec, Xerox Co.)

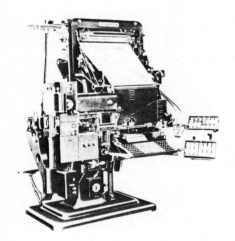

FIG. 4-12 Intertype Fotosetter was among the earliest of the phototypesetters for text composition. The machine is no longer marketed by Intertype. (Courtesy Intertype Co.)

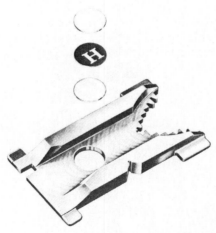

FIG. 4-13 Exploded view of a Fotosetter matrix called a *Fotomat*. (Courtesy Intertype Co.)

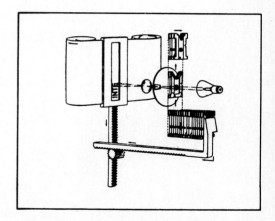

FIG. 4-14 Schematic drawing illustrates how each Fotosetter matrix is exposed. (Courtesy Harris Corp., Composition Systems Div.)

type, which is similar to a Linotype. The Monophoto was essentially a Monotype. In these machines the master character image was carried on a matrix. The matrix contained a negative of the character (Fig. 4-13). As the matrices were composed into full lines, they were photographed instead of cast into metal (Fig. 4-14). The

(A)   (B)

FIG. 4-15 Justowriter impact typewriter recorder (A) and reproducer (B).

Justowriter impact typesetting machine (Fig. 4-15) was a forerunner of a first-generation device called the ATF Typesetter.

Instead of strike-on characters, the ATF Typesetter used a revolving disc containing characters that were flashed on photographic paper. All first-generation phototypesetters are basically mechanical and slow in operation.

Second-Generation Phototypesetters

Second-generation phototypesetting equipment includes some of the earlier systems that were designed for setting type photographically. These devices were not adaptations of earlier metal or nonmetal typesetting systems. These machines operate directly from a keyboard in which both the keyboard and photocomposition components are one unit (Fig. 4-16). Some machines operate from a

FIG. 4-16 Comp Set 500 is a second-generation phototypesetter. (Courtesy VariTyper Division of AM International.)

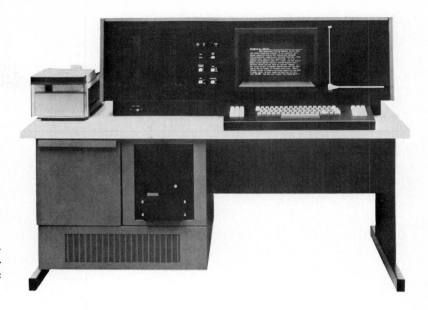

FIG. 4-17 Keyboard machine used to perforate tape that will be used to operate a phototypesetting unit. (Courtesy Compugraphic Corp.)

punched tape or magnetic tape prepared on a separate keyboard (Fig. 4-17). Before a tape is made, format data such as typeface, point size, set width, line length, and leading are entered into the keyboard mechanism.

Third-Generation Phototypesetters

Computerized photocomposition systems that utilize a cathode-ray tube (CRT) as part of an image-forming component are called third generation. Characters are formed on a TV-like screen by a series of tiny dots or lines (Fig. 4-18). The image on the screen is then transferred to photographic paper. Speed of CRT devices vary from approximately 250 characters per second to 3000 characters per second. In comparison, second-generation machines range in speed from 5 to 15 characters per second.

FIG. 4-18 Third-generation phototypesetter. The generation of a character (Garamond) on the cathode-ray tube. The character generates from left to right on a common base-line. The completely generated character appears exactly as shown at the right of the illustration. The small "a" (14 point) is a direct photographic reduction of the image on the tube. The "raggedness" is not apparent, but can be seen readily under magnification.

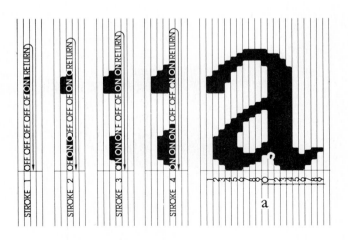

FIG. 4-19   This photodisplay machine produces single line strips of type composition. (Courtesy Photo Typositor ® Visual Graphics Corp.)

FIG. 4-20   This photodisplay machine produces multiple lines of composition. (Courtesy Compugraphic Corp.)

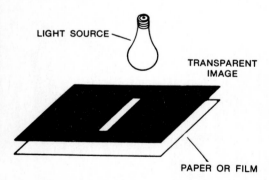

FIG. 4-21   Schematic drawing shows operating principle of photodisplay machine.

Photodisplay Units

Several different *photodisplay* units are available and are generally used to compose unjustified display type. The output is either in single line strips (Fig. 4-19) or in multiline composition (Fig. 4-20). The majority of these machines require hand operation for character selection and fitting. They are considerably slower than the phototypesetting systems to be discussed a little later.

The principle of operation among these machines is basically the same. The type font, carried on a filmstrip, grid, or disc, is installed on the machine. The operator manually moves the font so that the character desired is in exposing position. A button is pressed and a light beam exposes the character onto a photosensitive paper. Figure 4-21 illustrates the basic operating principle of photodisplay units. After the composition has been set, the paper is developed, fixed, and washed. This process is done either in the machine or outside in a separate device.

Some photodisplay units are operated from a keyboard (Fig. 4-22). These units are much faster and more versatile than the manually operated machines. A standard typewriter keyboard arrangement is used. Many newspapers and commercial printers use these machines for headline and display typesetting.

Photodisplay systems are divided into two basic groups. These include *manual letterspacing* and *automatic letterspacing*. In manual

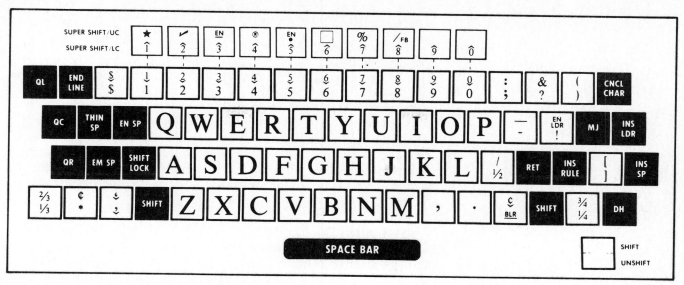

FIG. 4-22 Standard typewriter keyboard arrangement is used to operate this photodisplay unit. (Courtesy Compugraphic Corp.)

systems, the operator has a visual check on what is being set. This includes being able to control both letterspacing and wordspacing. In automatic systems, the operator cannot see the type being set. Letterspacing and wordspacing are done automatically according to the operator's machine instructions. In either manual or automatic systems, these machines can usually be adjusted to set type with normal, tight, loose, or overlapping letterspacing (Fig. 4-23).

Photodisplay units that operate on the *contact-printing* principle (Fig. 4-24) are usually limited to producing same-size (one-to-one) images of the film fonts available for each machine. Photodisplay units that operate on the *projection-printing* principle increase the range of type sizes possible from any one type font. This is possible because of a built-in enlarging mechanism or lens arrangement (Fig. 4-25).

FIG. 4-25 Schematic drawing illustrates the principle of photodisplay projection, allowing enlargement and reduction of type characters. (Courtesy Wang Laboratories, Inc.)

CHARACTER
CHARACTER
CHARACTER

FIG. 4-23 Loose, normal, and tight letterspacing is possible on manual or automatic photodisplay units. (Courtesy Compugraphic Corp.)

FIG. 4-24 Schematic drawing illustrates the principle of photodisplay contact printing. (Courtesy Compugraphic Corp.)

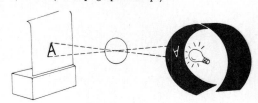

The basic elements in a phototypesetter:

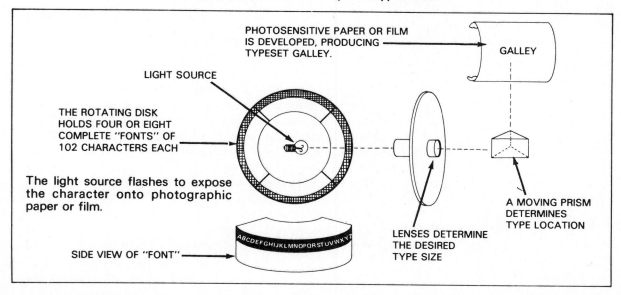

PHOTOSENSITIVE PAPER OR FILM IS DEVELOPED, PRODUCING TYPESET GALLEY.

GALLEY

LIGHT SOURCE

THE ROTATING DISK HOLDS FOUR OR EIGHT COMPLETE "FONTS" OF 102 CHARACTERS EACH

The light source flashes to expose the character onto photographic paper or film.

A MOVING PRISM DETERMINES TYPE LOCATION

LENSES DETERMINE THE DESIRED TYPE SIZE

SIDE VIEW OF "FONT"

Most photodisplay units can be operated under normal room-lighting conditions. With some machines, however, the operator must work under safe light conditions to avoid exposing the photosensitive paper to white light.

In most cases, photodisplay units set type as a continuous strip of paper approximately 2 inches wide. On the more sophisticated units, the type is set on rolls of paper, which allows lines to be set one under the other. Some of the more popular photodisplay machines are described below. These include machines ranging from manually operated to keyboard arrangements having full-word and letter-spacing capabilities.

STRIP PRINTER The Strip Printer (Fig. 4-26) is a photodisplay machine that is used to set display-size lines of type manually. Type sizes range from 6 to 96 point. A variety of type styles are available. The Strip Printer uses a *filmstrip* font (Fig. 4-27). Each font contains one size and style of type. The machine has no reduction or enlargement capabilities. The filmstrip is inserted through the exposure unit. This positions the font between the lamp and photographic paper.

After lining up the desired character over a preset point on the machine, the exposure is made by pressing a button. After all the exposures have been made, the paper is removed from the machine. It is then developed, fixed, washed, and dried.

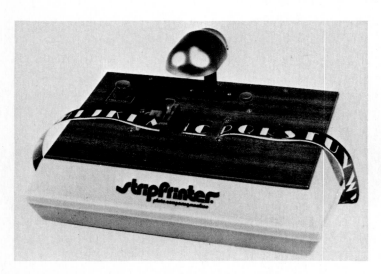

FIG. 4-26 Strip Printer. (Courtesy Strip Printer, Inc.)

FIG. 4-27 Strip Printer film strip font. (Courtesy Strip Printer, Inc.)

VARITYPER HEADLINER The VariTyper Headliner (Fig. 4-28) is a manually operated photodisplay machine. Type is set from plastic discs called Typemasters in sizes from 10 to 86 point (Fig. 4-29). Each Typemaster contains one font, and there are no reduction or enlargement capabilities. The Typemaster disc is about the size of a $33\frac{1}{3}$ rpm record. The type is set on a 35mm paper or filmstrip. Letterspacing can be adjusted manually for tighter setting. The machine can be operated under normal room-lighting conditions.

The operator selects the desired character by rotating the disc. The character is positioned between the lamp and photographic paper. The exposure is made by pressing a button. After all the

FIG. 4-28 VariTyper Headliner. (Courtesy VariTyper Division of AM International.)

FIG. 4-29 VariTyper Headliner Typemaster font. (Courtesy VariTyper Division of AM International.)

exposures have been made, the paper is cut and automatically fed into a three-compartment developing tank inside the machine. The exposed paper is developed, fixed, and washed. It emerges from the machine semi-dry.

FILMOTYPE The Filmotype machine (Fig. 4-30) sets lines of display type from 12 to 144 point. It will mix up to 20 fonts. Words or lines can be set to exact lengths. Each type font includes all characters such as capitals, lowercase, punctuation marks, numerals, and symbols. Other fonts include logotypes, trademarks, borders, and designs.

The operator uses a special dial when setting a word or whole line of copy to a specific length. Each type font has a built-in signal that automatically adjusts the spacing between letters. The machine can be operated under normal room-lighting conditions.

FIG. 4-30 The Filmotype is a manual display composing machine that uses the contact method of image production. (Courtesy Alphatype Filmotype Sales.)

PHOTO TYPOSITOR   The Photo Typositor (Fig. 4-31) is a manually operated machine that can compose single and multiple display lines. Type can be reduced or enlarged from 25% to 200%. Multiple film fonts are stored on font reels. This permits intermixing of type styles in a single line. Type can be set in a variety of styles such as backslant, italic, condensed, staggered, and with shadow effects or background tints (Fig. 4-32). The operator is able to control letterspacing manually.

The desired characters are positioned between the lamp and the photographic paper by turning the handwheels on the machine. After each exposure, the character is automatically developed inside the machine. The developed type composition is removed from the machine and then fixed, washed, and dried.

COMPUGRAPHIC CG 7200   The Compugraphic CG 7200 (Fig. 4-33) is a keyboard-operated display machine. The keyboard is similar to the layout on a standard typewriter. Type fonts are available in a wide variety of styles. These are contained on filmstrips. Each filmstrip holds two styles. Two filmstrips can be placed in the machine at the same time. It is possible to select any of the four different styles while setting type.

FIG. 4-31   Photo Typositor. (Courtesy Photo Typositor® Visual Graphics, Corp.)

FIG. 4-32   The Photo Typositor can produce type in a variety of styles and effects. (Courtesy Photo Typositor® Visual Graphics Corp.)

A A A A A A A A BACKSLANT ITALICS E E E E E E E E

repro camera system.

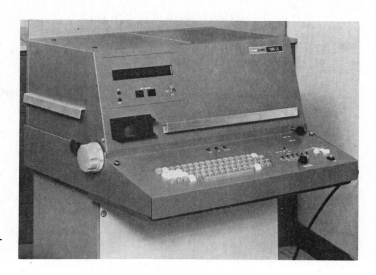

FIG. 4-33 Compugraphic CG 7200. (Courtesy Compugraphic Corp.)

Typeface selections are made by regulating the lens selection dial. Typefaces are available in eight different sizes for each font. By adjusting the lens, it is possible to set type up to 120 points in size. A visual display unit allows the operator to view the characters. By pressing a button, the line is automatically exposed inside the machine. The exposed photographic paper is then transferred to a lightproof cassette for processing. The composition can then be cut apart and pasted into position on a paste-up.

Text Phototypesetting Systems

A typical text phototypesetting system (Fig. 4-34) is made up of three units: (1) *keyboard* for input; (2) *computer* for making end-of-line decisions such as hyphenation and justification; and (3) *photo unit* for output, or typesetting.

FIG. 4-34 A phototypesetting system includes: (A) keyboard; and (B) computer with photographic unit. (Courtesy Harris Corp., Composition Systems Div.)

(A)

(B)

FIG. 4-35 Keyboard is the input unit of a phototypesetting system. (Courtesy Harris Corp., Composition Systems Div.)

KEYBOARD The input unit of a phototypesetting system is the keyboard (Fig. 4-35). All current systems use a keyboard that is similar to a standard electric typewriter. Instead of a strike-on character, however, each time a key is pressed an electrical impulse is produced.

On some keyboards the typed line is immediately sent to the computer control and image formation units. This is called *direct entry*. A popular method, called *indirect entry* or off-line, stores the typed lines on punched paper tape or magnetic tape. Efficiency and speed are gained by the use of tape. Several typists can prepare tape and these tapes can be placed on the computer for output at high speed. In this way, the computer and photo unit devices are more productive.

Paper tapes are narrow-width rolls in which holes are punched. Each hole corresponds to a certain keyboard character (Fig. 4-36). The computer can then "read" the holes and produce the correct character. Corrections can be made on the tape by punching a certain

FIG. 4-36 (A) Paper tapes are punched (perforated) with holes that correspond to various keyboard characters. (B) Tape is "read" automatically by a computer to produce correct photographic type characters. [(A) courtesy Mergenthaler Linotype Co.; (B) courtesy Compugraphic Corp.]

(A)

(B)

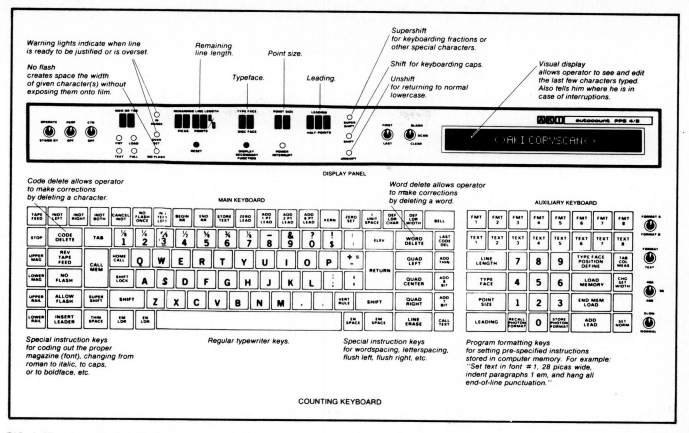

FIG. 4-37 Counting keyboard. (Courtesy AKI.)

code. The output device automatically deletes or adds the desired characters.

Magnetic tapes are either on a disc, drum, or cassette. These tapes can be read by the output device faster than paper tape. Corrections are easily made at any point on the tape. Characters can also be erased at any point, and two tapes can be easily merged to produce a new tape.

Counting Keyboard. With the *counting keyboard* (Fig. 4-37) all end-of-line decisions are made by the operator as the copy is typed. The operator must know the typeface, point size, line length, wordspacing, and so on. In addition, the operator must have a good understanding of the machine's controls.

As the copy is being typed, the unit widths of the individual characters are totaled and displayed on a scale. As the minimum line length is approached, the machine informs the operator by a light or audio signal that an end-of-line decision must be made. After making the end-of-line decision, the operator then presses a key that instructs the unit to expand the wordspace to fill out the line to the desired length. The tape is punched and the operator sets the next line. Since the end-of-line decisions are already made, the tape, called a *justified tape*, does not go through a computer. It goes directly to the photo unit for typesetting.

When direct-entry phototypesetters are used, there are no punched tapes involved. Instead, the typed characters are momentarily held in "memory" until an end-of-line decision is made. At this point the line is entered into the photo unit of the machine where each character is recorded on photopaper at high speed. The exposed photopaper is processed automatically—ready for paste-up.

Noncounting Keyboard. The *noncounting keyboard* system can be operated to make all end-of-line decisions. The operator must have the ability to type accurately at high speeds. The system can be adjusted to any desired line length, type style, and leading. All end-of-line decisions are made by the computer rather than by the keyboard operator. As the operator types the copy, an unjustified tape is produced. This tape is often called an "idiot tape."

Direct-entry phototypesetters do not have noncounting keyboards because there are no punched tapes involved. These machines have built-in controls that perform the end-of-line decision automatically or allow the operator the choice.

COMPUTER UNIT The *computer unit* is basically a machine that has a format program and memory (Fig. 4–38). Its job is to process the unjustified tapes and make end-of-line decisions. A format program contains written specifications of typesetting requirements called *logic*. It is written in a special language for the computer. The format sets up the basic rules from which the computer can arrange or compose the input data. The tape input data is in code. When this tape code is translated in the computer's stored format program, it processes a second, or output, tape. The computer automatically hyphenates, justifies, and makes up columns or even whole pages.

In some phototypesetting systems the computer unit is a built-in part of the photo unit. In this case, the unjustified tape is sent directly into the photo unit, and a minicomputer decides where line breaks will occur as the type is being set.

There are several methods by which computers can be programmed to decide what happens at the end of a line. These include: (1) logic; (2) exception dictionary; (3) discretionary; and (4) hyphenless.

Logic. The computer is programmed with rules of hyphenation called *logic*. All words covered by the program are hyphenated accordingly. If the rules cannot be applied to a word, the word is not hyphenated. In this case, the line is justified by adding wordspacing and/or letterspacing.

Some words in the English language that are permitted to be hyphenated according to logic nevertheless should be discouraged in this system. For example, the word *away* should not be hyphenated a-way. The word *bossing* should not be hyphenated bos-sing. These are exceptions to the rules of hyphenation. Many computers have an exception dictionary for this purpose.

Exception Dictionary. An *exception dictionary* is a built-in list available to the computer of all words not logically hyphenated. In operation, a line is composed until a word oversets or overruns the end of the line. The overset word is instantly checked by the computer's exception dictionary first.

If the word is not in the exception dictionary, it is checked in the computer's hyphenation logic. This is done first by prefix and suffix; then the root of the word is broken down according to logic rules. When the hyphenation point has been found, the part of the word that is to remain is sent back to the line with a hyphen added. The line is then justified automatically according to the amount of wordspacing and/or letterspacing required.

Discretionary. With *discretionary* hyphenation, the operator is called upon to help the computer. As the operator types the copy, words of three syllables and more are hyphenated. The computer

FIG. 4–38 Computer unit of a phototypesetting system contains program format and memory. (Courtesy Monotype International.)

then uses "discretion" to select only the hyphenation it needs. It disregards hyphenations that are not needed.

Hyphenless. A method of setting type in which no hyphenations are used is called *hyphenless*. The lines are justified by increasing or decreasing the wordspacing and/or letterspacing. Hyphenless composition often produces poor wordspacing and letterspacing, especially in short line lengths. It is sometimes necessary to reset certain lines to give a more pleasing typographic appearance.

PHOTO UNIT The output from photocomposition comes from the *photo unit*, or phototypesetter (Fig. 4-39). It is a combination of electronic, mechanical, and photographic components. The type font is carried as a negative image on an *image master* (Fig. 4-40). Depending on the system, the type font may be a grid, spinning disc, drum, or filmstrip (Fig. 4-41). The type is set using high-intensity light flashes through the character, projecting them onto photographic paper or film. If a grid is used, the entire grid is illuminated and the desired character is selected by means of a masking system. Only the character image selected passes through a series of prisms, enlarging lenses, and mirrors until it is positioned and exposed on photographic paper. Photo units that use a spinning disc or spinning drum produce type characters at greater speeds than those using grids or filmstrips.

In some photo unit systems, the image master remains stationary while the light source moves. In other machines, the image master rotates or spins while the light remains stationary. With some photo units, a different image master is used for each type size. More sophisticated units use a single image master that reduces and enlarges the type with a lens system. This makes it possible to produce a number of different type sizes.

FIG. 4-39 Photo unit of a phototypesetting system produces the type composition. This phototypesetter includes the computer. (Courtesy Harris Corp., Composition Systems Div.)

FIG. 4-40 Type font image master. (Courtesy Alphatype Corp.)

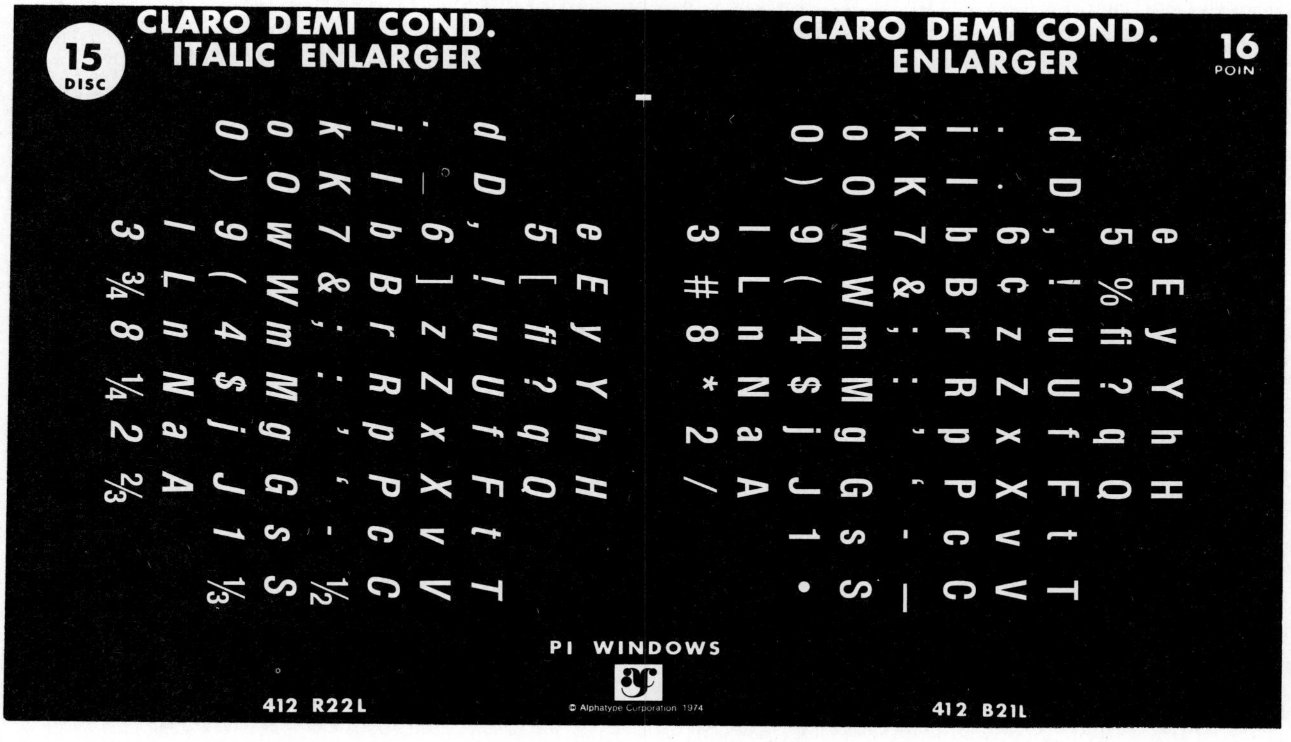

CLARO DEMI COND. ITALIC ENLARGER

15 DISC

CLARO DEMI COND. ENLARGER

16 POINT

PI WINDOWS

412 R22L

© Alphatype Corporation 1974

412 B21L

FIG. 4-41   Discs are commonly used as image masters for high-speed phototypesetting systems. (Courtesy Harris Corp., Composition Systems Div.)

When phototypesetting is completed, the film cassette containing the exposed material is removed from the photo unit. The exposed paper or film is passed through a *processor* (Fig. 4–42), which automatically develops and fixes the photographic images ready for the paste-up process.

FIG. 4-42   Processors (A) and (B) are used to develop and fix exposed phototypesetting paper. [(A) courtesy Eastman Kodak Co.; (B) courtesy Compugraphic Corp.)

(B)

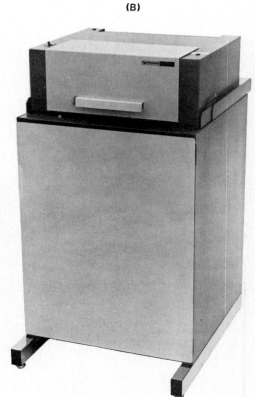

(A)

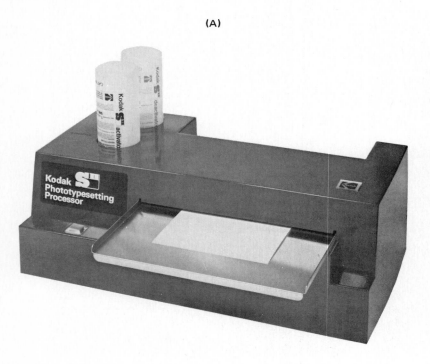

CORRECTIONS Making *corrections* can be more time-consuming and costly than the typesetting. The best and least expensive way to avoid this is by careful attention to the original typesetting process. Once the type is set, it becomes more difficult and expensive to correct.

Keyboard Corrections. In a *non-computer-assisted* photo-typesetting system, corrections must be keyboarded in machine-readable form and then processed through the phototypesetting unit and developed. Any corrections must be set, cut apart, and pasted over the incorrect lines. There is always a possibility that the reset type may not exactly match the original. As an example, the reset type may appear lighter, darker, fatter, or thinner.

Computer-Assisted Corrections. In a *computer-assisted* system, each line is numbered and stored in memory (Fig. 4-43). Once the material is proofread, incorrect lines are noted. These are reset, and the computer is instructed to find a certain line in its memory and add the corrected line. The computer then produces a "clean tape" (free of errors), which is reprocessed through the phototypesetting machine.

The latest systems use *visual display terminals* (VDTs) (Fig. 4-44). A screen is used to show words and allows an operator to view the contents of an input tape, and then to add, delete, or change copy. A new corrected tape is produced.

Designed originally as an editing device, the VDT has been made more flexible by recent technology. Operators can not only edit pre-

FIG. 4-43 The computer assigns a number to each typeset line and stores it in memory for future use. (Courtesy Autologic, Inc.)

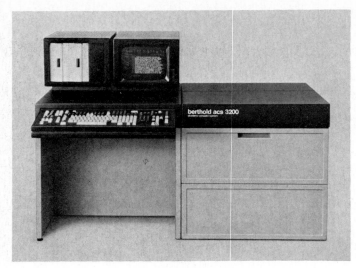

FIG. 4-44 A Visual Display Terminal called *VDT*. (Courtesy Berthold of North America.)

keyboarded copy but also do full-page make-up on the screen. This shows up exactly as it will when typeset, line for line. Editing and corrections are easily handled before actual typesetting takes place.

Many publication printers now use the VDT system to store large quantities of composition on *floppy discs*. These are magnetic discs that record millions of characters and store them for future use. Writers and journalists can keyboard their articles directly into a VDT machine, where they may see their article as it will appear in type. Editors can then recall this information on master VDTs and edit, format, and send it to typesetting machines. This procedure eliminates rekeyboarding.

OCR SYSTEMS One of the most recent input systems is called *optical character recognition* (OCR). With the OCR system, a special typewriter font is used to prepare unjustified characters representing the original copy. When the desired copy is prepared, it is placed on an optical scanning device (Fig. 4-45). This converts the typewritten information to a magnetic diskette. The diskette is used to automatically set the type (Fig. 4-46). The photo unit processes the dis-

FIG. 4-45 This unit scans typed pages and records the copy on a magnetic diskette. The unit is also adaptable to the preparation of perforated tape. (Courtesy VariTyper Division of AM International.)

FIG. 4-46 Copy contained on the magnetic diskette is typeset at the rate of 50-70 lines per minute on the phototypesetter shown in background. The unit is also adaptable to perforated tape input. (Courtesy VariTyper Division of AM International.)

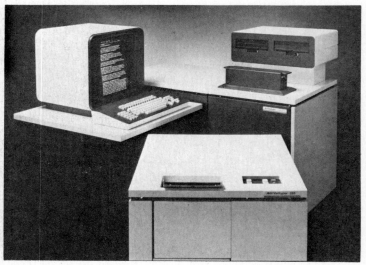

kette input, and a high-speed light passes through the image master characters of the film font. Each character is exposed on paper or film.

CRT SYSTEMS *Cathode-ray tube* (CRT) systems are high-speed phototypesetting machines. They use digital stored characters and display the computer processed data on a television-like tube. These systems are much more sophisticated than the image master machines discussed earlier. Characters are imaged from a series of small dots on a grid of "x" and "y" lines (Fig. 4–47). These are scanned by the machine from a type font plate. They may also be programmed and stored on magnetic tape in the memory of a computer. This is done at speeds anywhere from 1000 to 10,000 characters per second. These speeds are possible because there are no moving parts in a cathode-ray tube.

Most CRT systems are used to compose full-page layouts in preparation for typesetting. It is possible to combine type and illustrations in a process called *photocomposing* (Fig. 4–48). The page makeup can be done on paper, film, microfilm, or offset plates. Photocomposition also provides the flexibility of storing large quantities of manuscript until such time as it is needed for typesetting.

Automated Page Make-up. The most current and sophisticated photocomposition system available is the *Automatic Illustrated Documentation System* (AIDS). Manufactured by Information International, Incorporated, the equipment is capable of composing

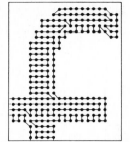

Enlargement of f formed by dots.

Enlargement of f made up of lines.

FIG. 4–47 Cathode ray tube (CRT) characters are imaged from a series of small dots on a grid of "x" and "y" lines. (Courtesy Harris Corp., Composition Systems Div.)

FIG. 4-48 Through the use of CRT systems, type and illustrations can be combined into full-page layouts. (Courtesy Compugraphic Corp.)

(A)

(B)

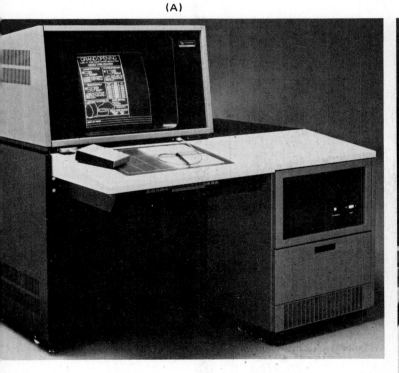

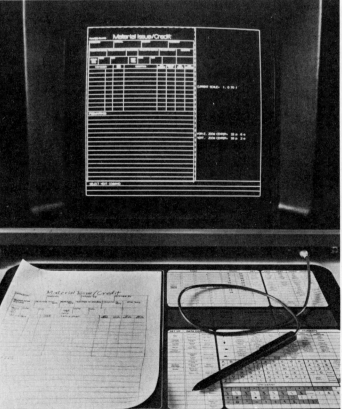

FIG. 4-49 J.C. Penney Co., Inc., used the Information International pagesetting system in producing the catalog where this page first appeared. (Courtesy Information International, Culver City, California.)

entire pages of text, line drawings, and halftones (Fig. 4-49). The system is primarily intended for publication printing. The system has the added capability of reducing page sizes to varying requirements.

In operation, original manuscript is keyboarded and automatically set into type on the *Text Editing and Composition System* (Fig. 4-50). All of the activities of a copy editing department involving repetitive cycles are quickly handled at this stage.

FIG. 4-50 Text Editing and Composition System. (Courtesy Information International, Culver City, California.)

FIG. 4-51 Illustration Scanner. (Courtesy Information International, Culver City, California.)

As typesetting takes place, continuous tone photographs and line artwork are automatically scanned by a computer-driven precision optics system called the *Illustration Scanner* (Fig. 4-51). Artistic and editorial judgments for determining size, style, format, and any other criteria governing the appearance of finished artwork can be translated into keyboard commands at this stage.

At this point, both the text and illustration copy are made up into complete pages. This eliminates the conventional method of preparing a paste-up. The *Page Makeup System* (Fig. 4-52) automates this process in its entirety. The computer program controls an electron beam that reproduces the typographic characters and half-tone dots as strokes of light on a CRT. The *Pagesetter* (Fig. 4-53) creates the completed pages containing text and artwork on photographic paper or film (Fig. 4-54). The finished photographic paper or film is then ready for platemaking and printing, usually by the offset process.

FIG. 4-52   Page Makeup System. (Courtesy Information International, Culver City, California.)

FIG. 4-53   Pagesetter. (Courtesy Information International, Culver City, California.)

FIG. 4-54 Pagesetter combines text and illustrations on photographic paper or film. (Courtesy Information International, Culver City, California.)

chapter 5

TYPE CLASSIFICATIONS

There are many different styles of lettering in modern typography. The paste-up artist is likely to become confused in choices of types unless an analysis is made of the various styles. To assist in the identification of various type styles, a classification system is in general use. With a basic knowledge of the several type classifications, the paste-up artist is better equipped to make intelligent decisions about job requirements, quality, economy, and printing process.

Chapter 4 was concerned with the nomenclature and methods of typesetting with an emphasis on photocomposition. Problems will often arise as to which typeface is best for a given job. This is difficult for the beginner and equally puzzling for many experienced layout and paste-up artists.

From the hundreds of type styles available, it is almost impossible to make type selections without some method of narrowing the choices. Effective printing depends upon appropriate type selection. To assist the layout and paste-up artist in making type selections, six major *type classifications* are in common use. These include: (1) Roman oldstyle; (2) sans serif; (3) square serif; (4) textletter; (5) script; and (6) decorative.

ROMAN OLDSTYLE

The most distinguishing characteristics of *Roman oldstyle* typefaces (Fig. 5-1) are the numerous serifs and the thin and thick strokes. Serifs are either rounded, angular, or rectangular (Fig. 5-2). Oldstyle typefaces were patterned after the classical Roman inscriptions. The characters are easily read because they are open, round,

---

CASLON OLD FACE

This is the roman letter cut by William Caslon in 1742 and is one of the most celebrated of all the old-face types. *The italic has decorative capitals called 'swash.' AEGMNT*

FIG. 5-1 Roman Oldstyle typeface design.

and wide. This provides a pleasing contrast between the thin and thick strokes. Oldstyle typefaces are adaptable to printing on rough finished papers.

Included under the Roman oldstyle classification are transitional and modern typefaces.

Transitional

The *transitional* typefaces (Fig. 5-3) have characteristics of both oldstyle and modern type designs. Transitional type designs historically were patterned after the oldstyle designs, but prior to modern types. The contrast between thin and thick strokes is not as great in modern as in oldstyle (Fig. 5-4). The serifs are somewhat long and contain rounded, smooth curves.

Transitional type designs are well suited to printing on smooth finished papers because of their detail and finer lines.

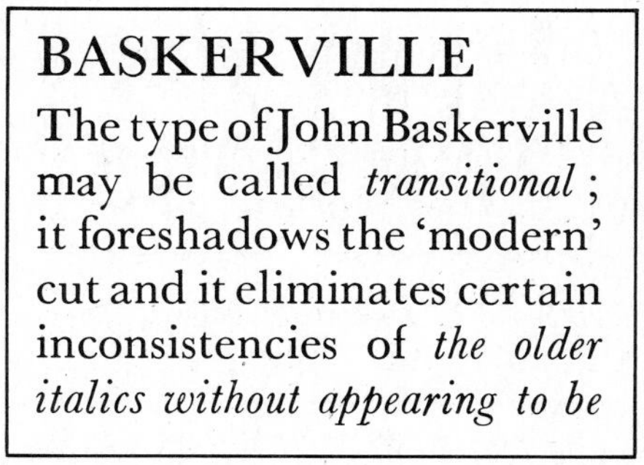

Modern

In comparison with oldstyle, *modern* type designs (Fig. 5-5) have a greater variation in thickness of strokes. The serifs are usually thin, straight, and somewhat rectangular (Fig. 5-6). There is some

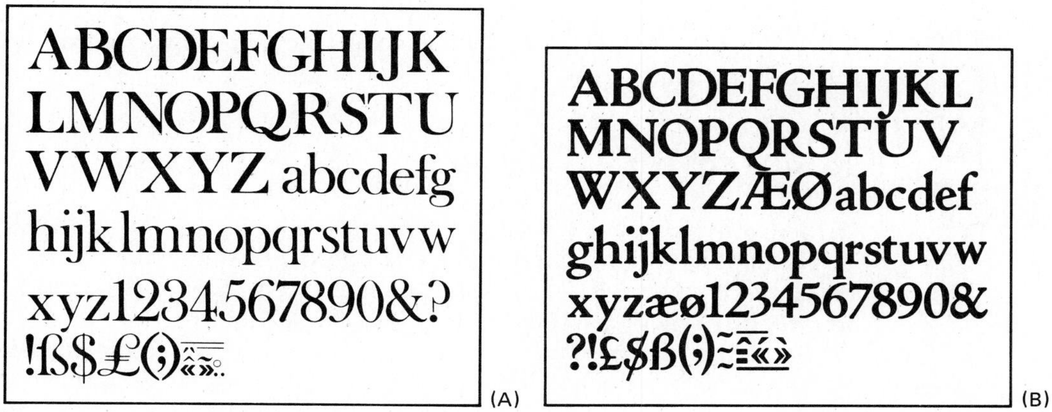

FIG. 5-2   Serifs are round, angular, or rectangular in shape.

BASKERVILLE
The type of John Baskerville may be called *transitional*; it foreshadows the 'modern' cut and it eliminates certain inconsistencies of *the older italics without appearing to be*

FIG. 5-3   Transitional typeface design.

ABCDEFGHIJK LMNOPQRSTU VWXYZ abcdefg hijklmnopqrstuvw xyz1234567890&? !ß$£()¡¿...

(A)

ABCDEFGHIJKL MNOPQRSTUV WXYZÆØabcdef ghijklmnopqrstuvw xyzæø1234567890& ?!£$ß()¡¿«»

(B)

FIG. 5-4   Transitional typefaces (A) contain more contrast between thin and thick strokes than Oldstyle typefaces (B). (Courtesy Letraset USA, Inc.)

FIG. 5-6   Modern typeface serifs are usually thin and straight and have a mechanical appearance. (Courtesy Letraset USA, Inc.)

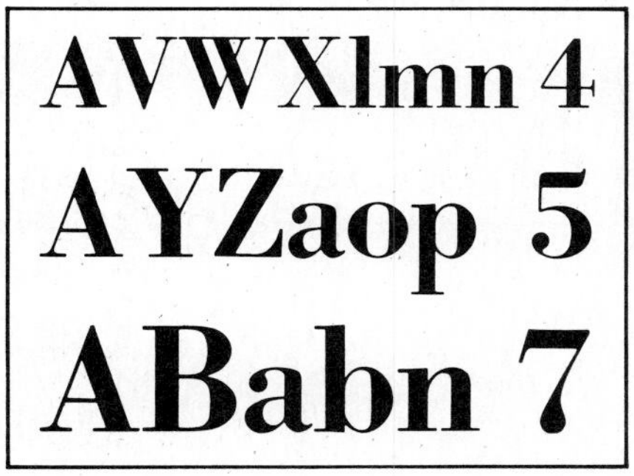

FIG. 5-5   Modern typeface design.

AVWXlmn 4
AYZaop 5
ABabn 7

ABCDEFGHI JKLMNOPQR STUVWXYZ abcdefghijklmn opqrstuvwxyz12 34567890&?!ß£ $();¡¿«

59

abcdefghijklmnopqrstuvwxyz

ABCDEFGHI
Expert wor
1234567$&

FIG. 5-8 Sans serif typeface design.

ABCDEFGHIJK
LMNOPQRST
UVWXYZ abc
defghijklmnop
qrstuvwxyz12
34567890&&?
!ß£$(-)《》≈

FIG. 5-9 Sans serif typefaces contain little or no contrast in the thickness of letter strokes. (Courtesy Letraset USA, Inc.)

rounding at the corners. Ascenders and descenders tend to be long (Fig. 5-7). The letter formations have a mechanical appearance.

Modern type designs are adaptable to printing on smooth finished papers. Most of the type used in magazines, books, and newspapers is composed with modern Roman type designs.

SANS SERIF

Type styles classified as *sans serif* (Fig. 5-8) have no serifs. Another characteristic is little or no contrast in thickness of letter strokes (Fig. 5-9). Because the strokes of the letters are all of the same weight or thickness, they are quite monotone. These faces are very popular today because of their simplicity of design and modern appearance. Sans serif type designs are well suited to printing on smooth finished papers.

Sans serif type styles are used to print magazines, books, and newspapers. They are also used in advertising, business cards, and stationery of all types. Sans serif is adaptable to printing on smooth finished papers.

SQUARE SERIF

Used mainly for display composition, *square serif* type is geometric in design (Fig. 5-10). The typeface is open, and the characters have square or blocked serifs and more or less uniform strokes (Fig. 5-11). Square serif types have limited usage as body or text matter.

Square serif type styles are good for display lines in advertisements, newspaper headlines, and some letterheads. Square serif prints equally well on rough finished and smooth finished papers.

FIG. 5-10 Square serif typeface design.

ALMaor2
ANast3

ABCDEFGHIJ
KLMNOPQR
STUVWXYZa
bcdefghijklm
nopqrstuvwx
yz1234567890
&?!ß£$(;)《》∴~

TEXTLETTER

Textletter (Fig. 5–12) is very difficult to read and therefore is used very little today. These type designs were patterned after the writing of the early scribes. The serifs are pointed and the strokes are angular (Fig. 5–13).

Textletter should never be composed in paragraph form or in all uppercase because it is so difficult to read. This type style is usually selected for certificates, diplomas, and religious occasions. It is well adapted to printing on rough finished papers.

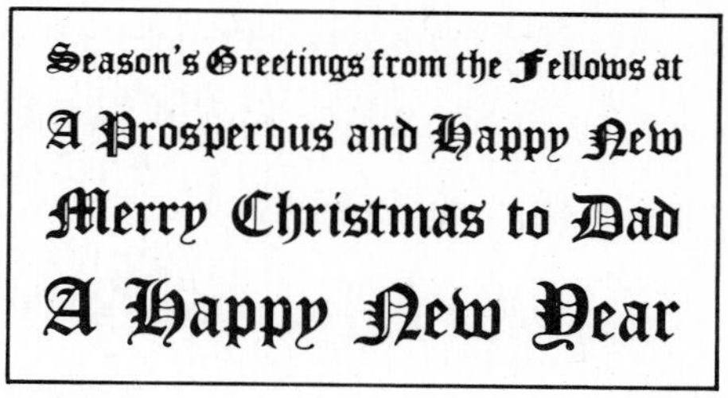

SCRIPT

Designed to imitate handwriting, *script* typefaces are divided into styles with letters that join and those that do not join. Script typefaces are designed so that each letter form connects as in handwriting (Fig. 5–14). The type styles that do not join are known as *cursive* (Fig. 5–15). Scripts and cursives contain thin and thick strokes. These variations result from pen designs and the natural pressure variations exerted in penmanship. Script type should never be set in all uppercase because the awkward letter combinations are difficult to read. In addition, these letter styles should never be letterspaced. This defeats the purpose for which they were intended—the imitation of handwriting.

Script and cursive typefaces are used primarily for commercial announcements and personal invitations. These type styles are adaptable to printing on either rough or smooth finished papers.

DECORATIVE

The *decorative* type classification contains those type styles that do not fit any other classification (Fig. 5–16). In most cases, these type styles are 24 point and larger and are used exclusively for display lines. Decorative types are adaptable to advertising since they attract attention. Decorative types are designed to express different moods

FIG. 5–12   Textletter typeface design.

FIG. 5–13   Textletter typefaces are recognizable by their pointed serifs and angular strokes. (Courtesy Letraset USA, Inc.)

FIG. 5–14   Script typefaces are designed so that each letter form connects as in handwriting.

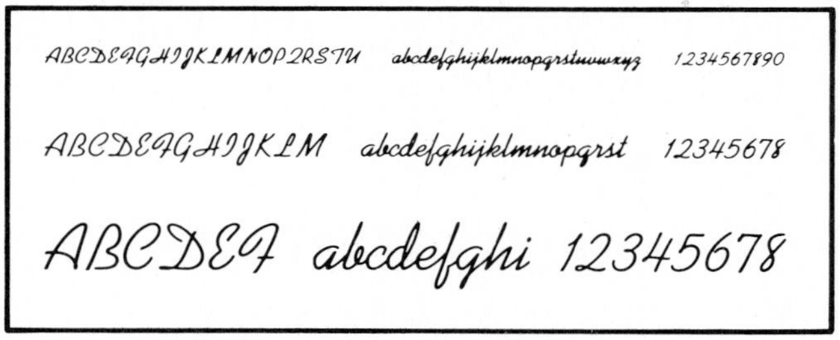

FIG. 5–15   Cursive typeface designs are recognizable by letters that do not connect.

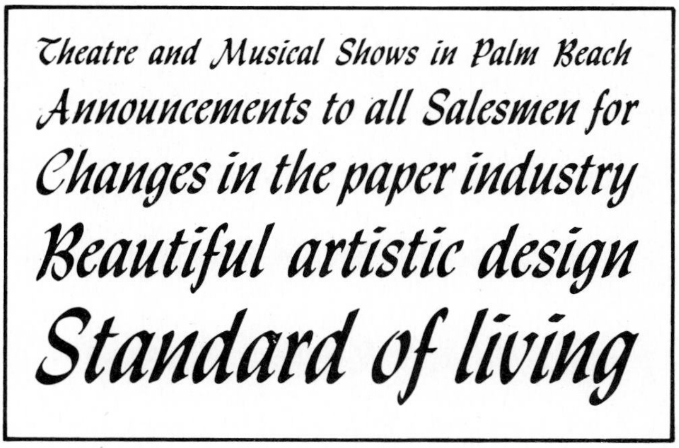

FIG. 5-16 Decorative typeface design.

and fashions. They are meant to be used with care and only as display. Depending upon their expression, decorative types print equally well on rough or smooth finished papers.

TYPOGRAPHIC SPECIMENS

There are literally hundreds of type styles available to the layout and paste-up artist. These include mechanical transfer lettering, strike-on, and photocomposition. Representative samples of popular typefaces are shown throughout this chapter. Type styles are normally shown in alphabetical order and are identified by the name given by the manufacturer (see p. 15).

chapter 6

ART AND COPY PREPARATION

This chapter deals with the preparation of artwork and copy for the offset printing process. It offers help to the paste-up artist in making the job requirements clear to the printer. After submission of layouts and dummies to the client and receiving OKs, there is the exacting job of making the finished artwork and properly marking it up for the printer. To prepare this artwork, it is important to familiarize yourself with all the steps in this translation of drawn artwork and photographs into the final printed result.

All material supplied to the printer for reproduction by the offset process is handled as *art and copy preparation*. The term *copy* includes all elements to be reproduced, including words, illustrations, photographs, borders, and other ornamentation.

After all the copy has been analyzed, the layout artist prepares a layout that will communicate the message in a pleasing and concise manner. For an intelligent and harmonious working relationship with the printer, the layout artist should become thoroughly familiar with the terms and procedures outlined in this chapter.

COPY PREPARATION

Design

The art and copy elements are assembled into a logical layout. This involves *design* as applied to the printed page. A pleasing design is illustrated in Fig. 6-1. In designing a printed page, the layout artist uses a set of design principles or rules. These include: (1) proportion; (2) balance; (3) harmony; (4) contrast; (5) rhythm; and (6) unity.

FIG. 6-1   A layout involves a pleasing design as applied to the printed page.

PROPORTION In design, *proportion* refers to the pleasing relationship of sizes and lengths of various parts on the printed page. First, proportion is applied to the general dimensions of the page itself. A page can be too long and narrow to be pleasing. It can be too near square to be interesting. A pleasing page shape is one in which the dimensions are about in a ratio of 2 to 3 (Fig. 6-2). Examples are 6″ × 9″ and 8″ × 12″.

When a single block of type is placed in the exact center of the printed page, the type will appear lower than it actually is. This is an optical illusion (Fig. 6-3). The area above and below the type, being equal, will lack interest. Moving the type to optical center will make the type appear balanced on the page. Optical center is a position approximately 5 units from the bottom and 3 units from the top (Fig. 6-4).

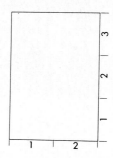

FIG. 6-2 A pleasing page shape is one in which the dimensions are in a ratio of about 2 to 3.

FIG. 6-3 A single block of type placed in the exact center of a printed page appears low.

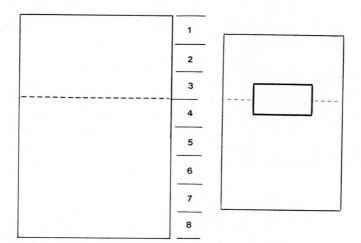

FIG. 6-4 Optical center.

FIG. 6-5 Formal balance. (Courtesy nu-Arc Company, Inc.)

FIG. 6-6 Informal balance. (Courtesy nu-Arc Company, Inc.)

FIG. 6-7 A layout that reflects harmony of elements. (Courtesy nuArc Company, Inc.)

BALANCE   There are two kinds of *balance:* formal and informal. In the case of *formal balance* (Fig. 6-5), the elements on the page are centered horizontally. An equal amount of each major unit is positioned on either side of an imaginary center line. This kind of balance gives a feeling of being strong, orderly, and dignified. *Informal balance* (Fig. 6-6) allows for elements to be placed at different positions on the page. This style is more modern than formal balance and allows for more movement in the placement of the elements.

HARMONY   The way in which a printed page is put together so that its elements do not clash with one another, or with the theme of the copy, is called *harmony* (Fig. 6-7). This includes choice of typefaces, shapes of the type elements, and the colors of ink and paper. These various elements should appear organized.

CONTRAST   In design, *contrast* (Fig. 6-8) adds interest, life, and attraction to the printed page. Contrast can be achieved by using different sizes and weights of type. Other ways of providing contrast include using a second color, underlining type, and using shaded backgrounds.

RHYTHM   The repetition of similar elements in a design creates *rhythm* (Fig. 6-9). Rhythm can be unplanned and accidental, or it can be used to add life and sparkle to a design. Rhythm can be achieved by selecting one element in a design and repeating it several times. This element might be an attention spot—for example, a dot or snowflake. Creating definite shapes in paragraph composition is another way of achieving rhythm.

UNITY   A design that combines all typographic elements and allows the reader's eyes to travel in a smooth way contains *unity* (Fig. 6-10). When all the type and illustrations in a design fit together and complement each other, unity is achieved. The elements of a design should not appear crowded. Instead, elements should have the look of belonging together.

FIG. 6-8 Design principle of contrast. (Courtesy nuArc Company, Inc.)

FIG. 6-9 Repetition of elements on a printed page creates rhythm. (Courtesy nuArc Company, Inc.)

FIG. 6-10 A design in which elements combine to allow the reader's eyes to travel in a smooth way consists of unity. (Courtesy nuArc Company, Inc.)

Layout Planning

Before a job of printing can be set in type, there must be a clear "blueprint" of its proposed style and form. The plan must show proportions, length of lines, choice of type styles, illustrations, and arrangement of the type.

THUMBNAIL SKETCHES The first step in designing a job is to make *thumbnail sketches* (Fig. 6-11). These are made small and of the same shape and proportion as the actual-size job. Several of these sketches are prepared and are done in pencil. Thumbnail sketches allow for the selection of the best of the many ideas that go into the job.

ROUGH LAYOUT The most promising thumbnail sketch is selected and then drawn as a *rough layout* (Fig. 6-12). The rough layout is usually prepared the same size as the proposed job. Space for type and position of drawings and pictures is shown on the rough layout. Since the rough layout is drawn in pencil, changes are less time-consuming.

COMPREHENSIVE LAYOUT The *comprehensive layout* (Fig. 6-13) is a detailed drawing of how the final printed product will look. It must show the styles, sizes of type, drawings, and pictures. These layouts are frequently drawn in colored pencils, felt pens, or tempera paints. In this way, the client is given a visual preview of how the printed product will appear. The comprehensive layout is the final step in planning before the actual setting of type and making of the camera-ready paste-up.

Mechanical. A *mechanical* (Fig. 6-14) is the same as a paste-up. It should not be confused with a comprehensive layout. The type is set and pictures and drawings are prepared so that all elements can be pasted up. The mechanical is also known as *camera-ready copy;* these terms mean the same and are used interchangeably.

FIG. 6-11   Thumbnail sketches. (Courtesy Hammermill Paper Co.)   FIG. 6-12   Rough layout. (Courtesy Hammermill Paper Co.)

DUMMY   A *dummy* is a set or collection of design layouts, such as a dummy for a magazine or booklet containing more than one page. The dummy serves as a visual preview of the final printed product. It shows drawings, display and body type, as well as all page numbers. Page numbers in book or magazine work are called *folios*. A dummy is useful to all production personnel because it gives a clear picture of how the job fits together. It also contains much of the technical data and instructions relating to its production.

Markup of Copy

The choice of type styles and sizes and length of lines involves *markup* (Fig. 6-15). Markup includes writing the following information on the layout: (1) size of type; (4) leading or spacing between lines; (3) name of the type style; (4) uppercase or uppercase and lowercase; and (5) width of type lines. This information is normally written as 10/12—20 picas, Spartan bold, c.&l.c.

In some instances, the layout artist who prepares the layout for a piece of printing may also specify (or "spec") the type styles and sizes. In other instances, a person in the copy preparation area is assigned the job of markup.

Other specifications that may be necessary in the markup process include: (1) amount of indentation for paragraphs; (2) whether body copy is to be set in italics or boldface; (3) typeface and size for display lines; (4) typeface and size for subheads; (5) whether

FIG. 6-13 Comprehensive layout. (Courtesy Hammermill Paper Co.)

FIG. 6-14 A mechanical is the same as a paste-up; and the terms are often used interchangeably. (Courtesy Hammermill Paper Co.)

FIG. 6-15 Markup of copy is done prior to typesetting. (Courtesy Stephen B. Simms, photographer.)

By E. Zimmerman --- 8

Film actor David Carradine (of "Kung Fu" TV fame) will star in the movie "Cloud Dancer," slated for release this month.

Set against the back drop of the American Southwest, the movie is reminiscent of a western, but instead of horses and stage coaches, the heroes ride Pitts Specials, a P-51 Mustang and a Piper Arrow.

Carradine accepted the challenge of his role in the movie and learned to fly, takng three months of flying lessons which that included aerobatics.

In "Cloud Dancer" the audience experience the same sights and sensations as the pilot and see things no man has ever seen before. This is the result of a new type camera and photographic

more

FIG. 6-16 Typewritten copy must be marked up for the printer.

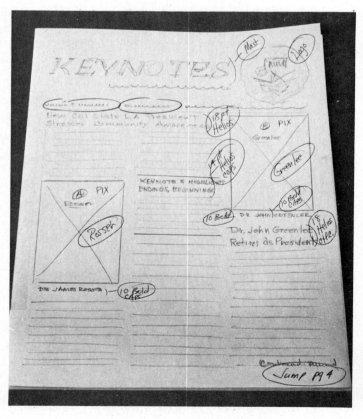

FIG. 6-17 Markup instructions are sometimes placed directly on the rough layout. (Courtesy Stephen B. Simms, photographer.)

display lines should be set flush left, flush right, or centered; and (6) whether subheads should be set flush left, flush right, or centered.

The detailed instructions covering the setting of the type from a piece of typewritten copy are marked in the margins of the copy before the type is set. Figure 6-16 illustrates how copy appears when marked up. Markup instructions can also be placed directly on the rough layout (Fig. 6-17).

ART PREPARATION

Enlargements and Reductions

Original copy of photographs or drawings can be *enlarged* or *reduced* if needed. Enlargements tend to magnify defects in the original. Reductions tend to reduce defects and in some instances improve sharpness in the original. For most purposes, the layout artist plans to reduce rather than enlarge original copy.

Enlargements and reductions are proportional. This means that if a photograph or drawing is narrow in width and long in depth, it will have these same proportions when it is reduced. A reduction will reduce the width and will also reduce the depth as illustrated in Fig. 6-18. An enlargement will increase the width and it will also increase the depth (Fig. 6-19).

FIG. 6-18   A camera reduction reduces the length and depth of artwork.

FIG. 6-19   An enlargement increases the width and depth of artwork.

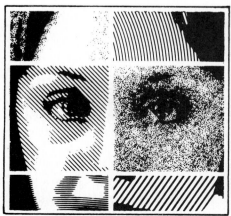

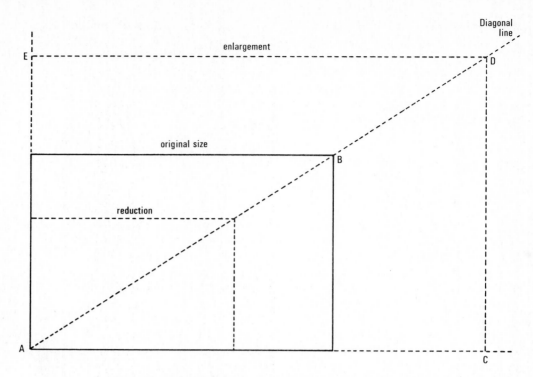

FIG. 6-20 Diagonal line method used to reduce and enlarge artwork. (Courtesy A.B. Dick Co.)

The diagonal of a rectangle or square can be used to see the final results of making an enlargement or reduction (Fig. 6-20). This is called the *diagonal line method*. The weight of a line in the drawing is decreased in a reduction and increased in an enlargement. For example, if a drawing is reduced to 50% of original size, the lines in the drawing will be thinner. Sometimes these fine lines are lost in the final printing.

When determining an enlargement or reduction of a photograph or drawing, only one of the two dimensions previously mentioned can serve for calculations. This is referred to as the *holding dimension*. If a photograph is being planned for a reduction to fit a space in a magazine column that is 20 picas wide (Fig. 6-21), the holding dimension is the width. Assume, however, that the width of the column is not the critical factor but that the depth of the photograph is. In this instance, the depth for reduction becomes the holding dimension.

Photographs and drawings should be covered with a sheet of tissue paper before writing the reproduction size. This allows for making pencil notations and protects the copy from dirt and fingerprints. The tissue is fastened to the back of the copy and folded over to cover the face of the photograph or drawing. Marks or indentations on the face of the copy are not acceptable because these will reproduce when photographed. Paper clips should never be used to attach notations to photographs. Instead, a production form is usually rubber cemented to the back of the copy (Fig. 6-22). The desired reproduction size in percentage is written on the tissue overlay. Any other needed instructions are noted on the production form.

FIG. 6-21 Holding dimension indicated on a piece of artwork. (Courtesy Formatt, Graphic Products Corp.)

```
┌─────────────────────────────────────────────────┐
│                                                 │
│   KEY _____  PAGE _____             │
│                                                 │
│   PERCENTAGE _____  LINE SHOT    ☐         │
│                                                 │
│   DROPOUT         ☐      DUOTONE      ☐         │
│                                                 │
│   SQ. HALFTONE    ☐         Heavy Color   ☐     │
│                             Heavy Black   ☐     │
│   SMALLER POS.    ☐                             │
│                          TRI TONE     ☐         │
│   Shoot Overlay   ☐                             │
│   For Color              SCREEN                 │
│                                                 │
│   FLOP            ☐         110       ☐         │
│                                                 │
│   POSTERIZE       ☐         133       ☐         │
│                                                 │
│      Step  1  2  3  4       150       ☐         │
│            ☐  ☐  ☐  ☐                           │
│            5  6  7  8  9     175       ☐         │
│            ☐  ☐  ☐  ☐  ☐                        │
│                                                 │
│                                                 │
│                                                 │
│   EXPOSURE _____  FLASH _____         │
│   In Seconds           In Seconds               │
└─────────────────────────────────────────────────┘
```

FIG. 6-22 Example of a production form used to indicate instructions required in photo department.

Another popular method of calculating enlargements and reductions is to use a *proportional scale* (Fig. 6-23). To find the percentage of enlargement or reduction, the present copy size on the "original size" scale (inside scale) is lined up opposite the desired new size on the "reproduction size" scale (outside scale). The percentage appears in the window opening.

To illustrate, assume that the original size of the photograph is 8 inches wide and 10 inches deep. The required reproduction size is 6 inches wide (the holding dimension). Line up the 8-inch mark on the original-size scale opposite the 6-inch mark on the reproduction-size scale, shown in Fig. 6-24 at (A). Next, read the percent of reproduction in the window opening on the scale (75%), shown at (B). To find the new depth of this same reduction, locate 10 inches (original depth) on the original-size scale, and read the new size that lines up on the opposite, reproduction-size scale (7½ inches), shown at (C).

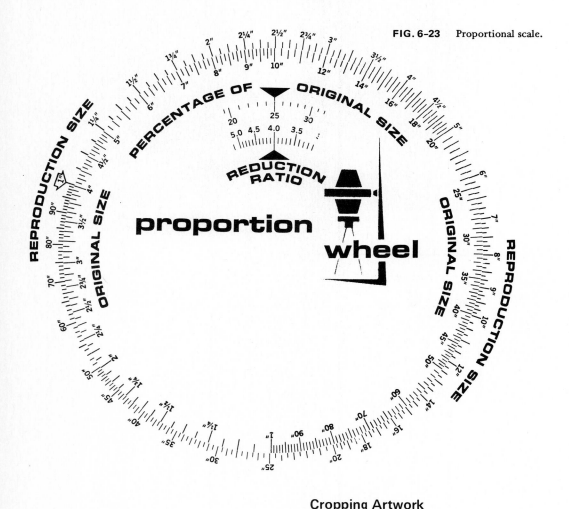

FIG. 6-23 Proportional scale.

Cropping Artwork

It is sometimes necessary or desirable to reproduce only a portion of an original photograph or illustration. This process is called *cropping* (Fig. 6-25). Creative cropping of photographs provides the layout artist an opportunity to improve the appearance of the artwork. Cropping is also done to make a piece of artwork fit the available space.

FIG. 6-24 Procedure for using a proportional scale: (A) set desired new width; (B) read percentage; and (C) read new depth in inches. (Courtesy GAF Corp.)

FIG. 6-25 Crop marks indicate only the area desired in this photograph. (Courtesy Stephen B. Simms, photographer.)

To prepare a photograph or line drawing for cropping, it may be necessary to mount it on a heavy piece of white illustration board with rubber cement to make it smooth. Cropping marks are then placed in the margins (not the image areas) with ink to show only the area to be reproduced. If it is not possible to mark in the margins, a sheet of transparent tissue paper is attached over the piece of artwork and lines are drawn to outline the part to be reproduced.

Kinds of Original Copy

There are several kinds of original copy images with which the layout and paste-up artist must be familiar. These are classified as to whether the copy is: (1) line; (2) continuous tone; or (3) combination.

LINE COPY *Line copy* (Fig. 6-26) includes type matter, pen and ink drawings, diagrams, and any artwork consisting of single tones. Line copy is photographed differently from continuous tone (halftone) copy.

of printing history. Th
of styles making easy tl

Line Copy

A WOL

Examples of reproductions from line copy. In the drawing of the apple, the artist suggested intermediate tones by random stippling with ink and brush.

FIG. 6-26   Examples of line copy. (Courtesy Eastman Kodak Co.)

FIG. 6-27   Example of continuous tone copy. (Courtesy Eastman Kodak Co.)

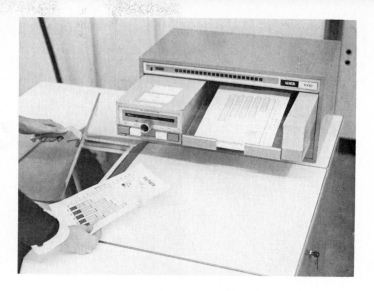

FIG. 6-28   Example of a halftone. (Courtesy Formatt, Graphic Products Corp.)

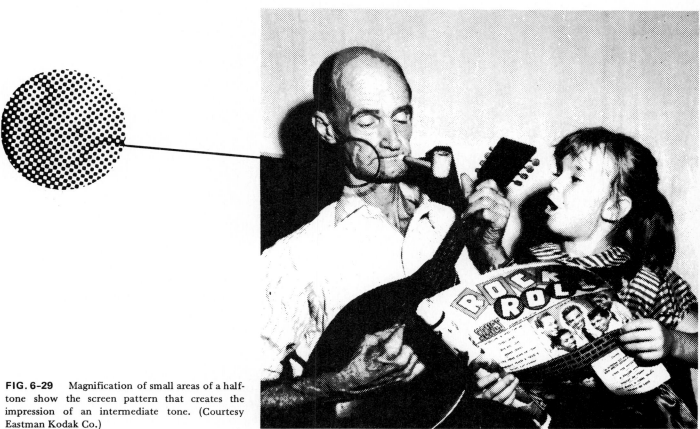

FIG. 6-29   Magnification of small areas of a halftone show the screen pattern that creates the impression of an intermediate tone. (Courtesy Eastman Kodak Co.)

CONTINUOUS TONE COPY   *Continuous tone copy* (Fig. 6-27) includes photographs, wash drawings, pencil or charcoal drawings, and airbrush renderings. This kind of copy contains intermediate tones of gray. Continuous tone images must be converted to dot pattern images called *halftones* (Fig. 6-28). This conversion produces a visual optical illusion; at normal reading distance, the small individual halftone dots appear to blend into continuous tone images because of the limitations of the human eye (Fig. 6-29). The preparation of a halftone requires a separate camera operation in which a screen is used to break the original copy into small dots of varying sizes (Fig. 6-30).

FIG. 6-30   Halftone screen is used to break the original copy into small dots of varying sizes. (Courtesy Eastman Kodak Co.)

COMBINATION COPY *Combination copy* refers to the combining of line and continuous tone copy into one printed unit (Fig. 6-31). This technique lends variety and interest to a printed page. A positive print is made of each element of copy requiring different treatment. The prints are then assembled into a single paste-up for the process camera. A single photographic negative can then be made of the completed paste-up.

FIG. 6-31 Combination copy has line and continuous tone elements combined into one printed unit.

Custom border widths can be created by cutting the border to desired size.

Special-Effects Copy

There are several materials and methods available with which to produce *special effects* (Fig. 6-32). This is the creative side of graphic arts darkroom photography. Special effects are produced to meet two general needs: (1) the reproduction of creative images from otherwise average copy; and (2) adherence to the limitations created by materials and equipment in order to produce effective and economical printing.

Line conversions, duotones, posterization, masking film, and screen tints are but a few of the special photographic techniques used. More information and procedures on these and other techniques can be obtained by contacting local graphic arts supply firms.

LINE CONVERSIONS The most common technique of making a halftone negative is to use a halftone contact screen. In addition, special-effect halftone screens can be used to convert continuous tone copy to *line conversions*. These special screens are used to create a variety of unusual effects. Among these are mezzotint, steel engraving, circular, wavyline, and vertical straightline (Fig. 6-33).

The layout artist can create unusual designs with special effect screened copy. The original copy is usually prepared on photoprint paper and attached directly to the paste-up. Figures 6-34 through 6-37 illustrate this technique.

FIG. 6-32 Special effects is the creative side of darkroom photography.

ROUND DOT (100)   SQUARE DOT (100)   ELLIPTICAL DOT (100)   MEZZOTINT (75)

STRAIGHT LINE (62)   SUNBURST (100)   MEZZOTINT (150)

STEEL ENGRAVING (50)   WAVY LINE (60)   CONCENTRIC CIRCLE (60)   STEEL ETCH (50)

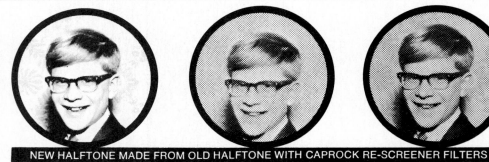

LINEN (50)

NEW HALFTONE MADE FROM OLD HALFTONE WITH CAPROCK RE-SCREENER FILTERS

Original 100 Line Halftone

(Made from Continuous Tone)

100 Line Halftone Re-Screened
With 60 Line Screen

(Made from 60 Line Halftone)

60 Line Halftone Not Re-Screened

(Made from Continuous Tone)

FIG. 6-33   Special effects such as those illustrated here are normally produced by using special halftone screens. (Courtesy Caprock Developments, Inc.)

FIG. 6-34 Ordinary continuous tone copy can be converted to special effects. (Courtesy Formatt, Graphic Products Corp.)

FIG. 6-35 A piece of special-effect, adhesive-screen material is positioned over the continuous tone copy. (Courtesy Formatt, Graphic Products Corp.)

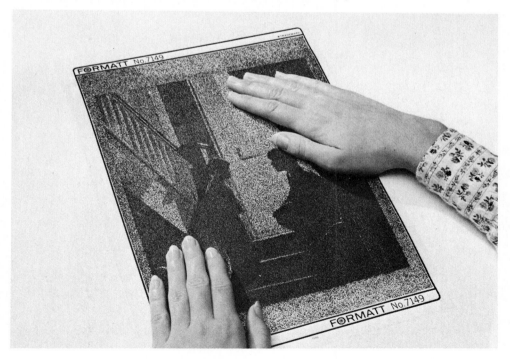

DUOTONES In contrast to simple color printing is the *duotone*. The term duotone means the use of two layers of tones to produce one final image. In this technique a black-and-white photograph containing good contrast is converted into an illustration of depth and beauty. Duotones involve the use of two halftones called *printers*.

FIG. 6-36 The screen material is trimmed to fit desired areas of the copy. (Courtesy Formatt, Graphic Products Corp.)

FIG. 6-37 Result of screen effect gives totally new look to otherwise ordinary continuous tone copy. (Courtesy Formatt, Graphic Products Corp.)

The two negatives are made to different specifications—one for highlights and one for shadow detail. Highlights are the lightest areas of the photograph and shadows are the darkest areas.

The duotone color combination is important. Most duotones are reproduced by using black or some other dark color ink and a light color ink. A two-color duotone will attract more attention than a single-color halftone. The entire printed piece must reflect the mood that the duotone is attempting to achieve.

POSTERIZATION The different tones of a black-and-white photograph can be converted to a *posterization* (Fig. 6–38). The different tones of the original are reproduced as line negatives. Posterizations are classified according to the number of colors and the number of different tones reproduced on the final press sheet. Only the number of different ink colors is counted. One negative is required for each tonal color.

Posterizations are prepared by increasing the exposure approximately three times the normal time of a line copy exposure. A second color may be added to the print by making a negative with the exposure reduced by approximately one-half. This records the middle tones of the original copy and adds detail to the print. Middle tones are in between highlight and shadow tones. More colors may be added to record the highlight areas of the original. However, for each color it is necessary to prepare a negative.

The layout artist can create interesting and pleasing reproductions by using the posterization technique. The original copy for this application must be contrasty. In addition, the copy selected must also be in keeping with the theme of the printed product.

FIG. 6–38 Posterization is a special-effect technique. (Courtesy A.B. Dick Co.)

MASKING FILM A number of red "light-safe" stripping materials called *masking films* are available to the paste-up artist. These materials photograph as if they were black images. Masking films have a coated emulsion on a polyester backing sheet. A sharp X-acto® knife is used to cut the film. A special adhesive between the emulsion and polyester allows unwanted areas to be removed from the backing by peeling away (Fig. 6-39).

Although the examples in Figs. 6-40 through 6-42 are in one color, masking films can be used to make manual color separations. As an example, the bird in Figs. 6-43 and 6-44 could be printed in a separate color to add interest.

Masking film is also useful when combining line and halftone elements (Fig. 6-45). The line work (solid lines such as type) and halftones (photographs that have a dot formation) must be made separately. The halftone negative is attached to the underside of the line negative in the "window opening" created by the masking film on the paste-up.

SCREEN TINTS Materials called *screen tints* are used by the paste-up artist to provide emphasis and special effects to certain parts of the layout. Screen tints differ from regular halftone screens in that there is no tonal variation within an area. Tints are designated in percentage, with 0% representing white and 100% representing solid black. The range from 0% to 100% is usually in multiples of 10

FIG. 6-39 Unwanted areas of masking film are removed by peeling away.

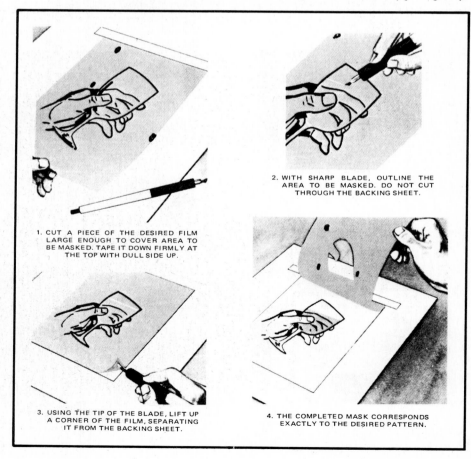

1. CUT A PIECE OF THE DESIRED FILM LARGE ENOUGH TO COVER AREA TO BE MASKED. TAPE IT DOWN FIRMLY AT THE TOP WITH DULL SIDE UP.

2. WITH SHARP BLADE, OUTLINE THE AREA TO BE MASKED. DO NOT CUT THROUGH THE BACKING SHEET.

3. USING THE TIP OF THE BLADE, LIFT UP A CORNER OF THE FILM, SEPARATING IT FROM THE BACKING SHEET.

4. THE COMPLETED MASK CORRESPONDS EXACTLY TO THE DESIRED PATTERN.

FIG. 6–40 Preparing copy on the paste-up base for two-color job. (Courtesy Dynamic Graphics, Inc.)

FIG. 6–41 Adding masking film and register marks for a second color. (Courtesy Dynamic Graphics, Inc.)

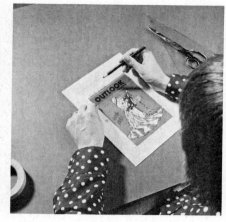

FIG. 6–42 Indicating percentage size desired for a second color. (Courtesy Dynamic Graphics, Inc.)

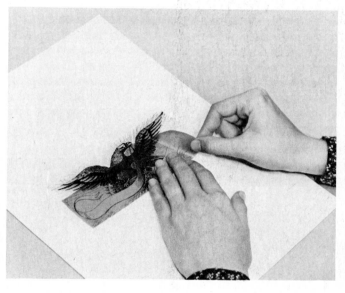

FIG. 6–43 Preparing single piece of artwork for a second color. (Courtesy Chartpak® Inc.)

FIG. 6–44 Masking film is trimmed to conform to area of a second color. (Courtesy Chartpak® Inc.)

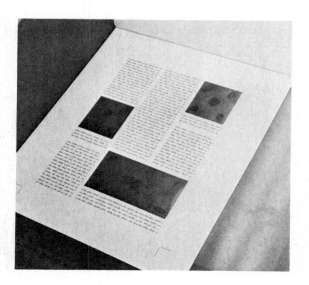

FIG. 6–45 Using masking film on the paste-up to create window opening for a halftone. (Courtesy Stephen B. Simms, photographer.)

150 LINE	5		10	10	15	15	20	20	25	25	30	30	40	40	50	50	60	60	70	70	80	80		90
133 LINE	5		10	10	15	15	20	20	25	25	30	30	40	40	50	50	60	60	70	70	80	80		90
120 LINE	5		10	10	15	15	20	20	25	25	30	30	40	40	50	50	60	60	70	70	80	80		90
110 LINE	5		10		15	15	20	20	25	25	30	30	40	40	50	50	60	60	70	70	60	80		90
100 LINE	5		10	10	15	15	20	20	25	25	30	30	40	40	50	50	60	60	70	70	80	80		90
85 LINE	5		10	10	15	15	20	20	25	25	30	30	40	40	50	50	60	60	70	70	80	80		90
65 LINE	5		10		15		20		25		30	30	40	40	50	50	60	60	70	70	80	80		90

ByCHROME PERCENTAGE-CALIBRATED SCREEN TINTS (Stable base)

FIG. 6-46 Screen tints are used for special effects. Tints are designated in percentage. The camera department prepares the tint through the use of a screen similar to that of a halftone screen. (Courtesy ByChrome Co.)

FIG. 6-47 Screen tints are used by the paste-up artist to add emphasis and special effects. (Courtesy Letraset USA, Inc.)

(Fig. 6-46). In addition, conventional-dot screen tints are designated by the number of screen rulings per linear inch. These range from 65-line to 150-line. When artwork and type are screened, the printed result is a pattern of dots (Fig. 6-47).

There are two basic methods used to provide screen tints on copy. These include: (1) film positives prepared by the photo department; and (2) adhesive shading materials applied directly to the paste-up copy elements.

Film Positive Method. Screen tints are generally prepared by inserting a screen between a negative or positive and the offset plate. A positive is the opposite of a negative. The image on a positive is opaque on a transparent background. On a negative the image is transparent on an opaque background.

HINTS FOR USE OF FILM POSITIVE SCREEN TINTS

The following should be kept in mind when using screen tints prepared by the photo department:

• When using positive copy, background tints should be light enough to keep the copy legible.

• When using reverse copy, the background tint should be dark enough to carry the copy.

• Screen tints tend to print 5% to 10% darker than specified.

• Screen tints are difficult to butt together because the variation in angle produces a ragged edge. A black line can be used to separate adjacent screen patterns.

• It is not advisable to superimpose one screen on another. The result is usually a moiré pattern—an objectionable wavering pattern that lacks tonal uniformity.

• Tint screens should not be used behind type that is less than 8 points in size. The dots tend to obliterate the letter structures of type that is extremely small.

In making an offset printing plate requiring a screen tint, the screen is placed between the negative or positive and the plate before exposure. In most instances, a positive screen tint film is used in which the dots are black. If the desired tint is to be 70%, a 30% positive tint screen film is used. If the desired tint is to be 30%, a 70% positive tint screen film is used. These film tints are taped or otherwise positioned behind the designated copy areas of the master film negative or positive.

It is important that each area of the paste-up that is to receive screen tint be carefully marked with the desired percentage of tint and color of ink. This is done in blue pencil on a tissue overlay or, if possible, on the art itself.

Adhesive Shading Method. Screen tints can also be applied directly on the paste-up with shading materials. These designs are printed on adhesive-backed transparent material mounted on a paper base (Figs. 6–48 and 6–49). They are available in a variety of

FIG. 6–48 Applying adhesive screen-tint material directly to the paste-up. (Courtesy Formatt, Graphic Products Corp.)

FIG. 6–49 Screen-tint material is easily cut along edges to conform to the image outline. (Courtesy Formatt, Graphic Products Corp.)

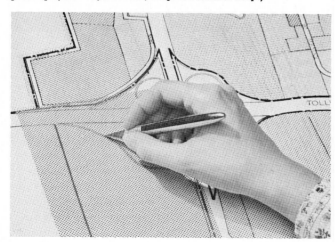

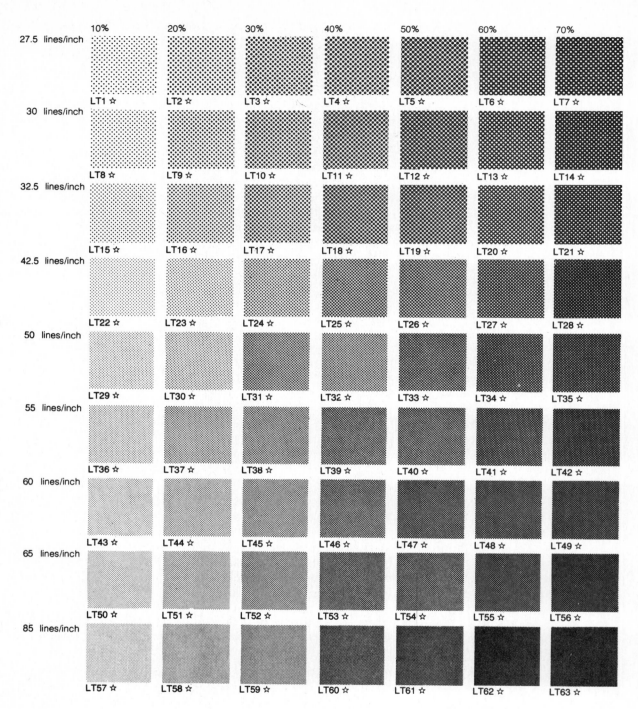

FIG. 6-50 Adhesive shading material is available in various patterns and screen densities. (Courtesy Letraset USA, Inc.)

patterns and screen densities (Fig. 6-50). A light tint might be 10% and a dark tint (almost solid) 90%. For offset lithography, screens ranging from 65 to 100 lines produce good reproductions without loss of dot detail. Screen rulings over 100 lines are difficult to photograph because of the smaller dots.

In using screen tints directly on the paste-up, the screen tint film is placed over the artwork. It is then cut to the desired shape (Fig. 6-51) and secured by burnishing with a small hand-held tool (Figs. 6-52 and 6-53). Screen tint material is most commonly applied to

HINTS FOR USE OF ADHESIVE SCREEN TINTS

The following procedures are recommended when attaching screen tint film to the paste-up:

- Carefully inspect all screen tint film sheets for imperfections prior to use.
- Check to see that there are no pencil lines or dirt under the screen tint film. The adhesive backing of the film attracts dirt easily.
- Do not attach screen tint film over cut edges of artwork or type. When burnished, the edges distort the pattern and are picked up by the camera.
- With the exception of single-line patterns, screen tint films cannot be effectively applied on top of each other. The result is a moiré pattern.
- If a camera reduction in the paste-up size is planned, make sure that the screen tint dot sizes will accommodate the reduction without filling in, causing loss of dot.

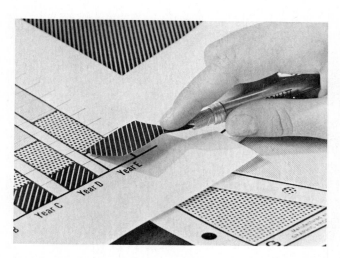

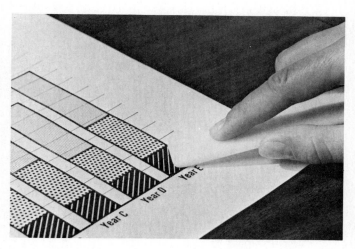

FIG. 6–51 (*Above*)   Adhesive shading is applied to the desired area of the paste-up. (Courtesy Formatt, Graphic Products Corp.)

FIG. 6–52 (*Above, right*)   After positioning the adhesive material, it is burnished tightly to the paste-up base. (Courtesy Formatt, Graphic Products Corp.)

FIG. 6–53   Adhesive shading material is easy to use and adds dramatically to finished design of product. (Courtesy Formatt, Graphic Products Corp.)

line illustrations and outline type. By using adhesive shading materials, the paste-up can be presented for approval in the exact form in which it will appear when printed. A sharp X-acto® knife is used to cut around the desired image or letter area. The knife should not penetrate the protective backing sheet. When cutting is complete, the X-acto® knife is used to lift the tint cutout from the backing.

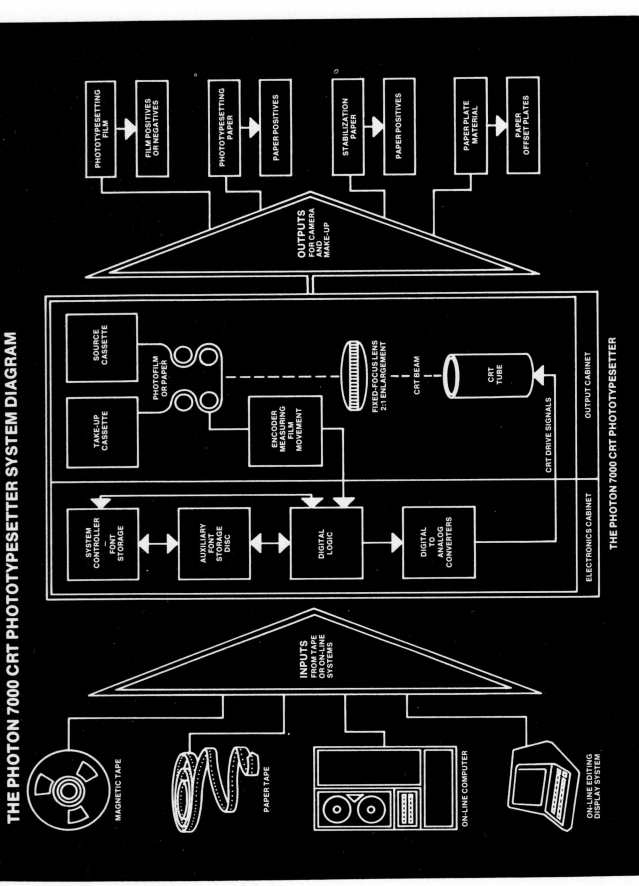

FIG. 6-54 Reverse print. (Courtesy Photon, Inc.)

The tint is positioned directly on the art and burnished lightly. Any unwanted tint is trimmed off and the material is burnished firmly.

A *reversal* has the same characteristics as any other kind of line copy. The difference between conventional line copy and reversal line copy is that selected areas are reproduced in white instead of black (when printing black ink on white paper). In a reversal print (Fig. 6-54), the reversed image area becomes the color of the paper on which the job is printed.

A common method used to prepare reversal copy is the overlay technique. The type is composed and pasted up in the desired position over the base element on an acetate overlay. It is necessary to include register marks on both the illustration board and the overlay to ensure accurate alignment during the photography process.

The overlay copy is then photographed to produce a line negative. The base element (in this example a line drawing) is reproduced as a line negative. The negative containing the type matter and the negative containing the line drawing are used to prepare an offset plate. The line drawing negative is placed over the unexposed offset plate and exposed. The negative containing the type is then placed over the same plate, aligned per the register marks, and a second exposure is made, thus creating a reversal effect.

SURPRINTING Printing a solid image over a lighter background is called *surprinting* (Fig. 6-55). Surprints are frequently combined with photographs to achieve special effects. A surprint is most effective when combined with a light background. A surprint usually consists of one or more lines of type matter. The type is composed and pasted up in the desired position over the base elements on the acetate overlay. The overlay is photographed to produce a line negative. A film positive is made from the negative. The base element (either a photograph or screen tint) is photographed. The positive

FIG. 6-55 Surprint is a solid image over a lighter background area of the copy. (Courtesy Formatt, Graphic Products Corp.)

containing the type matter and the negative containing the halftone or screen tint are combined and used to prepare an offset plate. A single exposure is made in the case of a reverse. The plate is then processed in the usual manner.

Photomechanical Transfer (PMT)

Kodak *Photomechanical Transfer* (PMT) materials are intended for use in simplifying production methods of paste-up and for making proofs. They are designed to produce photographic positive copies with a process camera. The resulting paper positives are suitable for preparing paste-ups, camera proofs, resized typography, halftones, and reverses.

With the use of PMT, each element of a reproduction that requires a different reduction or enlargement can be reproduced in the form and size required. The process is suitable for combining line work with halftones and makes it possible to assemble a single paste-up for making either a negative or a positive.

The Kodak PMT system consists of a negative and receiver paper. The photo negative paper is used for making same-size, enlarged, or reduced copy in a process camera. Receiver paper is used in conjunction with photo negative paper. After the light-sensitive negative paper has been exposed (Fig. 6–56), it is processed with a piece of receiver paper (Fig. 6–57), producing a right-reading print that is ready for use (Fig. 6–58). The processing is quickly and automatically done in a diffusion transfer processor using a solution of activator.

FIG. 6-56 Photo Mechanical Transfer (PMT) negative paper is exposed to the desired copy. (Courtesy Eastman Kodak Co.)

FIG. 6-57 Exposed negative paper and receiver paper are processed automatically. (Courtesy Eastman Kodak Co.)

FIG. 6-58 Right-reading PMT print is ready for paste-up or further camera application. (Courtesy Eastman Kodak Co.)

chapter **7**

PASTE-UP FOR PROCESS PHOTOGRAPHY

After the layout has been approved, a paste-up is prepared. The paste-up assembly includes all the type and illustrative elements of the layout. These elements are pasted on a sheet of illustration board. The entire assembly is then photographed on a graphic arts process camera. The result is a film negative or positive suitable for making a printing press plate.

The paste-up process involves assembly of various copy elements once the design layout has been completed. The copy elements used in paste-up are prepared for the single purpose of being reproduced (photographed) very precisely on a graphic arts process camera. In most cases, paste-ups are prepared for the photo-offset lithography printing process. All kinds of printed matter are prepared as paste-ups, including magazines, newspapers, brochures, letterheads, and business forms.

The final printed product will only be as good as the accuracy and quality of the paste-up. Cleanliness and sharp paste-up copy elements are most desirable. Good conditions for the mechanics of photo-offset printing will ensure quality results for the client.

The best way to become proficient at doing paste-ups is to do some. In this way, you can see the various steps involved and understand the reasons for them. As you study this chapter, you should follow through with the preparation of a simple paste-up that combines type with screened photoprints (also called Veloxes). In addition, a number of paste-up assignments are provided at the end of the book.

TOOLS FOR PASTE-UP

In preparing a paste-up, several kinds of small tools are necessary. Figure 7–1 illustrates many of the basic tools needed to perform the tasks involved in paste-up. Among these are such items as the following:

1. Light table, drawing table, or drawing board
2. T-square
3. Triangles (45° and 30°–60°)
4. Measuring scale, line gauge
5. Curves, irregular and French
6. Compass
7. Dividers
8. Ruling pen or technical drawing pen
9. Opaquing brushes
10. Nonreproducing light-blue pencil or pen
11. X-acto® knife
12. Scissors
13. Burnishing tool
14. Proportional scale
15. Magnifier
16. Percentage screen tint guide
17. Black drawing ink
18. Opaque white-out fluid

Depending on local conditions, there are many other tools and materials that may be required for paste-up. For purposes of this chapter, only the most common tools are needed.

FIG. 7–1 Basic tools including work surface are necessary in the preparation of paste-ups. (Courtesy Agfa-Gavaert, Inc., Graphic Systems Div.)

BEGINNING THE PASTE-UP

A light table, drawing table, or drawing board is needed as a work surface. The *working edge* (left side as you sit at the table) must be straight. Some table tops and most light tables are supplied with a steel insert on the working edge. This ensures a better wearing surface.

Base Material

As a *base material* for the paste-up, hot-press illustration art board that has a smooth white surface is recommended. In some instances, a lighter weight material, such as 110-pound index bristol, may be used. However, the surface of index bristol separates easily when copy elements must be repositioned for any reason. The board should be cut approximately 3 inches to 4 inches larger on all four sides than the finished size of the printed piece being pasted up (Fig. 7-2).

To start a paste-up, the top edge of the paste-up base material should be aligned with a T-square. The top edge must be aligned horizontally with the top edge of a T-square. After the illustration board has been aligned, it should be held down and taped to the drawing surface with masking tape at all four corners (Fig. 7-3).

Guidelines

The next step in paste-up is to draw *guidelines* with a light-blue nonreproducing pencil or pen. Light-blue pencils or pens are used to make guidelines and notes on the illustration board. The reason for using blue is that with the usual kind of photographic film used in the process camera blue is photographed as though it were white, and thus the guidelines and notes do not require erasing. These lines should include *vertical center* and *horizontal* lines, as well as *finish size* and *image area* lines (Fig. 7-4). Light-blue nonreproducing lines should be drawn to the size of the elements to be pasted down. These lines help to align material along the margins. Thin black *crop marks*

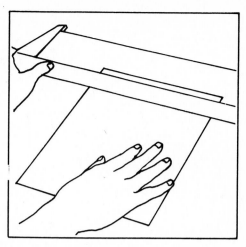

FIG. 7-2 Illustration board must be larger on all four sides than finished size of paste-up copy.

FIG. 7-3 Illustration board is fastened to the drawing surface with masking tape at all four corners.

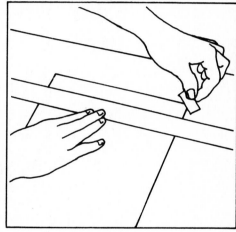

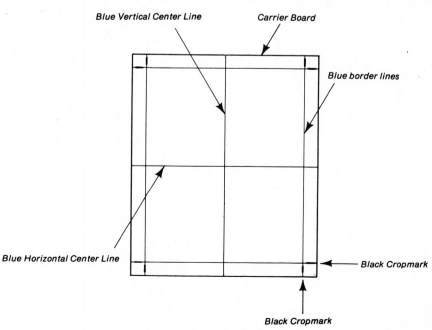

Blue Vertical Center Line   Carrier Board

Blue border lines

Blue Horizontal Center Line

Black Cropmark

Black Cropmark

FIG. 7-4 Nonreproducing light blue pencil or pen is used to indicate guidelines on the paste-up.

The NEW in SHOES

For Spring or Summer

Spring really starts from the ground up—as any flower could tell you. And YOUR new spring look starts with the lovely new patents, butter-soft calf creations, suede and fabric dreams to be found here.

Deliciously supple and pliant calf. Touched with a band of classic incised ornament that reveals its beauty more fully.

$21.50

Here's a gloriously simple classic pattern with a line Hogarth would envy The little tie is an irresistable touch.

$17

The soft, lustrous sheen of this sandal with its dainty lines makes beautiful the foot of any woman lucky enough to wear it.

$19.75

Shown at the shoe salon of

JCPenney

1000 W. Main Street

FIG. 7-5 Crop marks are drawn in black ink ½-inch long to indicate finish size.

ruled about ½–inch long at right angles in the corners should be used to show finish size (Fig. 7–5).

When an image area of the paste-up is planned to extend off the edge(s) of the final printed page, *bleed* is involved (Fig. 7–6). Bleed is designed to eliminate white spaces between the printing and the trimmed edges of the printed job. It is not necessary to bleed on all four sides of the page. If one side of a printed page is to be bound or folded, it is not necessary to indicate bleed. Normal bleed allowance is from ⅛ inch to ¼ inch.

FIG. 7–6 Image areas that are planned to extend off the edge(s) of the final printed page are referred to as bleed. Normal bleed allowance is ⅛–¼ inch.

Copy Elements

Type for the paste-up may come in the form of a *reproduction proof*. This is a high-quality print made from hand-set or machine-set metal type. In the majority of cases, however, cold-type composition is provided. This will usually be in the form of *photocomposition*.

Preprinted transfer lettering, borders, and ornaments (designs) can be used for some kinds of work (Figs. 7–7 and 7–8). These materials are either of the rub-off variety (Fig. 7–9) or adhesive (Fig. 7–10).

FIG. 7–7 Preprinted transfer lettering. (Courtesy Formatt, Graphic Products Corp.)

FIG. 7–8 Preprinted transfer borders and ornaments. (Courtesy The C-Thru Ruler Co.)

FIG. 7-9 Transfer letters of the rub-off variety. (Courtesy The C-Thru Ruler Co.)

FIG. 7-10 Adhesive transfer lettering contains a backing that sticks to the paste-up base. (Courtesy The C-Thru Ruler Co.)

Rub-off letters are easily applied to the paste-up by first locating the exact position for the letter and then placing the transfer lettering sheet in position over the spot. A special burnishing tool is used to rub the letter onto the paste-up (Fig. 7-11). The sheet is then lifted and moved into position for the next letter (Fig. 7-12).

Adhesive letters are handled differently from rub-off letters. The desired adhesive letter is cut from the lettering sheet and then positioned on the paste-up along a predrawn light-blue line. A special tool is available that can be used to position individual letters accurately, thus making letterspacing and wordspacing easier. The procedure for positioning, aligning, and burnishing letters on a paste-up is illustrated in Figs. 7-13 through 7-15.

FIG. 7-11 Burnishing tool used to rub lettering onto the paste-up base for tight bond. (Courtesy Chartpak® Inc.)

FIG. 7-12 Using rub-off transfer lettering requires perfect alignment and letter fit. (Courtesy Chartpak® Inc.)

FIG. 7-13 (*Above*)   Positioning an adhesive letter on the paste-up base. (Courtesy Formatt, Graphic Products Corp.)

FIG. 7-14 (*Above, right*)   Aligning an adhesive letter on the paste-up base. (Courtesy Formatt, Graphic Products Corp.)

FIG. 7-15   Burnishing an adhesive letter on the paste-up base. (Courtesy Formatt, Graphic Products Corp.)

Many different kinds of borders are available [Figs. 7-16 and 7-17(A) and (B)], which are easily applied to the paste-up by hand or with the aid of a special applicator (Fig. 7-18). Borders are cut to the desired length with an X-acto® knife. The technique used to miter (square) a corner using border material is illustrated in Figs. 7-19 through 7-21.

Ornaments of various designs are normally available in adhesive form. These materials are applied directly to the paste-up in much the same way as border material (Figs. 7-22 through 7-24).

In working with transfer materials, the layout artist normally indicates the exact position on the paste-up by drawing light-blue guidelines. These act as a reference mark for the actual application of the images.

Illustrations can be drawn directly on the paste-up base. They can also be drawn on another material and then attached to the main paste-up base. Sometimes it is necessary to enlarge or reduce illustrations to fit the proportions of the job layout. In this case, a *photoprint* is prepared.

All *continuous tone* copy must be photographed separately from line copy because continuous tone copy must be separated into a series of fine dots of various sizes. The result is a tonal effect resembling the original continuous tone copy. Because of this, original photographs are not placed directly on the paste-up base. Three methods commonly used to locate photographs on the paste-up

RULES AND BORDERS

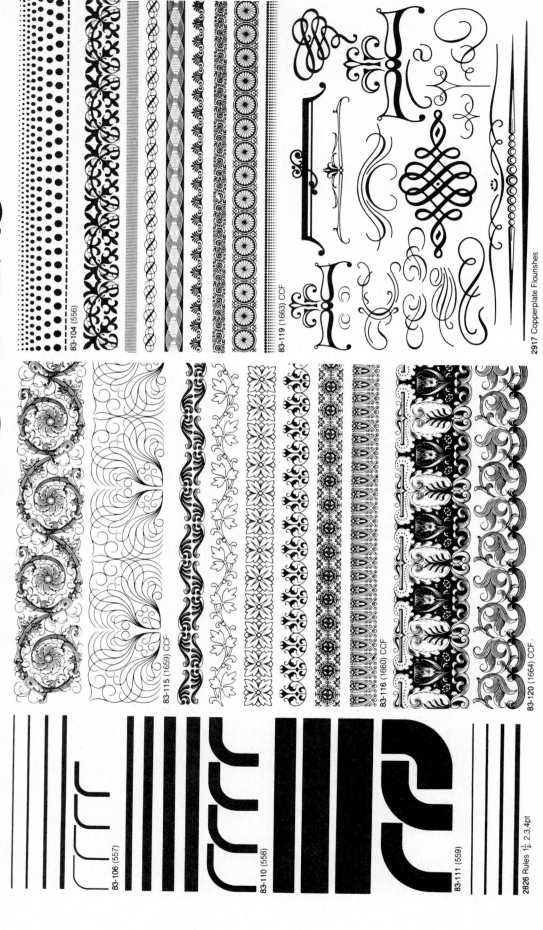

83-104 (556)

83-119 (1663) CCF

2917 Copperplate Flourishes

83-106 (557)

83-110 (558)

83-111 (559)

2826 Rules 1½, 2, 3, 4pt

83-115 (1659) CCF

83-116 (1660) CCF

83-120 (1664) CCF.

FIG. 7-16 Rules and borders are available in a variety of designs. (Courtesy Letraset USA, Inc.)

100

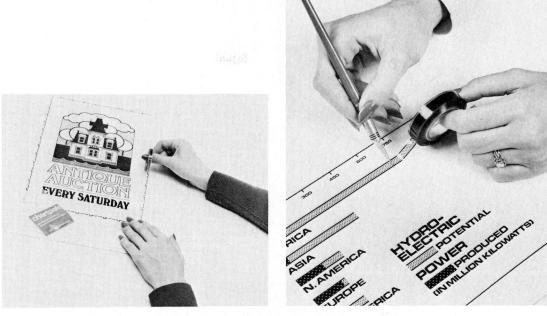

FIG. 7-17   Border can be applied to the paste-up by hand. (Courtesy Chartpak® Inc.)

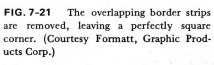

FIG. 7-18   Borders can be applied to the paste-up using a special applicator. (Courtesy Chartpak® Inc.)

FIG. 7-19   To miter (square) an adhesive border corner, the strips are positioned along a light blue guideline and allowed to overlap about 1 inch at the corners. (Courtesy Formatt, Graphic Products Corp.)

FIG. 7-20   A straight edge is used to cut a 45-degree angle through both border pieces. (Courtesy Formatt, Graphic Products Corp.)

FIG. 7-21   The overlapping border strips are removed, leaving a perfectly square corner. (Courtesy Formatt, Graphic Products Corp.)

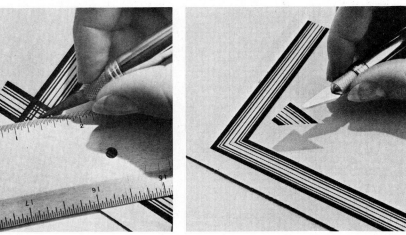

FIG. 7-22 The desired adhesive border material is removed from the border carrier sheet with an X-acto® knife. (Courtesy Formatt, Graphic Products Corp.)

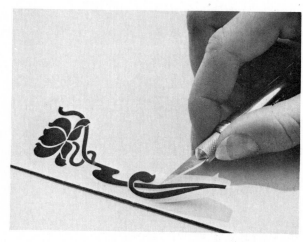

FIG. 7-23 Border elements are carefully positioned on the paste-up base. (Courtesy Formatt, Graphic Products Corp.)

FIG. 7-24 Several border elements can be used to create attractive design formations. (Courtesy Formatt, Graphic Products Corp.)

base include: (1) outline; (2) block; and (3) screened print or Velox (halftone print).

OUTLINE METHOD   In using the *halftone outline* method, the location of the photograph is marked on the paste-up by four thin black or red lines (Fig. 7-25). Separate negatives are made of the paste-up and continuous tone copy. When the two negatives are prepared, a window opening is cut into the paste-up line negative where

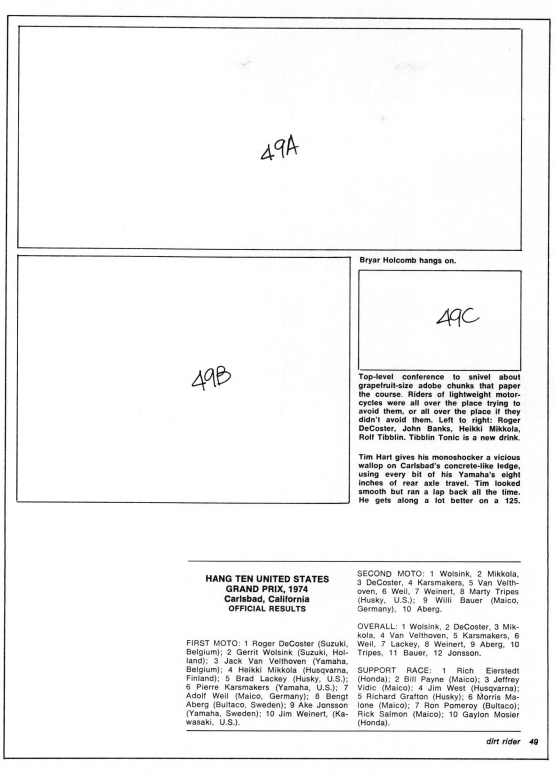

Bryar Holcomb hangs on.

Top-level conference to snivel about grapefruit-size adobe chunks that paper the course. Riders of lightweight motorcycles were all over the place trying to avoid them, or all over the place if they didn't avoid them. Left to right: Roger DeCoster, John Banks, Heikki Mikkola, Rolf Tibblin. Tibblin Tonic is a new drink.

Tim Hart gives his monoshocker a vicious wallop on Carlsbad's concrete-like ledge, using every bit of his Yamaha's eight inches of rear axle travel. Tim looked smooth but ran a lap back all the time. He gets along a lot better on a 125.

**HANG TEN UNITED STATES GRAND PRIX, 1974
Carlsbad, California
OFFICIAL RESULTS**

FIRST MOTO: 1 Roger DeCoster (Suzuki, Belgium); 2 Gerrit Wolsink (Suzuki, Holland); 3 Jack Van Velthoven (Yamaha, Belgium); 4 Heikki Mikkola (Husqvarna, Finland); 5 Brad Lackey (Husky, U.S.); 6 Pierre Karsmakers (Yamaha, U.S.); 7 Adolf Weil (Maico, Germany); 8 Bengt Aberg (Bultaco, Sweden); 9 Ake Jonsson (Yamaha, Sweden); 10 Jim Weinert, (Kawasaki, U.S.).

SECOND MOTO: 1 Wolsink, 2 Mikkola, 3 DeCoster, 4 Karsmakers, 5 Van Velthoven, 6 Weil, 7 Weinert, 8 Marty Tripes (Husky, U.S.); 9 Willi Bauer (Maico, Germany), 10 Aberg.

OVERALL: 1 Wolsink, 2 DeCoster, 3 Mikkola, 4 Van Velthoven, 5 Karsmakers, 6 Weil, 7 Lackey, 8 Weinert, 9 Aberg, 10 Tripes, 11 Bauer, 12 Jonsson.

SUPPORT RACE: 1 Rich Eierstedt (Honda); 2 Bill Payne (Maico); 3 Jeffrey Vidic (Maico); 4 Jim West (Husqvarna); 5 Richard Grafton (Husky); 6 Morris Malone (Maico); 7 Ron Pomeroy (Bultaco); Rick Salmon (Maico); 10 Gaylon Mosier (Honda).

dirt rider **49**

FIG. 7–25 In using the halftone outline method, thin black or red lines are drawn on the paste-up base to indicate the halftone position. (Courtesy *Dirt Rider* Magazine.)

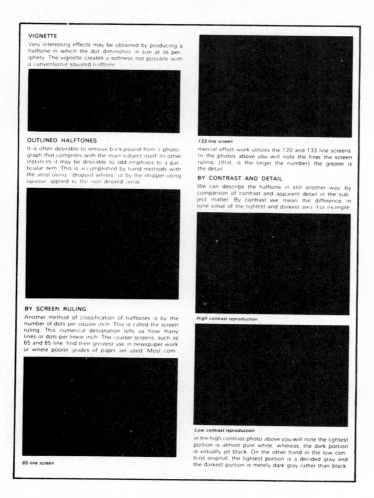

VIGNETTE

Very interesting effects may be obtained by producing a halftone in which the dot diminishes in size at its periphery. The vignette creates a softness not possible with a conventional squared halftone.

OUTLINED HALFTONES

It is often desirable to remove background from a photograph that competes with the main subject itself. In other instances it may be desirable to add emphasis to a particular item. This is accomplished by hand methods with the artist using "dropout whites" or by the stripper using opaque applied to the non desired areas.

BY SCREEN RULING

Another method of classification of halftones is by the number of dots per square inch. This is called the screen ruling. This numerical designation tells us how many lines or dots per linear inch. The coarser screens, such as 65 and 85 line, find their greatest use in newspaper work or where poorer grades of paper are used. Most com-

65 line screen

133 line screen

mercial offset work utilizes the 120 and 133 line screens. In the photos above you will note the finer the screen ruling, (that, is the larger the number) the greater is the detail.

BY CONTRAST AND DETAIL

We can describe the halftone in still another way, by comparison of contrast and apparent detail in the subject matter. By contrast we mean the difference in tone value of the lightest and darkest area. For example,

High contrast reproduction

Low contrast reproduction

in the high contrast photo above you will note the lightest portion is almost pure white, whereas, the dark portion is virtually jet black. On the other hand in the low contrast original, the lightest portion is a decided gray and the darkest portion is merely dark gray rather than black.

FIG. 7–26 In using the halftone block method, black paper or red masking film is cut to desired size of the reproduction and adhered with rubber cement to paste-up base.

the lines were drawn. The halftone negative is then taped behind the window on the line negative.

BLOCK METHOD Black paper or red masking film is used in the *halftone block* method. It is cut to the desired size of the reproduction and adhered with rubber cement to the paste-up base (Fig. 7–26). The masking film is cut in proportion to the final desired size of the continuous tone copy. As in the outline method, separate negatives are made of the paste-up and continuous tone copy. The black paper or red masking film becomes an "open window" in the negative when photographed and processed. The halftone negative of the continuous tone copy is then taped behind the clear window opening of the paste-up line negative.

SCREENED PRINT METHOD OR VELOX* This method, also called the *halftone print* method, starts with the preparation of a halftone negative from the original continuous tone copy. A photographic contact print is then made from the halftone negative. The screened print or Velox is pasted directly on the paste-up base. The entire paste-up is photographed as line copy because the screened print is made up of dots and the film will record them. Veloxes or screened

---

*Eastman Kodak's trademark.

prints of finer than 120-line should not be used because the fine dots will be lost in the final preparation of the line negative.

The major disadvantage of the screened print method is that halftone quality is reduced because of the two extra steps involved. In preparing a conventional halftone, the procedure is to go from continuous tone copy to a halftone negative. In preparing screened prints, the procedure is to go from continuous tone copy to a halftone negative to a screened print and then back to a line negative of the already screened copy. A slight amount of quality is lost at each step in the screened print process.

A much faster process of preparing a halftone print uses Kodak Photomechanical Transfer (PMT). This one-step procedure involves preparing a halftone print that can be used directly on the paste-up base. An 85- to 100-line PMT halftone screen is generally used. Processing is exactly the same as for line PMT work.

Rescreening a Halftone

Sometimes it is necessary to rephotograph an already printed halftone. This process is called *rescreening*. Rescreening may be necessary if a printed halftone has an indistinct screen pattern, if a screen pattern is too fine, or if a large reduction in size is required.

The closer the printed piece is to the original, the better the quality will be. When a halftone must be rephotographed from a newspaper or magazine, a screen having a ruling either 50 lines finer or 50 lines coarser than the screening on the original (at its new size) should be used. When rescreening, the copy or screen should be angled so that the result is exactly 30° more than the original angle. This angle must be accurate to minimize the possibility of producing a disturbing pattern on the negative, which is called *moiré* (Fig. 7-27).

The final reproduction of a rephotographed printed halftone is often slightly inferior to that obtained by the other methods just described.

FIG. 7-27 A moiré pattern results from improper screen angle when rescreening a halftone print. (Courtesy Eastman Kodak Co.)

ATTACHING COPY ELEMENTS

There are two basic methods of attaching type elements and illustrations to the paste-up base. These include: (1) waxing; and (2) rubber cement.

Waxing

A waxing machine (Figs. 7–28 through 7–31) or hand-held waxer (Fig. 7–32) is used in this method. *Waxing* is the most popular method because of the speed of preparation and cleanliness of the finished paste-up. A special kind of wax has been manufactured for use in waxing equipment (Fig. 7–33). The elements can easily be removed from the surface of the paste-up base if changes are required. The elements to be waxed are coated with a thin film of wax applied to the back of the copy sheet. The simplest procedure is to wax the back of the entire sheet and then place it face up on a piece of stiff cardboard. The individual elements are cut out as needed with an X-acto® knife (Fig. 7–34).

Individual elements are picked up as needed with the X-acto® knife and lifted into position on the paste-up base (Fig. 7–35). Using

FIG. 7–28   Daige waxer. (Courtesy Daige Products, Inc.)

FIG. 7–29   Portage table-top waxer. (Courtesy Portage Paste-up Products.)

FIG. 7–30   Portage pedestal waxer. (Courtesy Portage Paste-up Products.)

FIG. 7–31   Dent-X   waxer.   (Courtesy Dent-X Corp., North American Philips Co.)

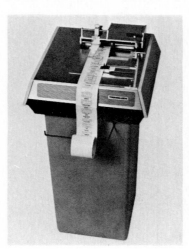

FIG. 7-32 Lectro-Stik hand-held waxer. (Courtesy Lectro-Stik Corp.)

FIG. 7-33 Special wax is used for waxing machines and hand-held waxers. (Courtesy Daige Products, Inc.)

FIG. 7-34 Individual image elements are cut from copy sheet after having been waxed. (Courtesy Stephen B. Simms, photographer.)

FIG. 7-35 X-acto knife is used to lift individual image elements into position on paste-up base. (Courtesy Dynamic Graphics, Inc.)

FIG. 7-36 Image elements are checked for squareness before being pressed to the paste-up base with a burnisher. (Courtesy Dynamic Graphics, Inc.)

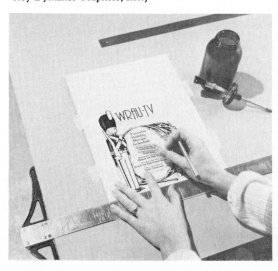

a T-square or straight-edge ruler, the paste-up artist places the individual elements in final position and checks for squareness before pressing the elements to the illustration board with a burnisher (Fig. 7–36). This procedure keeps small pieces of type from being lost and acts as a check to make certain that all of the type has been transferred to the paste-up base.

Rubber Cement

One of the most familiar adhesives used in paste-up is *rubber cement* (Fig. 7–37). It is applied to both surfaces and allowed to dry before being joined. Material placed on the paste-up while it is still wet has a tendency to shift and may become stained because the trapped cement does not always dry properly. When dry, the reproduction proof or other copy element is placed face up on a sheet of stiff cardboard. The blocks of type are cut out with an X-acto® knife and a T-square as needed. The dried rubber cement will hold the elements on the cardboard until they are ready to be transferred to the paste-up.

FIG. 7–37 Rubber cement can be used to adhere image elements to the paste-up base. (Courtesy Chartpak® Inc.)

CHECKING PASTE-UP ALIGNMENT

The T-square (Fig. 7–38) and the triangle are used to achieve perfect alignment of all copy elements (Fig. 7–39). When all elements on the paste-up board have been positioned and checked for alignment, a sheet of clean white paper is placed on top of the elements (Fig. 7–40). A hand roller or other type burnisher is then used to burnish tightly.

Sometimes type matter is not square, even when photocomposition systems are used to produce the type. This must be checked and, if necessary, the problem lines cut apart to make certain that they are aligned accurately. The paste-up artist is responsible for checking and repairing smudged or broken type. Obvious cases of

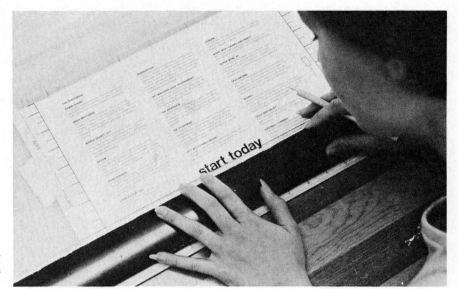

FIG. 7-38 Using T-square to check copy elements for alignment. (Courtesy Joseph Gross.)

FIG. 7-39 The layout artist is responsible for checking to see that all copy elements are square. (Courtesy Formatt, Graphic Products Corp.)

FIG. 7-40 The paste-up is covered with a sheet of clean white paper prior to final burnishing. (Courtesy Stephen B. Simms, photographer.)

damaged type should be returned to the typesetter. Even though the type has been proofread, the paste-up artist should be alert for errors.

PASTE-UP CLEANLINESS

All excess wax, rubber cement, pencil lines (other than light blue), eraser residue, and dirt must be removed from the surface of the paste-up. It is easy to see unremoved rubber cement if the paste-up is held at an angle to the light. This part of cleanup is important since unwanted elements, if left for the camera department, will be photographed along with the type and illustrations.

FINAL ASSEMBLY

Before the paste-up is sent to the camera department, it must be prepared for conversion to negative form. Continuous tone photographs provided with the paste-up are marked with the letters "A," "B," "C," etc. for identification. This process is referred to as *keying*. The halftones are keyed in on the paste-up in the exact spaces that the halftones will occupy (Fig. 7–41).

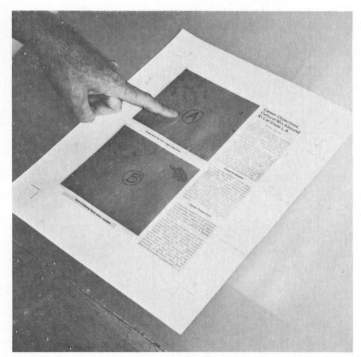

FIG. 7–41 Keying is done on the paste-up to indicate the exact position of halftones. (Courtesy Stephen B. Simms, photographer.)

If the outline method is used, a letter is written in the space provided for the halftone or illustration. If the block method is used, the letter is written on top of the black paper square. In the case of red masking film, the letter is placed underneath the square on the paste-up base. This allows it to be picked up later by the stripping department. In addition, the same letter is written on the reverse side of the photograph or illustration to match its position on the paste-up. Identifying or keying each continuous tone photograph is

PASTE-UP CHECK LIST

The paste-up should be checked for the following points before it is submitted to the camera department:

- All copy should be proofread.
- Type should be checked for correct sizes.
- The paste-up should be clean. Excess wax, rubber cement, dirt, fingerprints, and pencil lines should be carefully removed.
- Line paste-up copy should be prepared in black, regardless of the color of ink that will be used to print the job. The black should be black and not gray.
- Broken type should be repaired or replaced. Smudged type should be replaced.
- Elements should be squared on the paste-up by using a T-square and triangle. Type should be aligned against both square edges.
- Any overlay material should be accurately registered.
- Separate continuous tone photographs and illustrations should be keyed for position identification. The required enlargement or reduction of every piece of separate artwork should be indicated.
- Any windows for halftones should be of correct size and in the proper position.
- Screen tint areas should be marked with the tint percentage and the color and number of ink desired on the tissue overlay.
- Instructions for all desired operations should be written on the base paste-up and separate artwork. All instructions should be written in light-blue pencil.
- The paste-up should be covered with a protective tissue or vellum overlay along with a sheet of text or book paper.

the only way the elements can be correctly combined after the negatives have been prepared.

A blank sheet of tissue or vellum paper should be attached to the paste-up. This provides a surface for marking corrections and prevents the temptation to mark on the paste-up base. It is also used to show the reproduction size desired. The paste-up should also be protected with a paper flap (Fig. 7-42). A piece of colored book paper is suitable for the purpose.

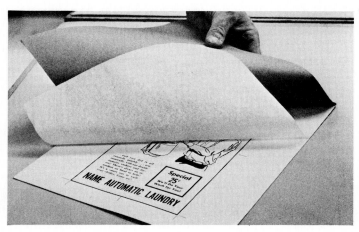

FIG. 7-42 Completed paste-up is covered with a sheet of tissue and paper flap. (Courtesy Stephen B. Simms, photographer.)

FLAT COLOR PASTE-UP

Much of the printing done today is single color. This means that it is printed in only one color, whether black, red, green, or blue, etc. In the graphic arts industry, black is considered a color. *Flat color* is any color the layout artist chooses for reproduction. Each color requires a separate printing plate and in some cases a separate run on the press. Many presses are equipped to run two or more colors at a time (Fig. 7-43). Flat color is not the same as color separation. This process is used to reproduce full-color continuous tone copy such as color prints, paintings, and transparencies.

FIG. 7-43 Two-color offset printing press. (Courtesy Rockwell International, Graphic Systems Division.)

The addition of a second color provides a number of design variations. Not only can the two colors be used individually, but they can also be combined as solids and screened tints to produce a variety of colors and tones. The use of additional colors on a job increases the range of design possibilities and aesthetic effects. Most flat color work uses from one to four colors. Two-color printing is the most popular choice.

Specifying Flat Color

Two methods are used to specify flat color. The first is to ask the printer to mix a color that is part of a color-matching system. The second method is to ask the printer to match a color that is not part of a color-matching system. The first method is the most practical because it allows the printer to mix inks using preestablished instructions for every color. The second method is more difficult for the printer, since the color requested is mixed through a hit-or-miss technique. There are several color-matching systems in use throughout the printing industry. The most widely used by layout and paste-up artists is the Pantone Matching System® (PMS).

FIG. 7–44 Pantone Matching System® ink color book. (Courtesy Pantone®, Inc.)

PANTONE MATCHING SYSTEM® This system is made up of 10 Pantone colors, which include 8 basic colors plus transparent white and black. These colors are mixed in varying amounts (a total of 500 possible different colors can be obtained). These colors are numbered and arranged in an ink color book (called a swatchbook) (Fig. 7–44) available from art and printers' supply stores.

To specify an ink color, the layout artist refers to the swatchbook, chooses the desired color, and indicates its number on the paste-up. Normal practice calls for the layout artist to attach a sample of the color to the paste-up. This prevents any possibility of error. The Pantone swatchbook contains sheets of numbered tear-out samples for this purpose.

KINDS OF REGISTER

In preparing a paste-up when two or more colors of ink are to be printed, *register* of the different color images on the paste-up is critical. There are three kinds of register: (1) commercial; (2) hairline; and (3) nonregister.

The use of *commercial register* allows for slight variations in color images amounting to approximately plus or minus $\frac{1}{64}$ inch.

When copy elements must be extremely precise where colors meet, *hairline register* is necessary. In this case, no overlap or white space is allowed to show where elements touch.

The least exacting flat-color registration set-up is that of *nonregister*. Allowance is made for several different colors to be completely independent of each other. Thus, exacting register is not necessary.

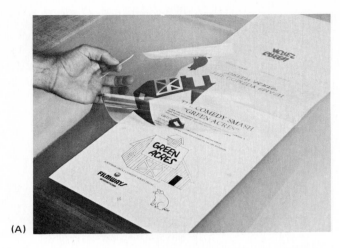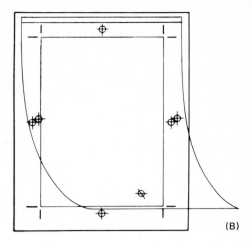

(A) (B)

FIG. 7–45 The overlay method is used on the paste-up to achieve second-color register. [(A) courtesy Stephen B. Simms, photographer; (B) courtesy A.B. Dick Co.]

Overlay Method

The simplest kind of paste-up prepared for color involves a design layout in which the body type prints in one color and the display type prints in another color. Since no type area touches any other type area, there is no problem of hairline register. It is a simple matter to paste all of the type that is to print in one color (usually black) on the paste-up base. All the display type that is to print in the second color is positioned in register on an *overlay* (Fig. 7–45). The overlay is attached at the top of the paste-up base.

Register Marks

The overlay must be in register with the material on the paste-up base. Register consists of providing markings that allow the overlay to be removed and then replaced in the identical location. *Register marks* (Fig. 7–46) are thin 90° cross lines drawn with a ruling or technical drawing pen. They are first drawn on the paste-up base on at least three sides. These should include the top, left, and right. Register marks are never placed in a planned bleed area of the paste-up.

FIG. 7–46 Register marks are drawn in black ink on the paste-up base and overlay. (Courtesy Stephen B. Simms, photographer.)

Register marks are drawn on the overlay exactly on top of those on the paste-up base. The register marks on each overlay should be slightly shorter than the ones on the paste-up or on the overlay below. This allows the paste-up artist to make sure that the marks are directly on top of each other. The thinner the marks, the more exact the register will be.

Register marks preprinted on transparent adhesive tape are also available (Fig. 7–47). These are convenient to use and easy to apply to most surfaces. A magnifier is helpful when applying register marks to overlays.

FIG. 7-47 Roll-type preprinted register marks have adhesive backing for easy application to the paste-up and overlays. (Courtesy Chartpak® Inc.)

USE OF SOLIDS

Any solid or screened pattern area intended for a multicolor job is indicated on the tissue overlay in the same way it would be for a one-color pasteup. Red *keylines* (Fig. 7–48) are used to indicate the size, shape, and position of all halftones, tint, and color areas on the paste-up base. Red lines drawn on the paste-up base appear on the film negative as transparent openings. Later these areas are removed along the lines in the negative to accept the artwork which is taped in behind the window cut-out.

FIG. 7-48 Red keylines are drawn on the paste-up to indicate position for halftone. (Courtesy Stephen B. Simms, photographer.)

FIG. 7-49 Red masking film is used for solid-color areas where hairline register is required. (Courtesy Stephen B. Simms, photographer.)

Hairline register of solid color areas is done with red masking film material (Fig. 7-49). It is possible to cut a more accurate edge on masking film than can be ruled or drawn with a pen. If a panel or shape for artwork is cut slightly out-of-register, it can be easily picked up and placed in position. The masking film can be trimmed or patched to produce more accurate register. Some masking films are manufactured so that the color can be peeled off the plastic base.

When using masking film, a piece should be cut that is approximately 2 inches to 3 inches larger on all four dimensions than the finished size of the job. It is attached to the paste-up base at the top with a single piece of cellophane tape. The emulsion or dull side of the masking film should face up. The design area is then outlined with an X-acto® knife and the unwanted or nonimage areas of film removed (Fig. 7-50). When using such film, care must be taken to avoid scratching or damaging the emulsion in any way.

FIG. 7-50 Design area is outlined with an X-acto® knife, and the unwanted or nonimage areas of film are removed.

ORIENTATION TO PASTE-UP

You are now ready to begin work on an actual paste-up. Review the following information relating to this assignment. You will find a Project Evaluation Checklist included. It is important that you follow the procedures carefully since instructor evaluation of the project can only be completed when all materials have been submitted.

Materials Required

T-square
45° and 30°–60° triangles
Line gauge
X-acto® knife
Nonreproducing blue pencil
Masking tape
11″ × 14″ illustration board
12″ × 14″ tissue paper
13″ × 14″ cover flap paper
Scissors
Magnifying glass
Technical drawing pen
Black India ink
Waxer
Burnishing roller

Procedure

1. Square a sheet of 11″ × 14″ white illustration board on the drawing surface.
2. Hold the T-square on the left edge of the drawing table and align the bottom of the 14″ side with the top edge of the T-square (Fig. 7–51).
3. Tape the white illustration board to the drawing table using 1″ pieces of masking tape at all four corners (Fig. 7–52).
4. Find the exact center of the illustration board (Fig. 7–53). Using a straight edge, draw a light-blue diagonal line from the top left corner to the lower right corner. Draw another diagonal line from the top right corner to the lower left corner. The intersection of the two diagonal lines will locate the exact center of the page.
5. Use a T-square to draw a light-blue horizontal line across the board through the center point formed by the two diagonals. This is the horizontal center line of the layout.

FIG. 7-51 Bottom edge of 14-inch side of illustration board is aligned with T-square.

FIG. 7-52 Tape illustration board at all four corners with 1-inch pieces of masking tape.

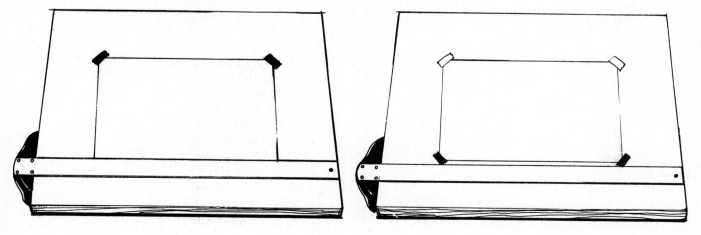

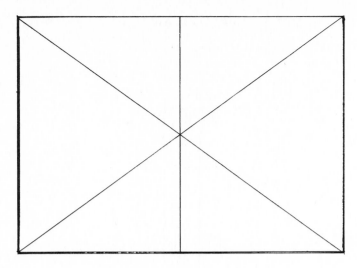

FIG. 7-53 Locate exact center of illustration board by using a line gauge or ruler.

6. Use the triangle and T-square to draw a light-blue vertical line through the exact center of the paper. This is the vertical center line of the layout.

7. Measure up $4\frac{1}{2}''$ from the center point along the vertical line and make a small reference point with the light-blue pencil. Do the same measuring down $4\frac{1}{2}''$ from the center on the vertical line.

8. Measure from the center point $5''$ along the horizontal center line to the right and make a reference point with the light-blue pencil. Do the same measuring $5''$ to the left of the center along the horizontal center line.

9. You have now located the outside edges of the paste-up area. Using a light-blue pencil, triangle, and T-square, draw four lines connecting the reference points into the shape of a rectangle, making sure the corners form right angles (Fig. 7-54).

10. These lines and the center lines should extend past the reference points and paste-up area at least $\frac{1}{2}''$.

11. The extending $\frac{1}{2}''$ lines are used as guides for the corner marks and should be inked in with a technical drawing pen up to, but not touching, the corner. In addition, ink in both horizontal and vertical center lines $\frac{1}{2}''$ long outside the paste-up area (Fig. 7-55).

FIG. 7-54 Use a light blue pencil, triangle, and T-square to draw lines that connect reference points into the shape of a rectangle.

FIG. 7-55 Ink corner marks and center lines with thin black lines $\frac{1}{2}$–inch long outside the paste-up area. Use a light blue pencil to draw a rectangle $8\frac{1}{2}'' \times 9''$ within the paper size area.

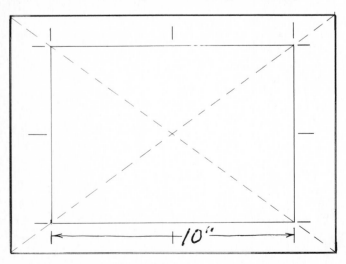

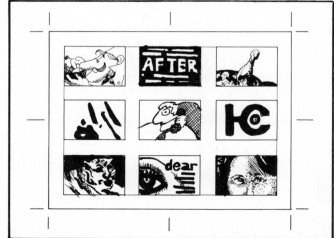

12. You have now located and inked in the corner marks (crop marks) and center marks. The distance between the corner marks should measure 9″ × 10″. To indicate this, measure and draw a horizontal line between the lower two corner marks with the light-blue pencil, being certain to leave a ½″-space somewhere near the vertical center line. Write in 10″ in the ½″-space, and where the line touches the corner marks draw arrows toward those marks. This measurement will tell the camera operator, platemaker, and press operator what the final dimensions are to be. This may also indicate any enlargement or reduction from the original paste-up.

The second half of this assignment involves the placement and adhering of copy elements that comprise the paste-up. Neatness and cleanliness are important factors to consider in this phase of paste-up.

1. Remove and wax the reproduction proof (Fig. 7–56) and place it on a piece of stiff cardboard beside your work area. Use a sharp X-acto® knife to cut out each element, leaving from ¹⁄₁₆″ to ⅛″ white space (margin) on each side of every element. Leave the elements in place on the cutting board until they are needed.
2. Using a light-blue pencil, draw a rectangle 8½″ × 9″ within the paper size area.
3. This rectangle represents the image size area.
4. Study the layout carefully before attempting to position and adhere the elements. Note that there are three columns and that the outside columns are flush left and flush right, respectively. The middle column is centered between the outside two. Vertically, the elements are equally spaced so that the top and bottom rows are flush on the image lines. Remember to include the label lines (1, 2, 3, etc.) with each element.
5. Use your T-square, light-blue pencil, and ruler or line guage to mark the paste-up board for positioning the copy elements. Accuracy is very important.
6. Begin "lifting" the copy elements to the paste-up board with the X-acto® knife. Use the alignment and reference marks made previously.
7. Using the T-square and X-acto® knife, square each element. Be careful not to move positions.
8. Place a piece of clean white paper over the paste-up elements and burnish the entire surface. Recheck with the T-square to make certain that no elements have moved.
9. Using a black ink pen, label each of the elements as to what kind of copy it is. You may need your instructor's help in identifying the examples. Do a neat job of lettering (all capitals). Remember that the purpose of a paste-up is to be photographed with a graphic arts process camera. Any flaws or dirty copy will turn up on the negative.
10. Cut a sheet of tissue paper 12″ × 14″. Lay the tissue over the paste-up even with the bottom edge of the paste-up board and turn the paste-up face down with the tissue underneath and extending 1″ above the top edge of the board. Using your X-acto® knife, cut each end of the tissue from the corner of the paste-up toward the center of the tissue at a 30-degree angle. Adhere the top edge of the board and tissue paper with a piece of clear cellophane tape approximately 11″ long. Be sure that the tissue is folded back over the top edge of the paste-up board smoothly and squarely.
11. Cut a sheet of colored text or book paper 13″ × 14″. Follow the same procedure used with the tissue paper. Cut the corner angles at 30-degree angles. Fold the cover paper over the top edge of the paste-up and adhere it with masking tape.
12. Remove all excess wax from the paste-up. Write your name on the back of the paste-up and indicate the total number of hours you spent on this assignment. Examine the Evaluation Check list to determine if you have completed all required tasks.
13. Turn the assignment in to your instructor for evaluation.

PROJECT EVALUATION CHECK LIST
ORIENTATION

This check list is designed to assist you in identifying the specific points upon which this assignment will be evaluated. Your instructor will indicate by the use of a check mark those areas that need additional attention.

PASTE-UP PLANNING

_____ One 11″ X 14″ illustration board
_____ 9″ X 10″ paper size area
_____ 8½″ X 9″ image area

PASTE-UP PREPARATION

_____ Elements trimmed smoothly
_____ Elements trimmed to correct dimensions
_____ Elements positioned according to the rough layout
_____ Elements aligned accurately
_____ Uniform application of adhesive and burnished
_____ Blue guidelines (light and thin)
_____ Crop marks in black ink approximately ½″ long
_____ Center marks in black ink approximately ½″ long
_____ Overall cleanliness and attention to neatness
_____ Protective tissue overlay attached correctly
_____ Colored cover flap attached correctly
_____ All copy elements labeled as to type of copy
_____ Name and time required to complete assignment included

COMMENTS:

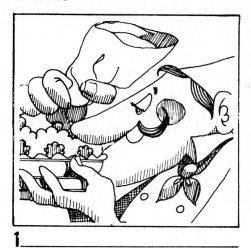

1 _____

2 _____

3 _____

4 _____

5 _____

HECHT CUSTOM PHOTO LAB

6 _____

7 _____

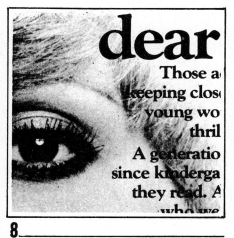

8 _____

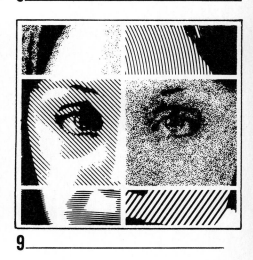

9 _____

Kinds of Copy You Will Be Assembling and Pasting Up

After you have completed the paste-up, write in on the appropriate copy lines: outline copy, line resolution, line with screen, logotype, halftone, photo conversions, reverse copy, overprint or surprint, and line copy.

chapter 8

CAMERA AND DARKROOM OPERATIONS

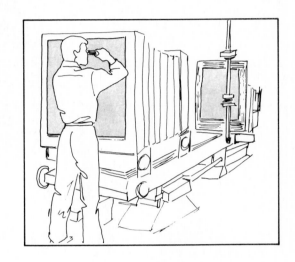

The process camera is not an ordinary home-type camera. It is a large camera that has special features that make it suited to its use in graphic arts. For most forms of printing, the process camera must produce a sharp film negative consisting of completely opaque and completely transparent parts. The parts are either in line form for things like type or in dot form for things like photographs. In addition to the process camera, there must be a darkroom where film processing takes place. The darkroom must be arranged so that everything in it is convenient to use. This chapter discusses the process camera, darkroom requirements, and some of the various operations that are normally carried on in this area of the graphic arts.

The graphic arts process camera differs in design from a small snapshot camera. The process camera is equipped with a lens of the *process* type. A process lens is made to give best results with flat (two-dimensional) copy. The lens on a snapshot camera is intended for three-dimensional subject matter. Process cameras are usually located in the darkroom itself. These are called *darkroom cameras*. Cameras located and used outside the darkroom are called *gallery cameras*. The two basic kinds of process cameras are the horizontal and vertical. Both cameras contain the same main parts and operate on the same principle.

HORIZONTAL PROCESS CAMERA

A *horizontal process camera* (Fig. 8-1), as its name implies, is constructed in a horizontal line. The parts of a horizontal process camera are illustrated in Fig. 8-2. Most horizontal cameras are installed through a wall and are used as darkroom cameras. The part of the camera that holds the film is in the darkroom. The major portion

FIG. 8-1   Horizontal process camera. (Courtesy Consolidated International Corp.)

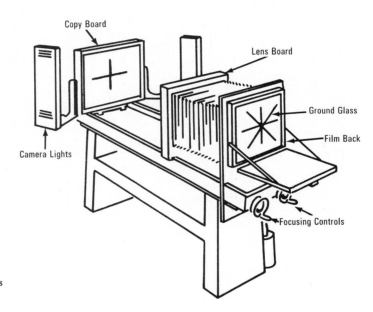

FIG. 8-2   Major parts of a horizontal process camera. (Courtesy A.B. Dick Co.)

of the camera remains in a lighted room. This arrangement makes it possible to load and unload film within the darkroom. As a result, film processing can be carried on without interruption.

VERTICAL PROCESS CAMERA

All *vertical process cameras* are constructed with the parts in a vertical line (Fig. 8-3). The parts of a vertical process camera are

FIG. 8-3 Vertical process camera. (Courtesy Consolidated International Corp.)

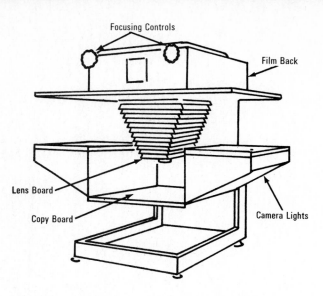

FIG. 8-4 Major parts of a vertical process camera. (Courtesy A.B. Dick Co.)

illustrated in Fig. 8-4. These cameras can be used either in the darkroom or in the gallery. Vertical cameras also save space.

PARTS OF A PROCESS CAMERA

Regardless of camera size or design, the method and function of the controls are basically the same. There are a number of parts common to all cameras. These include: (1) copyboard; (2) copyboard lights; (3) lensboard; (4) bellows extension; (5) ground glass; (6) vacuum back; and (7) focusing controls.

Copyboard

The *copyboard* (Fig. 8-5) is the part of the process camera on which the copy to be photographed is positioned. It has a large flat surface with a hinged glass cover to hold the copy during exposure. The copyboard is mounted on a track so that it can be moved forward and backward for enlargements and reductions.

Copyboard Lights

Copyboard lights (Fig. 8-6) act as a source of illumination for the copy. On most cameras the lights are mounted in conjunction with the copyboard. This allows for the same distance between lights and copyboard regardless of enlargement or reduction settings. The lights are generally positioned at a 45-degree angle to the copyboard (Fig. 8-7).

Lensboard

The *lensboard* is mounted on a track so that it can be moved forward and backward. This is necessary in order to maintain the proper distance relationship between copyboard and lensboard during enlargements and reductions. The primary function of the lensboard is to act as a carrier for the *lens* (Fig. 8-8). The process camera lens is the most delicate part of the entire camera.

FIG. 8-5 Copyboard holds the copy to be photographed. (Courtesy nuArc Company, Inc.)

FIG. 8-6 Copyboard lights illuminate copy to be photographed during exposure. (Courtesy nuArc Company, Inc.)

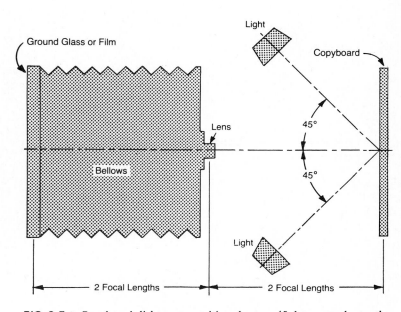

Ground Glass or Film

Light

Copyboard

Lens

45°

45°

Bellows

Light

2 Focal Lengths

2 Focal Lengths

FIG. 8-7 Copyboard lights are positioned at a 45-degree angle to the copyboard.

FIG. 8-8 Lensboard and lens. (Courtesy nuArc Company, Inc.)

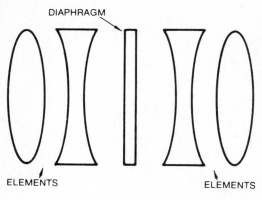

FIG. 8-9 A process camera lens is constructed of several optical glass elements assembled into a barrel. (Courtesy Goerz Optical Company, Inc.)

FIG. 8-10 The process camera diaphragm is located within the lens assembly. (Courtesy Goerz Optical Company, Inc.)

FIG. 8-11 Relationship of f-stops to the size of opening produced by the diaphragm.

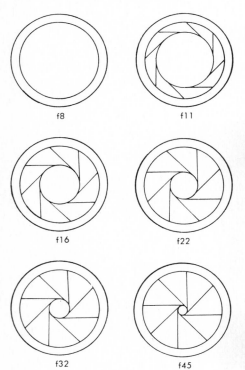

f8   f11

f16   f22

f32   f45

The lens is made up of several optical glass elements assembled into a barrel (Fig. 8-9). The entire assembly is threaded into the lensboard. Within the lens assembly is an adjusting device called a *diaphragm* (Fig. 8-10). The diaphragm is an arrangement of metal blades that allow varying amounts of light to pass through the lens. The size of opening produced by the diaphragm is referred to as the *f-stop*. A series of f-stops is f-8, f-11, f-16, f-22, and f-32 (Fig. 8-11). A diameter of f-11 is larger than a diameter of f-16, and so on down the line. The f-32 opening is the smallest.

Bellows Extension

The *bellows extension* is attached to the lensboard (Fig. 8-12). The bellows is an accordion-shaped part that forms a light tunnel from the lens to the film plane. The accordion arrangement of the bellows is designed so as to allow the lensboard to be moved for enlargements and reductions.

Ground Glass

Most cameras are fitted with a *ground glass* to assist the camera operator in positioning and focusing the image (Fig. 8-13). The ground glass is attached to the rear camera case. It is usually mounted in a hinged frame so that it can be swung out of the way when not in use. When it is in the viewing position, the glass surface is on the same plane as the film during exposure.

Vacuum Back

The *vacuum back*, like the ground glass, is hinged to the rear case (Fig. 8-14). The dull, black-colored vacuum back has markings on it to show the proper position for standard film sizes. A series of

FIG. 8-12 The accordian-shaped bellows extension. (Courtesy nuArc Company, Inc.)

FIG. 8-13   The ground glass is used for focusing the image. (Courtesy nuArc Company, Inc.)

FIG. 8-14 (*right*)   Film is held in position on the vacuum back during exposure. (Courtesy nuArc Company, Inc.)

FIG. 8-15   Copyboard and lensboard controls. (Courtesy Stephen B. Simms, photographer.)

FIG. 8-16   Copyboard and lensboard controls run sliding tapes with percentages printed on them. (Courtesy nuArc Company, Inc.)

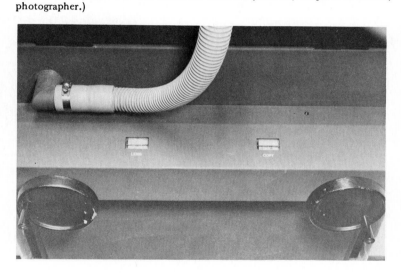

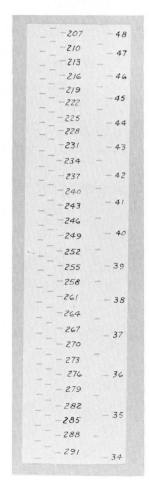

holes or narrow channels in the vacuum back connect to a vacuum chamber. When the vacuum pump is turned on, the photographic film is held in place during exposure.

Focusing Controls

The *copyboard* and *lensboard controls* are located at the rear camera case (Fig. 8-15). Each control consists of a dial that runs a sliding tape with percentages printed on it (Fig. 8-16). When enlarging or reducing copy size on a process camera the copyboard and lensboard tapes must both be set at the same percentage size. For a reduction, the lensboard moves closer to the vacuum back to reduce the image size. For an enlargement, the lensboard moves away from the vacuum back to enlarge the image size.

DARKROOM OPERATIONS

In the graphic arts, a negative made in the process camera is used to prepare a printing plate. The plate is used on a printing press to reproduce the image in quantity. The kind of copy prepared governs how it will be handled in the process camera. The basic kinds of copy are divided into line and continuous tone.

Line Copy

All *line copy* is either black or white; there are no intermediate gray tones (Fig. 8-17). This kind of copy is converted into a film negative (or positive) by simple exposure and proper development (Fig. 8-18).

When a piece of line copy is photographed in a process camera, the image is formed by the contrast between the white paper and the black type matter or inked drawings (Fig. 8-19). The white areas of the copy reflect light through the lens of the process camera. The light then strikes the film emulsion, thus exposing it. The result is the negative (Fig. 8-20). When fully processed, the nega-

Line Copy

Examples of reproductions from line copy. In the drawing of the apple, the artist suggested intermediate tones by random stippling with ink and brush.

Line Negative

FIG. 8-17 Examples of line copy. (Courtesy Eastman Kodak Co.)

FIG. 8-18 Line copy is converted into a film negative by exposure and development. (Courtesy Eastman Kodak Co.)

FIG. 8-19 When line copy is photographed, the image is formed by the contrast between the white paper and the black image matter. (Courtesy Ulano® Corp.)

FIG. 8-20 Film negative of a piece of line copy. (Courtesy A.B. Dick Co.)

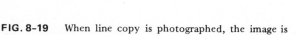
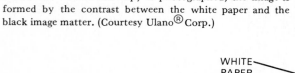

BLACK IMAGE AREAS

WHITE PAPER BACKGROUND

FILM NEGATIVE

A

FILM POSITIVE

FIG. 8-21 Film positive. (Courtesy A.B. Dick Co.)

FIG. 8-22 Contact printing frame is used to produce positives and negatives on film or photographic paper. (Courtesy Iconics Control, Inc.)

FIG. 8-23 Light source and control panel used for contact printing. Light housing on right is attached to ceiling directly over contacting frame. (Courtesy Iconics Control Inc.; inset illustration courtesy nuArc Company, Inc.)

tive is dark (opaque) in the areas that were light on the copy. The negative is light (transparent) in the areas that were dark on the copy.

Film Positive

A film positive is the opposite of a film negative. The black areas of a film negative correspond to the white areas of the copy, and the clear areas of the negative correspond to the black areas of the copy. A film positive is clear in the areas that correspond to the white areas of the copy and black in the areas that correspond to the black areas of the copy (Fig. 8-21).

The usual way to produce a film positive is to make a contact print of a negative on a piece of film or photographic paper. The negative is held in tight contact with a piece of film or paper by using a contact printing frame (vacuum printing frame) and a light source (Fig. 8-22). A light source similar to the one shown in Fig. 8-23 is used to make the exposure.

CONTINUOUS TONE COPY

Camera copy that has intermediate tones of gray is referred to as *continuous tone copy*. Wash drawings and photographs are examples of continuous tone copy (Fig. 8-24). In making a negative of such copy, the camera operator must produce a film image made up of small dots of various sizes. This is called a *halftone* image. Halftone photography makes the printing of continuous tone photos, paintings, or drawings possible. This is done by converting the continuous tone image into a pattern of very small and clearly defined "dots" of varying sizes (Fig. 8-25). When the image is printed on a press, the dots and the white paper between the dots fuse visually and create an optical illusion in which the eye sees intermediate tones. The tones range all the way from white to black.

FIG. 8-24   Examples of continuous tone copy: (A) pencil and charcoal; (B) wash drawing; (C) black-and-white photograph. [(A) and (B) courtesy Kimberly-Clark Corp.; (C) courtesy Kooh-I-Noor Rapidograph, Inc.]

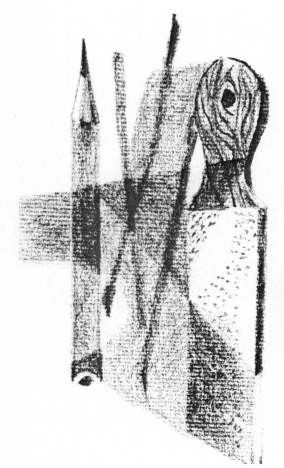

(A)

(B)

(C)

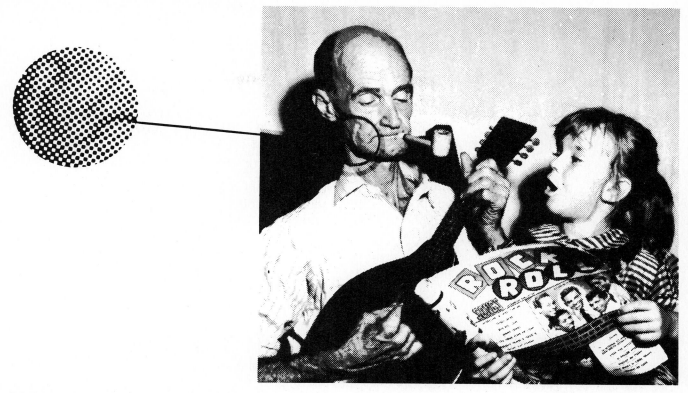

FIG. 8-25 Enlargement of halftone dots. (Courtesy Eastman Kodak Co.)

Halftone Screens

In making a halftone negative, the camera operator places a *halftone screen* in the camera in front of the film. This is done before making the exposure. The halftone screen is a precise grid pattern of lines. There are two basic kinds of screens: (1) glass screen; and (2) contact screen.

GLASS SCREEN A *glass screen* consists of two pieces of glass, with each piece containing a given number of grid lines per linear inch (Fig. 8-26). The two pieces of glass are cemented together at right angles to each other. In use, the glass screen is mounted in an adjustable holder, just in front of the film in the process camera. The screen and film do not come in direct contact. The screen and film are precisely spaced to obtain dots of the desired size and character.

Enlarged pattern of
glass halftone screen

FIG. 8-26 A glass screen consists of a given number of lines per linear inch. (Courtesy Eastman Kodak Co.)

CONTACT SCREEN A *contact screen* is made on a flexible film base. The dots are vignetted (shaded off gradually into the surrounding area) and vary in density. Density is greatest at the center and lightest at the outer edges of each dot. The screens are placed in direct contact, emulsion to emulsion, with the film in the camera. Contact screens are available with various kinds of dot formations (Fig. 8-27).

Two commonly used contact screens are the *magenta* and the *gray*. Magenta is a reddish, blue color. The magenta screen is suited for black-and-white halftone photography. The gray screen is used for either black-and-white or color halftone photography. Contact

FIG. 3

SQUARE DOT

The square dot is the most straight forward screen pattern. Its symmetrical appearance is easy to evaluate. Its primary application is newsprint and commerical photo engraving where complex etching processes are used. The square dot pattern, however, has disadvantages in the printing process. An abrupt jump in the tonal scale occurs where the four corners of the dot join at 50%. This discontinuity prevents smooth midtone transitions often evident as "banding" in flesh tones.

FIG. 4

ELLIPTICAL DOT

The elliptical dot pattern is mainly used in modern offset printing. This dot shape allows a much smoother tonal gradation than the square dot in the 50% area. Two opposite corners of the diamond shaped dot join the adjacent dots first at approximately 40% while the two remaining dots join near 60%. With the dots joining in two steps a much smoother tonal transformation is achieved. To avoid an increased moire pattern the magenta is angled perpendicular to its normal 75 degrees resulting in a 165 degree angle.

FIG. 5

HRS TRIPLET DOT

The Triplet Dot pattern offers several unique features. It allows the full potential of modern presses, plates and papers to be realized for a superior printed product. Contrast, detail rendition and smoothness are achieved without compromises in dot quality or printability. The tonal gradation curve is kept nearly ideal for optimum reproduction. The unique dot configuration with its satellite dots appearing gradually throughout the whole tonal range allow easy dot percentage evaluations. Read the adjoining article for more information.

FIG. 8-27 Halftone screens are available with several kinds of dot formations. (Courtesy Beta Screen Corp.)

screens are available in a variety of screen rulings (lines per linear inch) and sizes.

Kinds of Halftones

Continuous tone copy can be handled to produce unusual effects in a printed job. Although the square halftone (Fig. 8-28) is the most popular, there are also oval and round halftones (Fig. 8-29). The camera techniques used to produce these kinds of halftones are basically the same as for conventional square halftones. The particular use of these halftone treatments is dictated by the job's aesthetic and functional considerations.

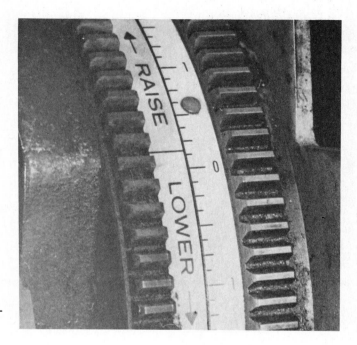

FIG. 8-28 Square halftone. (Courtesy Stephen B. Simms, photographer.)

FIG. 8-29 Oval and round halftone shapes lend variety to a printed piece. (Courtesy Stephen B. Simms, photographer.)

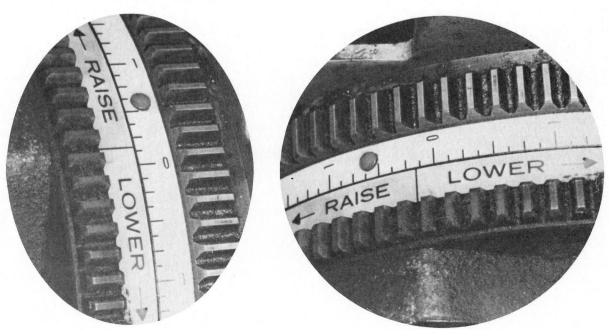

STRAIGHT LINE **BULLSEYE** **CROSS LINE** **CONTOUR LINE**

WAVY LINE

SCREENLINES

Screenline is an all inclusive term applied to screen techniques that make use of lines rather than dots. Screenlines can come in a variety of forms. The small group of illustrations here demonstrate and label those that are commercially available in contact screen form.

Not only do these line screens find application in single color but very interesting variations of Two, Three, and Four Color process; Duotones; and Triotones may be created. It requires only the substitution of the line contact screen for the conventional dot screen to create these special effects.

FIG. 8–30 Special-effect screens are handled similarly to a conventional halftone screen. Careful use of special-effect screen patterns can lend interest to a printed product. (Courtesy Hammermill Paper Co.)

Special-Effect Screens

In addition to the conventional dot halftone screens, *special-effect screens* are available that provide pleasing aesthetic effects (Fig. 8–30). Special-effect screens are handled in approximately the same manner as conventional screens. As with conventional screens, the layout artist must in all cases specify which screens are to be used.

Duotones

A *duotone* involves a two-color halftone process. Two halftone negatives are made of the same photograph. Before the second negative is exposed, the contact screen is turned to an angle of 30° to the first exposure. The two negatives are used to print the duotone in two colors—usually black for detail and a lighter color for accent. The duotone treatment is excellent for printed matter in which two or more colors are planned.

THE DARKROOM

The *darkroom* is where the majority of process camera work takes place. It must be a light-tight room so that it can be completely darkened. To make it convenient to enter and leave the darkroom without admitting light, special doors are installed (Fig. 8-31). The major components of a darkroom include developing sink, film storage cabinet, safelights, timer, vacuum contacting frame, and miscellaneous equipment. A typical layout of an efficient darkroom is shown in Fig. 8-32.

FIG. 8-31 Revolving darkroom door makes entering and leaving the darkroom convenient and does not disrupt operations inside. (Courtesy Consolidated International Corp.)

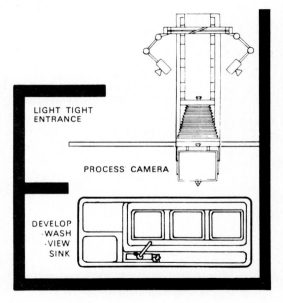

FIG. 8-32 Film processing productivity is directly related to a well-designed darkroom. (Courtesy nuArc Company, Inc.)

PHOTOGRAPHIC FILM

The term *film*, when used in photography, refers to a transparent plastic base that has a coating that is sensitive to light. The coating is a photographic emulsion containing gelatin and silver salts. The sensitivity of the silver salts to light is the basis of the photographic process. The most widely used films are orthochromatic and panchromatic. Orthochromatic film is the type used for most of the line and halftone work in photo-offset lithography. The major use of panchromatic film is for color separation work.

Film Structure

Film is a photographic emulsion coated on a transparent plastic base. In manufacture a problem arises because the emulsion will not adhere to the plain plastic base. As a result, the base is first coated with a subcoating on both sides. This can be compared to the primer used when painting metal. The primer adheres to the metal and the final coat of paint adheres to the primer. With film, the emulsion is coated on one side of the subcoated base and then an *antihalation coating* is applied to the back side. The antihalation coating prevents light from reflecting back to the emulsion side of the film. Figure 8-33 illustrates the several layers that make up a piece of film.

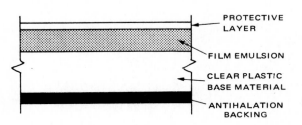

PROTECTIVE LAYER

FILM EMULSION

CLEAR PLASTIC BASE MATERIAL

ANTIHALATION BACKING

FIG. 8-33 Schematic drawing of a piece of photographic film illustrating its several layers. (Courtesy A.B. Dick Co.)

Film Processing

Exposure of the film on a process camera causes a *latent image* in the emulsion. A latent image is an invisible image. To make this image visible, it must be processed with special chemicals. Film processing involves four basic steps: (1) developing; (2) stop bath; (3) fixing bath; and (4) washing bath. The trays used for processing are positioned left to right in a sink (Fig. 8-34).

DEVELOPING The action of the *developer* is somewhat complex. It involves a chemical reduction of the silver salts in the emulsion.

FIG. 8-34 Darkroom trays are normally positioned in the sink so that the operator works from left to right. (Courtesy nuArc Company, Inc.)

The white areas of the paste-up copy reflect light through the lens of the camera and expose the film. The black areas of the copy absorb (do not reflect) the light, thereby producing no exposure on the film. The exposed areas of the film react with the developer to form black metallic silver. The developer does not affect the areas that are not exposed to light. During development the antihalation coating starts to dissolve. Developing time is approximately 2½ minutes.

STOP BATH With development completed, the film is placed in a *stop bath* solution for approximately 10 seconds. This bath consists of a weak solution of acetic acid and water. Since the bath is acid, it has the effect of immediately stopping the action of the developer.

FIXING BATH After stopping the developing action in the stop bath, the film is then placed in a *fixing bath*. The fixing bath serves three purposes: (1) it dissolves the remaining emulsion in the unexposed areas (black areas of the original); (2) it hardens the emulsion so that it resists scuffing and scratching when it is dry; and (3) it dissolves any unused dye remaining in the antihalation coating. Fixers are available in both liquid concentrate and dry powder form. Most films used in graphic arts photography fix in approximately 1 to 3 minutes.

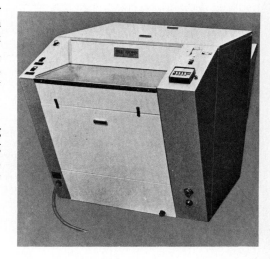

WASHING BATH After the film is fixed, it is washed in running water for approximately 10 to 30 minutes to dissolve the remaining processing chemicals. When washing is complete, the film is squeegeed to eliminate excess water. The film is then hung to dry in a dust-free area of the darkroom or is processed in an automatic film dryer.

FILM PROCESSORS

When volume is required, automatic *film processors* (Fig. 8-35) are used to develop, stop, fix, and wash film. Processors maintain quality and accuracy of development. They are useful in operations where medium to high volume film processing is required.

FIG. 8-35 Film processors are used for automatic development, fixation, and drying of film where medium to high volume is necessary. (Courtesy Direct Image Corp., Monterey Park, California.)

chapter 9

PRINTING PROCESSES

The paste-up artist must have a thorough knowledge of the major printing processes used in the graphic arts industry. Each printing process has its own advantages and limitations. Knowing these, the paste-up artist is better equipped to adequately select type, illustrations, and paper for any given piece of printing. This in turn leads to better quality and cost control of a job. This chapter covers each of the four major printing processes. These include letterpress, offset lithography, gravure, and screen process. The information is intended to assist you in the task of preparing copy with the end result a printed page.

Several methods are used to produce printing. The four major printing processes discussed in this chapter include: (1) letterpress; (2) offset lithography; (3) gravure; and (4) screen process. Each of the printing processes involves the transfer of ink from printing plate to paper or other similar materials.

LETTERPRESS

The printing process known as *letterpress* (relief) involves the transfer of ink from a raised surface through direct pressure. The image to be printed is on a raised surface. The nonprinting area is lower than the printing surface. The image area is inked and a piece of paper is then placed over the inked image. By means of pressure, the ink is transferred from the relief surface to the paper (Fig. 9-1). This method of printing had its origin in Germany around 1450, when Johann Gutenberg invented movable metal types.

Although letterpress is gradually being replaced by other printing processes, it is still used for printing magazines, newspapers, packaging,

FIG. 9-1 Letterpress printing involves the transfer of ink from a raised surface through direct pressure to the paper. (Courtesy A.B. Dick Co.)

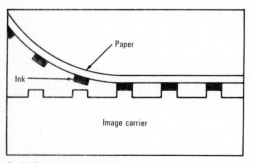

Relief printing (letterpress)

138

PRINTING CHARACTERISTICS OF LETTERPRESS

● Letterpress is recognizable by the fact that the type elements reveal a slight amount of ink squeeze around the edges due to the pressure applied to the elements during printing.

● Among the uses of letterpress is short-run printing from type and engravings. Letterpress is adaptable to jobs requiring numbering, imprinting, die-cutting, slotting, perforating, embossing, and hot stamping.

● This process lays down an ink film thicker than offset but not as thick as gravure or screen process.

● Exceptionally long press runs can be made by using duplicate printing plates.

● Printing plates are usually more expensive than offset, but they are less expensive than gravure.

● Letterpress is capable of printing from hand-set or machine-set type as well as from original or duplicate printing plates.

● Duplicate printing plates are expensive. The most commonly used duplicate plates are electrotypes, plastic, rubber, and stereotypes.

● Letterpress prints best on book papers. When printing halftones, the paper must be calendered or coated. Paper of almost any thickness can be used, from onion skin to cardboard.

● When printing from original metal types or engravings, any part of the job can be changed without the expense of preparing new plates. The exception is when printing from one-piece duplicate plates or from curved (rotary press) plates.

● Longer press makeready times are required to compensate for the slight variation in thicknesses of plates and engravings and height of type.

and other similar products. Inasmuch as letterpress is the only process in which printing can be done directly from metal type, it is most appropriate for jobs consisting mainly of type matter. Type matter can be changed easily, and it can be stored ready to be used again for reprints.

A great deal of time is consumed in *makeready* for the letterpress process. Makeready involves building up of the various type areas so that both heavy and light areas print with equal impression. It often happens that type and plates (illustrations and pictures) are of slightly different heights.

The makeready process provides the necessary pressures required by the different parts of the type form. Light parts of a printing form of type and plates require less pressure than others to print well. For example, a hairline-faced rule usually takes less pressure than does type matter. The dark areas of a halftone are usually built up to increase the printing pressure slightly more than the light areas of the halftone. The solid areas of plates and very heavy large types often need more pressure to the paper than smaller type faces.

Although type height is 0.918 inch, and theoretically all plates and type would print well at this height, it does not work out this way in letterpress presswork practice.

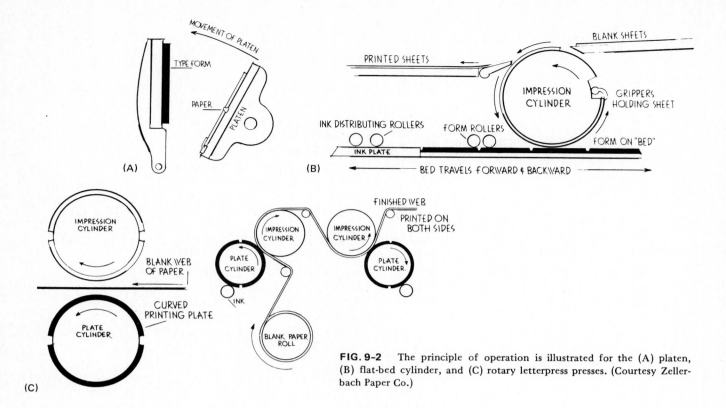

FIG. 9-2 The principle of operation is illustrated for the (A) platen, (B) flat-bed cylinder, and (C) rotary letterpress presses. (Courtesy Zellerbach Paper Co.)

Types of Letterpress Presses

There are three types of letterpress printing presses: (1) platen; (2) flat-bed cylinder; and (3) rotary. The principle upon which each operates is illustrated in Fig. 9-2.

PLATEN PRESS One of the oldest letterpress printing presses is called the *platen press* (Fig. 9-3). The type form is held in a metal frame on a flat bed. Impression is obtained by the impact of a flat platen or plate that holds the piece of paper. The entire surface of the platen meets the type form squarely in a single thrust. The type form is inked by a set of rubber rollers. The rollers pick up ink from a disc and distribute it evenly over the type surface.

Most of the platen presses used today are of the automatic variety. This means that sheets of paper are fed into the press by an automatic feeding system. Most of the earlier presses were fed by hand.

FLAT-BED CYLINDER PRESS The *flat-bed cylinder press* is a letterpress (Fig. 9-4) in which the type form is held on a large flat bed that moves backward and forward on a track beneath an impression cylinder. Sheets of paper, fed in at the top, are carried around the cylinder and receive their impression by a rolling contact with the type. Only a small area of the cylinder touches the form at one time.

Most cylinder presses are of the two-revolution variety. This means that the cylinder prints while it is making one revolution, and it rises during the second revolution to allow the form to make its return trip. Inking rollers ink the form during its return trip. The printed sheets are delivered to the front of the press and are stacked with the printed side up.

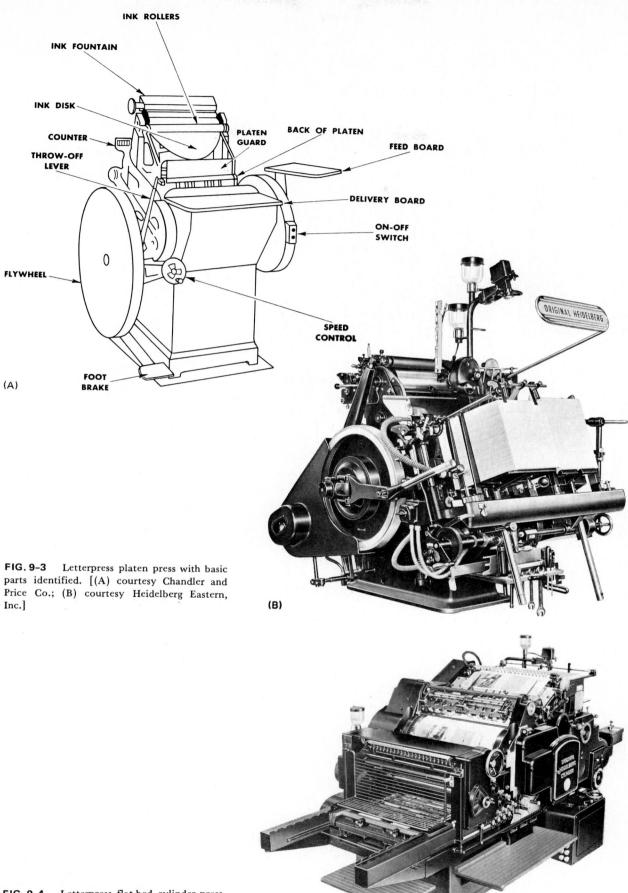

INK ROLLERS

INK FOUNTAIN

INK DISK

COUNTER

THROW-OFF LEVER

PLATEN GUARD

BACK OF PLATEN

FEED BOARD

DELIVERY BOARD

ON-OFF SWITCH

FLYWHEEL

SPEED CONTROL

FOOT BRAKE

(A)

(B)

FIG. 9–3 Letterpress platen press with basic parts identified. [(A) courtesy Chandler and Price Co.; (B) courtesy Heidelberg Eastern, Inc.]

FIG. 9–4 Letterpress flat-bed cylinder press. (Courtesy Heidelberg Eastern, Inc.)

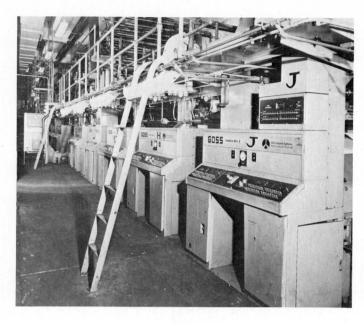

FIG. 9-5 Letterpress rotary presses print from a continuous roll of paper. (Courtesy Rockwell International, Graphic Systems Division.)

ROTARY PRESS The *rotary press* (Fig. 9-5) is a letterpress printing press that uses an impression cylinder to press the paper against a printing cylinder. The printing plates for the rotary press are curved to fit the contour of the printing cylinder. Most of these presses print on both sides of the paper in a single pass through the press. They are known as *perfecting* presses. Rotary presses generally print from a roll of paper and are called *web-fed*. *Sheet-fed* presses print from individual sheets of paper. Some web-fed presses are equipped to cut the paper into individual sheets immediately after printing.

OFFSET LITHOGRAPHY

Alois Senefelder (Fig. 9-6) developed the lithographic process in 1796. *Offset lithography* is a planographic (flat) process (Fig. 9-7). It is based on the principle that water and grease do not readily mix. The image area that prints and the nonimage area that does not print are both on the same plane or surface. This means that the image to be printed is neither raised above the surface nor engraved below the surface (Fig. 9-8). These distinct areas of the plate make the printing area receptive to ink and the nonprinting area receptive to water. The plate is created by a combination of photomechanical and photochemical processes.

In the actual printing process, the plate (which is attached to a cylinder) is dampened first with water and then immediately by ink. This creates the desired image in the ink-receptive area. The image area repels moisture (it does not become wet) and is receptive to ink. The image area picks up the ink while the nonimage area, which is moist with water, repels the ink. The image is then transferred from the plate to a rubber blanket, which is a rubber mat stretched tightly around a cylinder. The rubber blanket in turn transfers (offsets) the image onto the paper. The term *offset* is frequently used to describe this printing process. (Fig. 9-9).

FIG. 9-6 Alois Senefelder developed the lithographic process in 1798. (Courtesy A.B. Dick Co.)

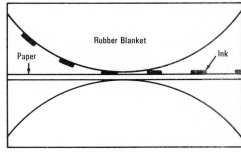

Offset Lithography Process (offset)

FIG. 9-7 Offset lithography involves the transfer of ink from a flat surface and is based on the principle that grease and water do not readily mix. (Courtesy A.B. Dick Co.)

FIG. 9-8 Offset printing plate is completely flat on its surface. (Courtesy 3-M Co.)

FIG. 9-9 A rubber blanket on the offset press transfers the image to the paper. (Courtesy 3-M Co.)

One of the primary benefits of the offset process is that it can handle a wider range of surface roughness of paper than can letterpress or gravure. This is due to the resiliency and compressibility of the offset blanket to which the image is transferred from the plate before it is offset onto the paper. Another advantage of this process is that it allows quick and easy plate changes between and during press runs.

Types of Offset Presses

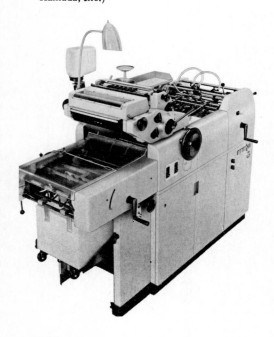

FIG. 9-10 Offset duplicator press. (Courtesy Hamada, Inc.)

Offset printing presses are of two basic types: those that print on sheets and those that print on continuous rolls of paper. The former are known as *sheet-fed* offset presses, the latter as *web-fed* offset presses. Magazines, catalogs, books, and newspapers are most commonly printed by web offset.

SHEET-FED OFFSET PRESSES Modern *sheet-fed offset presses* are made in many sizes, usually designated by the maximum sheet size the press will handle. Small offset presses are called duplicators and are used for relatively small printing jobs (Fig. 9-10). These presses commonly print on paper sizes up to 14″ × 20″. There are several different manufactured brands of duplicator-size offset presses.

Large offset presses, as distinct from duplicators, range in sheet size to approximately 55″ × 78″ at present (Fig. 9-11). Some of these presses are manufactured in standard units. The units can be assembled in any number up to six for printing from one to six colors (Fig. 9-12). Most short-run printing is produced on one-color equipment. Multicolor presses are generally used for long printing runs. Larger presses in the sheet-fed category which print on both sides of the paper at the same time are known as *perfectors* (Fig. 9-13). A schematic diagram of a typical perfecting press is illustrated in Fig. 9-14. These presses can print in any of the following config-

FIG. 9-11 Large offset press. (Courtesy Rockwell International, Miehle Products.)

FIG. 9-12 Units of an offset press are normally connected in tandem. Each unit is capable of printing one color. (Courtesy Rockwell International, Miehle Products.)

FIG. 9-13 Presses that print on both sides of the paper at the same time are known as perfectors. (Courtesy Royal Zenith Corp.)

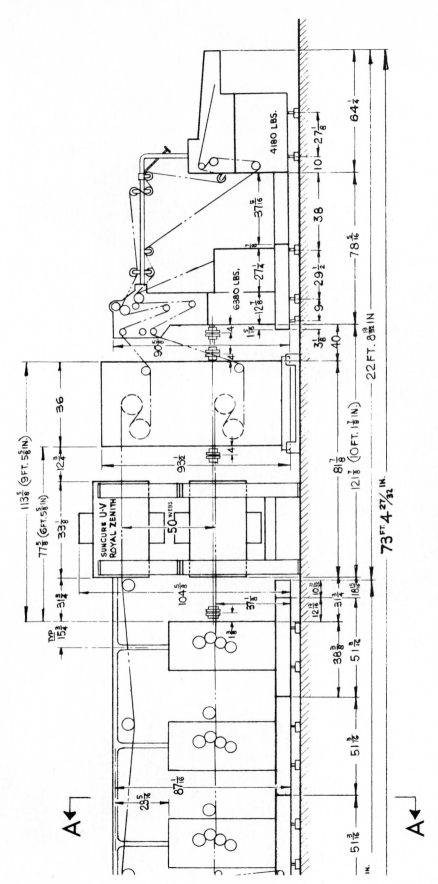

FIG. 9-14 Schematic drawing of a perfecting offset press. (Courtesy Royal Zenith Corp.)

urations: six colors on one side; five colors on one side, with one color one side; four colors one side, with two colors one side, etc.

WEB-FED OFFSET PRESSES *Web-fed offset presses* produce single color and multicolor printing for small-run and medium-run newspapers, magazines, and books (Fig. 9–15). In addition, web offset

FIG. 9–15   Web offset presses at: (A) San Diego Union Tribune; and (B) New York Times. (Courtesy Rockwell International, Graphic Systems Div.)

(A)

(B)

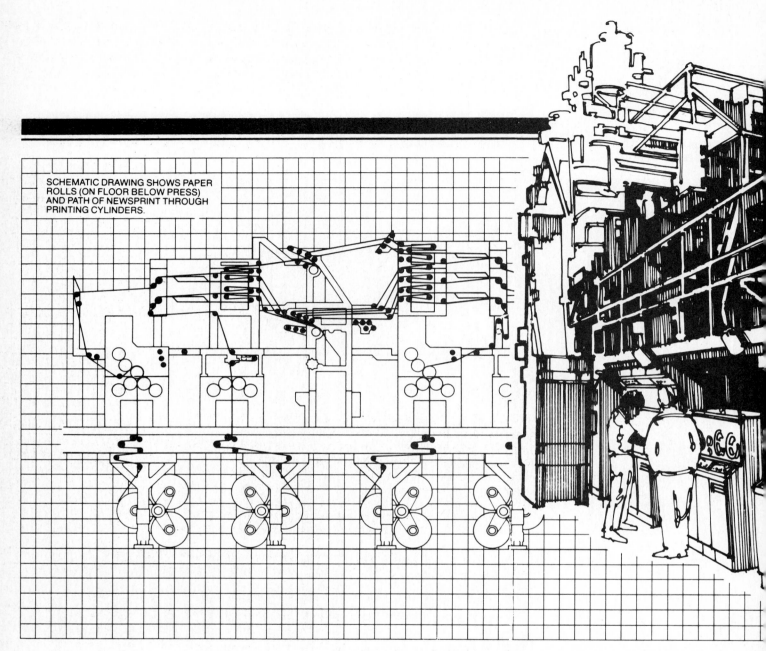

SCHEMATIC DRAWING SHOWS PAPER ROLLS (ON FLOOR BELOW PRESS) AND PATH OF NEWSPRINT THROUGH PRINTING CYLINDERS.

FIG. 9-16 Schematic drawing of a web offset press. (Courtesy Rockwell International, Graphic Systems Div.)

is used to produce business forms, catalogs, and commercial printing of all types. A schematic diagram of a typical web offset press is illustrated in Fig. 9-16.

Speed is by far the primary advantage of web offset. Much of the printing produced on web offset presses proceeds directly to a folder where various combinations of folds convert the web into finished products. Other operations that can be performed on the web press include numbering, cutting, slitting, perforating, and paste binding. All of these operations are possible while the presses run at high speeds, usually two to four times faster than the fastest sheet-fed offset. A typical setup for such an operation is shown in Fig. 9-17.

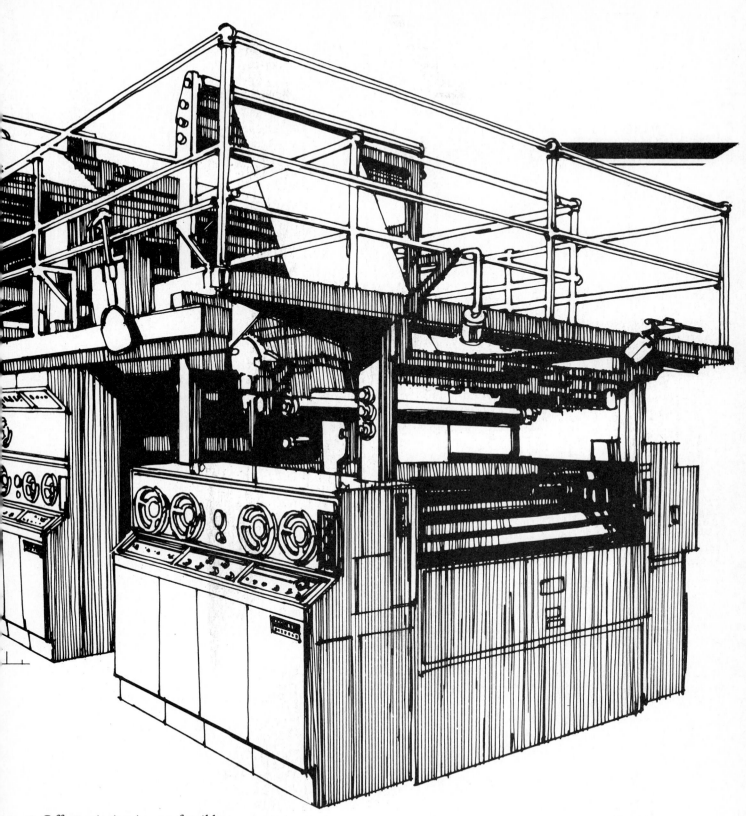

Offset printing is now feasible on large presses: the Rockwell-Goss Metroliner offers major daily newspapers improved speed, economy and reproduction.

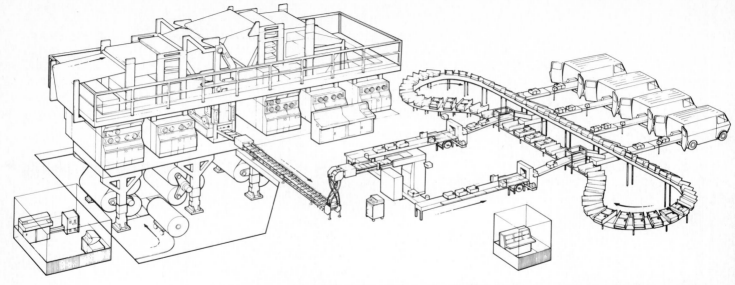

FIG. 9-17 High-speed web offset presses are capable of performing operations such as numbering, cutting, slitting, perforating, and paste binding. (Courtesy Rockwell International, Graphic Systems Division.)

GRAVURE

The *gravure*, or intaglio (etched), process of printing is very different from the other printing processes (Fig. 9-18) in that the image to be printed is etched or engraved into and below the surface of the printing cylinder (Figs. 9-19 and 9-20). The image areas consist of cells or wells etched into a copper cylinder or wraparound plate, and the cylinder or plate surface represents the nonprinting areas. The plate cylinder rotates in a bath of ink. The excess ink is removed from the surface by a flexible steel *doctor blade*. The image is formed by the excess of ink remaining in the thousands of recessed cells. Direct image transfer is made as the paper passes between the plate cylinder and the rubber-covered impression cylinder.

To provide the network of cells on which the doctor blade rides, the entire plate cylinder must be screened. This occurs even if the impressions consist entirely of type or line matter. A recognizable characteristic of gravure printing is the screen that covers the entire printed image. The deeper the indentations on the plate cylinder, the more ink they carry and deposit. The fine screened images are virtually invisible to the naked eye.

Intaglio process (gravure)

FIG. 9-18 Gravure printing involves the transfer of ink from sunken images in the plate cylinder. (Courtesy A.B. Dick Co.)

FIG. 9-19 Gravure printing involves the etching or engraving of an image into and below the surface of the printing plate cylinder. (Courtesy Motter Printing Press Co.)

FIG. 9-20 Excess ink is removed from the surface of the gravure plate by means of a scraping blade called the "doctor" blade. (Courtesy Motter Printing Press Co.)

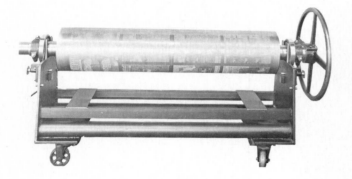

PRINTING CHARACTERISTICS OF GRAVURE

- Gravure printing is recognizable by the fact that the entire image area is screened, including the type. With the aid of a magnifier, the type elements are seen to have ragged outlines as a result of screening. For this reason, gravure is better suited to printing continuous tone images rather than type. This is especially true of type having fine serifs and in sizes of 8 point or below.
- Gravure is most economical for web-fed long runs at high speed. Short-run work can be printed at competitive costs and quality of letterpress.
- Gravure provides high-quality, high-speed printing in black and white or in full color.
- Gravure produces the richest blacks and the widest tonal range of all the printing processes.
- Copper printing cylinders are more expensive than either offset or letterpress plates.
- Gravure is capable of printing on a wide range of surfaces. Best results are attained on smooth or coated paper. Good quality work is also possible on inexpensive uncoated papers.
- Consistent quality can be maintained throughout the press run.

Gravure printing is considered outstanding for reproducing color pictures. However, high plate-making costs usually limit its use to long runs. By long run is meant over 100,000 copies of a printed piece. Gravure is widely used to print food wrappers, Sunday newspaper magazine and TV supplements, mail order catalogs, and color preprint inserts for newspapers.

Types of Gravure Presses

As with rotary letterpress, gravure presses (Fig. 9-21) are manufactured both for sheets (sheet-fed) or rolls (rotogravure) of paper. Components of a gravure press include: (1) gravure cylinder on

FIG. 9-21 Web-fed gravure printing presses are quite large; these presses require highly skilled operators. (Courtesy Motter Printing Press Co.; photography by J. David Allen.)

which the images to be reproduced are etched; (2) impression cylinder that brings the web of paper into contact with the gravure cylinder; (3) doctor blade that removes excess ink from the surface of the gravure cylinder; and (4) ink pan or reservoir in which the gravure cylinder is immersed.

SCREEN PROCESS

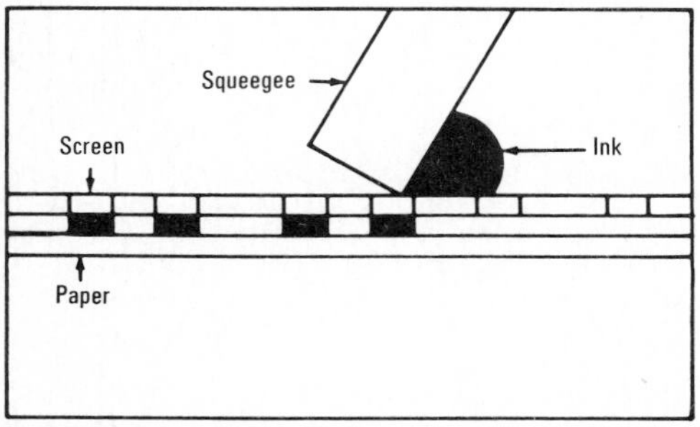

The *screen* (porous) *process* printing system (formerly known as silk screen) is a stenciling technique by which a heavy film of ink is applied through a mesh screen in the form of a design (Fig. 9–22). The original name was given since silk was extensively used to support the stencil. In recent years other fabrics have been developed—for example, nylon, organdy, and metal cloth woven of stainless steel.

The screen process is a simple one. The surface to be imaged is placed under a stencil. A mass of ink is drawn across the stencil surface with a rubber squeegee. The ink is forced through the open areas of the stencil and deposited on the imaging surface. Most commercial screen printing has been mechanized to speed production.

Stencils for screen process printing can be hand-cut or photographically prepared as a photosensitive emulsion applied to the screen mesh. Most commercial screen printing utilizes the photographic stencil preparation technique because it is faster and provides a wider range of image detail. Printed circuits used in electronic work are made by screen process utilizing photographically prepared stencils.

Screen printing can be recognized by the thick layer of ink applied to the printing surface. Any surface can be printed, including paper, metal, fabric, glass, wood, plastic, cork, etc. Virtually any

Screen process (silkscreen)

FIG. 9–22 Screen process printing involves the transfer of ink through a porous mesh screen into paper or fabric. Screen printing is basically a stenciling process. (Courtesy A.B. Dick Co.)

PRINTING CHARACTERISTICS OF SCREEN PROCESS

● Screen process printing is characterized by a thicker ink film transfer than other methods.

● It is widely used for reproducing artwork consisting of pictures alone or in combination with type matter.

● It can be done by hand printing, but it is more commonly done by automatic presses.

● Screen process is used for printing metal signs, short-run billboard posters, wallpaper, fabrics of all kinds, and decoration of thermoplastic sheets for subsequent vacuum forming.

● Screen process printing can be done with many different kinds of image carriers. The carrier material can be natural silk, artificial fibers, and metal cloth woven of copper, stainless steel, and other metal threads.

● Most frequently used stencil-making techniques include: (1) photographic; and (2) knife-cut made by manual skills.

● Almost any paper can be used. In addition to paper and paper boards, metal foils, plastic materials, sheet metal, glass, and wood are among the materials printed by this method.

● Since the ink film used in screen process is too thick for stacking printed sheets without individual drying, a number of drying shelves are required.

shape or design, any thickness, and any size up to a billboard can be printed. Screen process is excellent for outdoor posters and signs because the heavy film deposited provides longer service life.

Types of Presses for Screen Process Printing

Several types of presses are available for screen process printing. These include a simple wooden or metal hand press (Fig. 9–23) and a variety of automatic presses for commercial purposes (Figs. 9–24 through 9–27). Multicolor printing is easily done on presses equipped with two or more screens (Fig. 9–28). On a hand press printing is done by feeding paper under the screen and forcing ink through the fine mesh openings with a rubber squeegee. On an automatic screen process press the paper is fed, squeegeed, and delivered automatically.

Most of the screen printing done commercially is sheet-fed, but some of it is done by web. Web screening is used for more specialized results, such as the decoration of plastic and cloth products. Some screen process printing is done on sheet-fed cylinder presses.

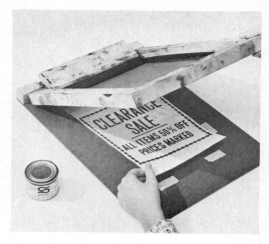

FIG. 9–23 Wooden screen printing press. (Courtesy Formatt, Graphic Products Corp.)

FIG. 9–24 American glider screen printing press. (Courtesy Advance Process Supply Co.)

FIG. 9–25 American Eagle screen printing press. (Courtesy Advance Process Supply Co.)

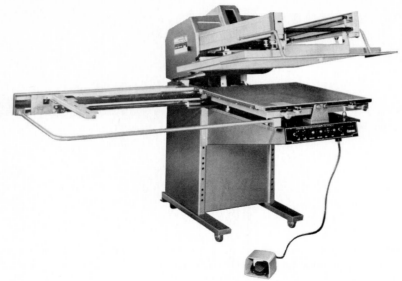

FIG. 9-26 American Cameo 30 screen printing press. (Courtesy Advance Process Supply Co.)

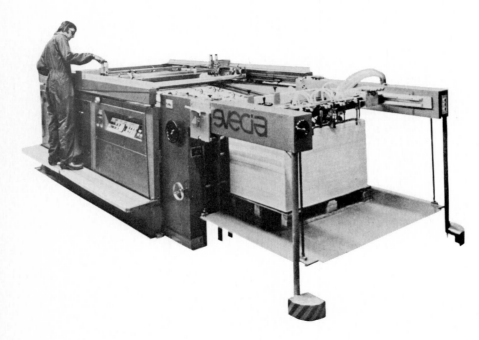

FIG. 9-27 Svecia high-speed cylinder screen printing press. (Courtesy Heidelberg Eastern, Inc.)

FIG. 9-28 Multicolor screen printing is done on presses equipped with two or more screens. (Courtesy Advance Process Supply Co.)

chapter 10

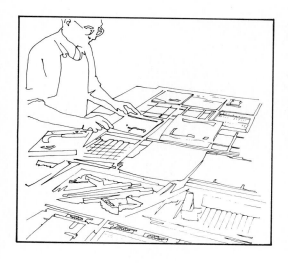

PRINTING IMPOSITIONS

The placing of pages so that they will be in proper sequence after the sheet is printed and folded is known as imposition. The matter of spacing and margins must be considered in the case of magazines, books, catalogs, and programs. Magazines and books are printed in units of several pages per sheet. A full sheet of paper is usually printed in units of 4, 8, 16, and 32 pages. The task of imposition is usually the responsibility of the layout or stripping department.

Laying out of pages in the proper sequence for printing is called *imposition* and is a special phase of graphic arts. There may be anywhere from 4 to 64 pages on each side of a printed sheet. It all depends on the size of each page and how large a sheet the press can print.

Folded printed sheets are called *signatures* (Fig. 10-1). This is a term used by the bindery and layout departments. A signature is a sheet that is printed on two sides and folded in a sequence of 4, 8, 16, 32, or 64 pages. Any number of these signatures when bound together will form a magazine, book, booklet, catalog, or program.

Imposition follows the same principle whether for offset, letterpress, or gravure printing. In offset and gravure, a *stripper* arranges the pages in sequence. The stripper works on a light table. The film negatives or positives are arranged and taped on a sheet of masking paper (Figs. 10-2 and 10-3). Once the film has been taped in place, the stripper cuts window spaces from the masking sheet. This allows light to pass through the film during exposure to the plate. In letterpress, the type or plates are arranged on an imposing stone (Fig. 10-4). This is a flat surface on which a person secures the material in a large metal frame for the press.

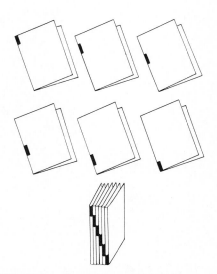

FIG. 10-1 Signatures are folded sheets usually printed on both sides. Marks printed along edge of signatures indicate correct sequence for assembly.

FIG. 10-2 Film negatives and positives are arranged and taped on a sheet of masking paper. (Courtesy Stephen B. Simms, photographer.)

FIG. 10-3 The stripper must arrange negatives and positives so that they are in the correct sequence for printing. This process is called *imposition*. (Courtesy nuArc Company, Inc.)

FIG. 10-4 In letterpress imposition, the type and plates are arranged on a steel imposing stone rather than on a light table. (Courtesy Times-Mirror Press, Los Angeles.)

Certain fundamentals are more or less standard procedure in imposition. After the page size has been determined, ⅛ inch to ¼ inch extra is added for *trim* on the top, side, and bottom of each page (Fig. 10-5). Trimming takes into consideration the amount of paper removed from the three outside edges after the signature is folded. In addition to trim allowance, provision must be made for *creep*. This allowance must be made when planning a thick saddle-stitched magazine or book. Creep occurs when the signature is

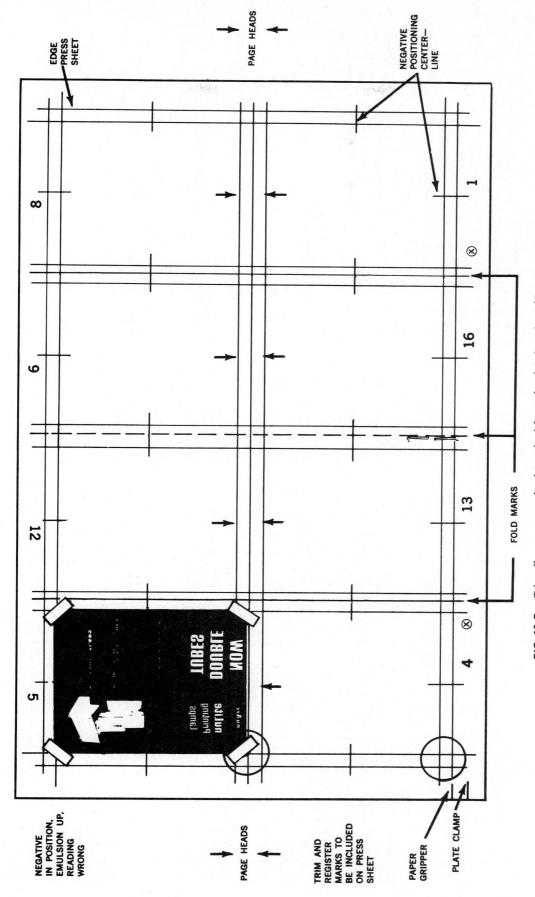

FIG. 10-5 Trim allowance must be determined for each printed product. (Courtesy nuArc Company, Inc.)

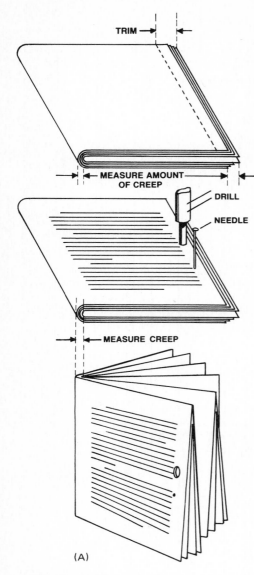

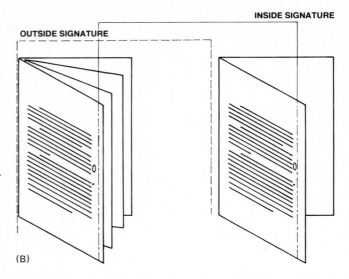

(B)

FIG. 10-6 Creep allowance is a critical factor when a book or magazine has many signatures.

FIG. 10-7 Four-page work-and-turn imposition.

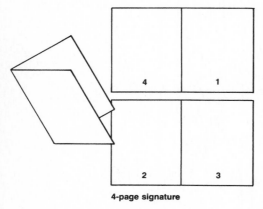

4-page signature

folded and the inside pages extend past the outside pages (Fig. 10-6). This means that the inside center pages will trim out smaller in size because they extend out farther than the outside signature pages.

TWO-PAGE IMPOSITION

A two-page imposition can be used for printing a single sheet on both sides. In this case, a double-sized sheet is printed on one side and then turned and printed with the same pages on the other side. The sheet is then cut in half, each full sheet making two complete copies. Two pages can be used to print one side of a four-page folder, the other side being printed with another two pages.

When a sheet is printed on both sides with the same pages and then cut in half, it is called a *work-and-turn* job. When it is printed on one side with one set of pages and then printed on the other side with a different set of pages, it is called a *sheetwise* job. Thus, two pages used to print a single sheet on both sides would be a work-and-turn job. A four-page folder that is printed two pages at a time would be printed sheetwise.

FOUR-PAGE IMPOSITION

When four pages are printed at a time, work-and-turn, two different impositions are possible (Fig. 10-7). This is the smallest signature possible. On one side of the sheet are pages 1 and 4; on the other side of the sheet are pages 2 and 3. Fold a sheet of paper once. Begin with the outside facing page and number 1 through 4. Open the sheet and lay it flat. This is how the pages are impositioned to print in the correct sequence.

EIGHT-PAGE IMPOSITION

Ordinary eight-page impositions are usually run either work-and-turn or sheetwise (Fig. 10-8). In addition to the space for margins, additional allowance must be made for trimming the pages after the signature is folded. An eight-page imposition is folded at the top (head) and at the binding edge (spine).

Fold a sheet of paper twice. Number the pages consecutively 1 through 8. Open the sheet and lay it flat. This is the sequence for an eight-page signature. The numbers are not in order, and some of the pages are upside down.

SIXTEEN-PAGE IMPOSITION

A 16-page signature is usually printed work-and-turn (Fig. 10-9). This can be visualized by folding a sheet of paper three times and numbering the pages consecutively 1 through 16. The same procedure can be followed to make 32-page and 64-page signatures.

DETERMINING IMPOSITION

It should be noted that imposition is determined by the printer, not by the layout and design person. The printer can best determine imposition on the basis of the equipment to be used and the job requirements.

A safe procedure for checking imposition of pages is to fold and mark a sheet of paper. If more than one signature is involved, a rectangular "door" should be cut and numbered (Fig. 10-10). The top of the right reading number establishes the top (head) direction

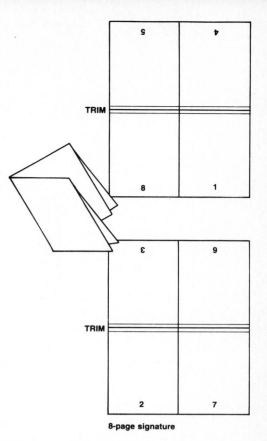

8-page signature

FIG. 10-8 Eight-page imposition can be printed work-and-turn or sheetwise.

FIG. 10-9 Sixteen-page imposition is normally printed work-and-turn.

FIG. 10-10 Checking imposition of pages should be done by marking, folding, and cutting a rectangular "door" through the middle of a dummy.

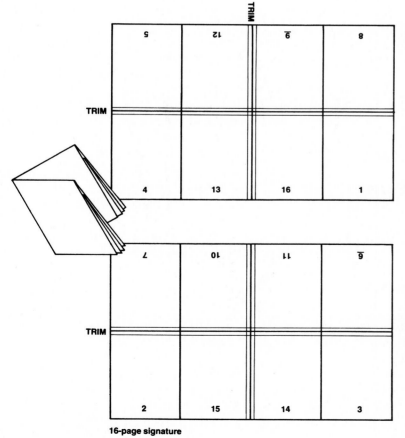

16-page signature

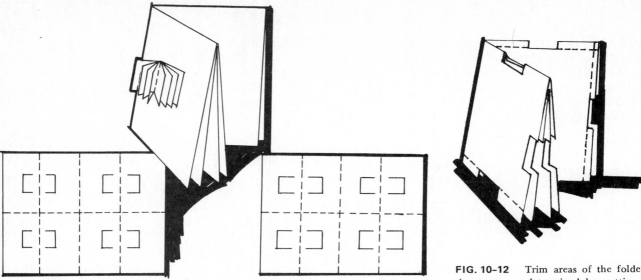

FIG. 10-11   Correct page imposition can be checked by opening the layout (dummy) and placing it on a table for inspection.

FIG. 10-12   Trim areas of the folded signatures are determined by cutting a rectangular-shaped notch at the top, right, and bottom sides.

of each page. The open layout (Fig. 10-11) clearly illustrates the correct page position.

To establish the correct trim areas of the folded signature, a rectangular-shaped notch is cut on the top, right, and bottom side (Fig. 10-12). The folded signature is then opened up flat and trim lines are ruled in (Fig. 10-13). The folded signature is then trimmed along the trim lines (Fig. 10-14).

FIG. 10-13   The folded signature, with notches in, is opened up flat and trim lines ruled in.

FIG. 10-14   The folded signature is trimmed along trim lines.

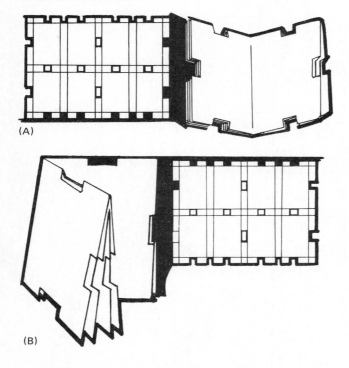

(A)

(B)

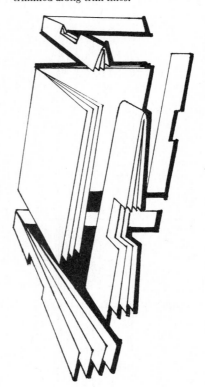

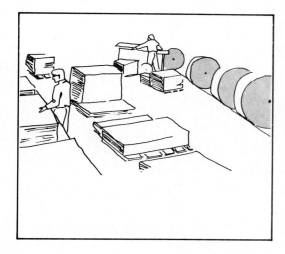

chapter 11

PRINTING PAPERS

The printer's product is made up of technical skill, type, ink, and paper. It would be difficult to determine which one of these four items is most important. However, in order to produce the best possible results, it is absolutely necessary that the paste-up artist have a thorough understanding of the characteristics of paper. Outstanding printing is brought about by the successful combination of type, ink, and paper. Paper can lift the final result to progressive heights of excellence by its own visual and textural qualities. Paper creates the mood and dramatic effect envisioned by the writer and the designer.

Most of the paper used by printers is made of wood pulp. Writing papers are made of cotton and linen rags. Almost all kinds of paper are manufactured in continuous rolls on modern paper machines.

PAPER MANUFACTURE

The manufacture of paper begins in the forest where trees are cut into logs for transport to the papermaking mill (Fig. 11-1). At the mill, bark is removed from the logs (Fig. 11-2). Giant debarkers strip the bark from the wood by friction (Fig. 11-3). Logs are then sent to a chipping machine (Fig. 11-4) that reduces the logs into chips the size of a quarter (Fig. 11-5).

The wood chips are fed into a tall digester where they are cooked in chemicals under pressure (Fig. 11-6). This process reduces the chips to a fiber form. The fibrous pulp is thoroughly cleansed and then passed through a chemical process that bleaches it a snowy white.

The pulps are mixed together in blenders (Fig. 11-7) with other papermaking materials. These include sizing, fillers, and dyestuffs. The materials are thoroughly mixed with water to the desired con-

FIG. 11-1 Trees provide the basic ingredient of most papers. (Courtesy Hammermill Paper Co.)

FIG. 11-2 Bark is removed from trees that have been cut into 4-foot logs. (Courtesy Hammermill Paper Co.)

FIG. 11-3 Debarkers remove bark from the wood by use of friction. (Courtesy Hammermill Paper Co.)

FIG. 11-4 Chipping machine. (Courtesy Hammermill Paper Co.)

FIG. 11–5   Logs are reduced to chips the size of a quarter. (Courtesy Hammermill Paper Co.)

FIG. 11–6   Wood chips are fed into a digester, where cooking and chemical action take place. (Courtesy Hammermill Paper Co.)

FIG. 11–7   The digester reduces wood to pulp after which it is mixed in a pulp blender. (Courtesy Hammermill Paper Co.)

FIG. 11-8   Pulp flows onto an endless bronze screen at the wet end of the Fourdrinier paper-making machine. (Courtesy Hammermill Paper Co.)

sistency. At this point, the mixture is about 0.5% fiber and 99.5% water.

The pulp, or *stock* as it is called, is allowed to flow onto an endless bronze screen at the wet end of the Fourdrinier papermaking machine (Fig. 11-8). The fine mesh screen moves and shakes to weave and mat the fibers together as the water drains off. The traveling web is passed over a succession of suction boxes and between rollers that further remove much of the water from the traveling web.

About halfway through the manufacturing process, the web is given a bath of sizing to seal the surface (Fig. 11-9). It is then dried again. At the end of the paper machine, the web of paper passes between polished steel rollers to give it a smooth, uniformly level surface.

FIG. 11-9   Sizing is added to the web to seal the paper's surface. (Courtesy Hammermill Paper Co.)

Toward the drying end of the papermaking machine, the web of paper is transferred to a felt blanket. It is carried through a succession of steam-heated drying cylinders to bring the final moisture in the paper to approximately 5% to 10% (Fig. 11-10). The web of paper is wound into huge rolls (Fig. 11-11). Most of the rolls are cut into single sheets (Fig. 11-12), wrapped, and shipped to printers (Fig. 11-13).

FIG. 11-10 Steam-heated drying cylinders help to reduce moisture content of newly formed paper. (Courtesy Hammermill Paper Co.)

FIG. 11-11 As paper is made, it is wound into rolls for processing at a later date. (Courtesy Hammermill Paper Co.)

FIG. 11-12 Most rolls of paper are cut into single sheets for printing on sheet-fed presses. (Courtesy Hammermill Paper Co.)

FIG. 11-13 Single sheets of paper are packaged and shipped to paper dealers and printers. (Courtesy Hammermill Paper Co.)

PAPER CHARACTERISTICS

There are a great many kinds and grades of paper. Paper manufacturers recognize the particular needs of each printing process. Lithography is more versatile than the letterpress, gravure, or screen processes. This is because a wider variety of kinds and surface finishes of papers can be used for production of fine-screen lithographic halftone images.

Coated Papers

Coated paper is surfaced with a special clay that is applied uniformly to the paper web. The paper web is then passed through a drying unit and against a highly polished chromium roller for smoothness. Coated paper is made in both glossy and dull finish and is the most ideal surface for printing.

Paper Finishes

Paper finish relates to smoothness. Paper can be used by the printer as it comes off the papermaking machine. However, most papers are finished by additional rolling and smoothing operations. The usual finishes are applied to uncoated book papers since this is the grade of paper most widely used. They are classified as: (1) antique finish; (2) eggshell finish; (3) machine finish (MF); and (4) sized and super calendered (S&SC).

ANTIQUE FINISH *Antique* paper has little calendering, which results in greater bulk and a velvety surface. It is not recommended for printing fine-screen halftones. Books or other lengthy reading matter are often printed on antique paper (sometimes called "text") because it reflects neither glare nor shine and it does not cause eyestrain.

EGGSHELL FINISH The texture of *eggshell* paper resembles the surface of an eggshell. In many respects, eggshell is similar to antique finish. Eggshell is produced on wet presses by special felts that create an irregular pattern of rounded hills and valleys. Eggshell is frequently used for programs and folders. It is not suitable for printing fine-screen halftones.

MACHINE FINISH *Machine finish* (MF) paper is similar to antique finish, but it is smoother and less bulky. The moderately smooth finish is applied to the paper in the paper machine. Typical uses for machine finish paper include magazines, books, booklets, and catalogs. It is not suitable for fine-screen halftones.

SIZED AND SUPER CALENDERED *Sized and super calendered* (S&SC) paper has a smooth and hard surface. Sizing is added to the paper web during manufacture. In addition, the paper passes through a number of metal rollers which add to its smoothness. This paper is suitable for fine-screen halftones.

WATERMARKS

While the paper is still wet and before the paper is calendered, a *watermark* (Fig. 11-14) is pressed into the paper by means of a *dandy roll*. A dandy roll is made of fine wire on which the wording or design of the watermark is in relief.

FIG. 11-14 A paper watermark is made by a dandy roll on the papermaking machine.

THE TWO SIDES OF PAPER

Paper has a *wire* side and a *felt* side because of the way paper is manufactured. The side directly in contact with the screen of the paper machine is called the wire side. The other side is called the felt side and usually has a closer formation of fibers. The felt side has less grain and better crossing of the fibers. The felt side of paper is the best printing side. On watermarked papers, the printing should be on the felt side. When a printed piece is held to the light, the printing should read in the same direction as the watermark.

PAPER GRAIN

Paper *grain* is an important factor in both printing and binding. It refers to the position of the paper fibers. During papermaking most of the fibers flow with their length parallel to that of the paper machine. Paper folds smoothly with the grain. Paper is stiffer in the grain direction (Fig. 11-15). Paper expands or contracts more in the cross direction when exposed to moisture changes. In books, magazines, catalogs, and programs the grain direction should be parallel to the binding edge.

Paper tears straighter with grain

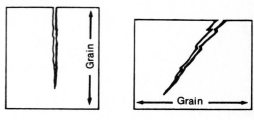

Paper folds more easily with grain

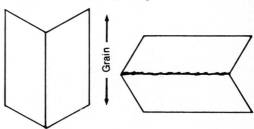

FIG. 11-15 Grain direction of paper is critical in the case of magazine and book printing.

DECKLED EDGES

Some book papers, especially those of antique finish, have *deckled edges*. These are feathery, ragged edges formed along the outer edges of the web as the paper is made. This finish appears either on one or on two opposite edges of the finished sheets of paper. Deckled edges give a pleasing, refined touch to some kinds of printing.

BASIS WEIGHT

In most cases, printing papers are manufactured and identified according to their *basis weight* (also called basic weight) as illustrated in Fig. 11-16. Basis weight is the weight in pounds of a ream (500 sheets) of paper in the *basic size* for that grade. For example, book paper has a basic size of 25″ × 38″. Basis 70 means that 500 sheets of 25 × 38 book paper weigh 70 pounds. The basic size is not the same for all grades.

Paper is commonly referred to in terms of its ream weight—for example, 20-pound bond, 60-pound book. However, most paper houses list prices of paper on a thousand sheet basis. The letter "M" means 1000. In practice, 25 × 38—120M for a 60-pound book paper means 1000 sheets of 25″ × 38″ that weigh 120 pounds.

BASIS WEIGHTS TABLE

	BOND, SPIRIT, MIMEO 17 x 22	BOOK (Offset) 25 x 38	COVER (Card Stock) 20 x 26	INDEX 25½ x 30½	BRISTOL (Post Card Stock) 22½ x 28½
BOND	* 9 (manifold)	23	13	19	16
	*12	30	16	25	20
	*16	41	22	34	28
	*20	51	28	42	34
	*24	61	33	50	41
	*28	71	39	59	48
	32	81	45	67	55
	*36	91	50	75	62
BOOK	16	**40**	22	33	27
	18	*45	24	37	30
	20	*50	27	41	34
	24	*60	33	50	41
	28	*70	38	58	47
	31	*80	44	66	54
	35	90	49	74	61
	39	100	55	82	68
	47	*120	66	98	81
	59	150	82	123	101
COVER	36	91	50	75	62
	47	119	*65	97	80
	58	146	80	119	99
INDEX	43	110	60	*90	74
	53	135	74	*110	91
	68	171	94	140	116
BRISTOL	55	140	76	114	*94
	58	148	81	121	100
	70	178	97	146	120

FIG. 11–16 Most printing papers are manufactured and identified by basis weight.

FIG. 11–17 Paper opacity can be tested by use of an opacity gauge. (Courtesy Oxford Paper Co.)

OPACITY

The degree of "show-through" of the printed image from the opposite side of the paper refers to *opacity*. It is affected by the thickness of the paper, ink coverage, and other chemicals added to the paper. This quality is important in magazine, book, and catalog work. A special instrument (Fig. 11–17) is used to measure the degree of opacity in paper. Opacity should be considered carefully in the planning stages of a printed job where show-through is a factor.

PAPER GRADES

There are a great many kinds and grades of paper. Each grade serves a specific printing purpose, usually suggested by its grade name. Some of the more common grades of printing papers include: (1) business; (2) book; (3) cover; (4) bristol; (5) label; (6) newsprint; and (7) paperboard.

Business (Bond)

The primary uses of *business papers* are financial and administrative rather than commercial. These papers are used as ledger sheets, money orders and bank checks, safety papers, stationery, and mimeograph and duplicating forms. Most letterheads and business forms are a standard 8½" × 11" size. Four pieces this size can be cut out of the 17" × 22" basic size of business papers. Weights of business papers generally range from 13 pound to 24 pound.

Book

Constituting the largest class of printing paper grades, *book papers* are used mostly for offset and letterpress. Book papers are available coated, uncoated, and enamel. Finishes include eggshell, antique, vellum, and super calendered. There are regular and dull coateds, semi-dull and glossy enamels, and mattes. The basic size of book paper is 25" × 38". Weights range from 30 pound to 100 pound.

Cover

The *cover papers* category, as with the book papers classification, includes a large family of grades, colors, and finishes. Cover papers primarily serve the important function of covering and protecting other printed materials. Paper manufacturers provide cover papers that are color-coordinated with their book grades in many finishes and textures. As with book papers, cover papers possess the properties essential to good printing. The basic size of cover paper is 20" × 26". Weights range from 50 pound to 130 pound.

Bristol

There are three types of *bristol papers*, all similar to an extent. *Printing bristols* are used primarily for posters and point-of-purchase displays, usually in a die-cut format. *Index bristols* are made not only to accept printing and writing but also to be extremely erasable. Index bristols are used as file cards, postcards, booklet covers, business forms, menus, and advertising pieces. *Wedding bristols* contain fancy vellum or antique plate finishes. They are manufactured in extreme thicknesses and are used for announcements, distinctive menus, and programs. The basic size of printing bristols is 22½" × 28½", and their weights range from 90 pound to 200 pound. The basic size of index bristols is 25½" × 30½", and their weights range from 90 to 170 pound. The basic size of wedding bristols is 22½" × 28½", with weights ranging from 120 to 240 pound.

Label

The first thing that needs to be pointed out about *label papers* is that they are not used just in the manufacture of labels. These papers are subjected to rigorous production processes. These include bronzing, embossing, multicolor printing, varnishing or lacquering, pressure-sensitive coating, die-cutting, and adhesive treatments. Label papers are used extensively for book and record jackets, candy wrappers, and multipurpose seals and bands. The versatility of these papers make them attractive surfaces on which to print. The basic size of label papers is 25″ × 38″. Weights range from 55 pound to 100 pound, with 60 pound the most popular sheet.

Newsprint

The standard paper on which newspapers are printed is *newsprint*. Newsprint has many properties that continue to make it desirable for newspapers of all sizes. Pulp yields from raw materials are almost double those of other papermaking processes. Over 90% of newsprint is supplied and used in rolls with common weights of 30 pound and 32 pound (24″ × 36″).

Paperboard

Aside from having adequate printing qualities, *paperboard* must be capable of being cut (die-cut), creased and folded, and formed into various shapes for its many end uses. Paperboard is manufactured in a wide range of densities. This makes paperboard very strong and durable. The thinner paperboards are usually printable by offset, letterpress, or rotogravure. The thicker paperboards are printed on platen or screen process flat-bed presses. Certain very heavy members of the paperboard family are called *blanks*. These are used in package printing, outdoor and transit advertising, point-of-purchase displays, and many commercial advertising endeavors. The basic size of paperboard is 22″ × 38″. Paperboard is manufactured in thickness up to 0.056 inch. The chart in Fig. 11–18 shows the many kinds and thicknesses of paperboard.

Number of Plies	Caliper	Approximate Wt. (1000 Sheets)
Plain Blanks		
3	.015	280
4	.018	330
5	.021	360
6	.024	420
8	.030	520
10	.036	600
Coated Blanks		
3	.015	340
4	.018	420
5	.021	460
6	.024	530
8	.030	650
10	.036	760
Railroad Board		
4	.018	400
6	.024	530
8	.030	650
Tough Check		
3	.012	310
4	.018	430
6	.024	550
8	.030	680
Thick China		
	.011	300

FIG. 11–18 Paperboard blanks—caliper and approximate weight (based on size 22″ × 38″). (Courtesy Boise Cascade Paper Group.)

ENVELOPES

Envelopes are manufactured in many styles and sizes (Fig. 11–19). Each style has a special use and is usually ordered by a designated number. For example, a No. 10 envelope for business use measures $4\frac{1}{8}'' \times 9\frac{1}{2}''$. A No. $6\frac{3}{4}$ commercial envelope measures $3\frac{5}{8}'' \times 6\frac{1}{2}''$. Envelopes containing a transparent window are used for statements and invoices.

Envelopes used for social invitations and wedding announcements are called *baronial*. A No. 5 baronial envelope measures $4\frac{1}{8}'' \times 5\frac{1}{8}''$. Invitational blanks are available for printing and inserting in baronial envelopes.

Heavy kraft or Manila envelopes are manufactured for mailing magazines, pamphlets, reports, books, and other similar materials. Two of the most common types are the Manila clasp envelopes that measure $8\frac{3}{4}'' \times 11\frac{1}{4}''$ and $9'' \times 12''$.

FIG. 11–19   Envelopes are available in many styles and sizes.

ENVELOPE STYLES

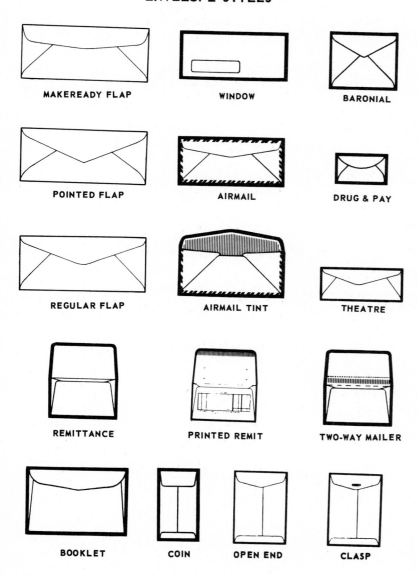

MAKEREADY FLAP	WINDOW	BARONIAL
POINTED FLAP	AIRMAIL	DRUG & PAY
REGULAR FLAP	AIRMAIL TINT	THEATRE
REMITTANCE	PRINTED REMIT	TWO-WAY MAILER
BOOKLET	COIN OPEN END	CLASP

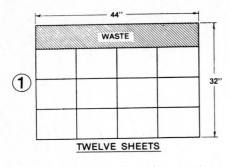

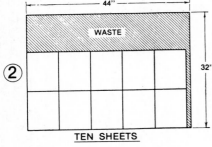

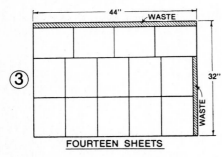

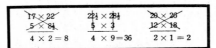

FIG. 11-20 Estimating the number of sheets needed for a printing job reduces the risk of costly waste.

Many types of envelopes are available in colors as well as plain white. They vary in thickness according to their construction and the weight of paper. Envelopes are usually sold in lots of 500 or 250 to a box, depending on style and size.

PAPER ESTIMATING

Estimating and cutting paper is an important operation performed by the printer. Paper is an expensive material and makes up a large percentage of the cost of a printed job. The printer plans the cutting of the paper in advance in order to avoid waste (Fig. 11-20).

The printer first determines the dimensions of the sheets needed for the job and then determines the size of the paper from which these sheets will be cut. The printer then calculates how many pieces for the job can be cut from one full sheet of basic size paper. Dimensions of the sheet to be printed are written under the dimensions of a full sheet of basic size paper. By using mathematical cancellation, the printer determines the maximum number of cuts obtainable each way out of each full basic size sheet (Fig. 11-21). The problem should always be checked by the cross-division method to determine if the maximum number of sheets is being obtained from the large sheet (Fig. 11-22).

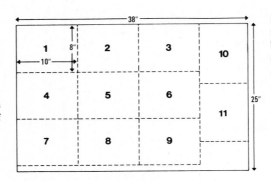

FIG. 11-21 The number of sheets that can be obtained from a full basic-size sheet is determined by drawing a cutting layout. (Courtesy A.B. Dick Co.)

17 × 22	22½ × 28½	20 × 26
5 × 8½	5 × 3	12 × 18
4 × 2 = 8	4 × 9 = 36	2 × 1 = 2

FIG. 11-22 Cross-division method is used to check original mathematical calculations.

FIG. 11-23 Cutting paper for a printing job requires that a few extra sheets be added for spoilage allowance.

25 × 38	(standard size of paper)
6 × 9	(size of printed piece)
4 × 4 = 16	(pieces per sheet)
1000	(number of finished printed copies required)
+ 75	(spoilage allowance for one-color, one-side offset)
1075	

$$\begin{array}{r} 67 \\ 16\overline{)1075} \\ 96 \\ \hline 115 \\ 112 \\ \hline 3 \end{array}$$ (full sheets required)

SPOILAGE

OFFSET SPOILAGE SCHEDULE

MAKEREADY (SHEETS)

	One Color Press One Color Work			Two Color Press Two Color Work			Four Color Press Four Color Work		
	1 Side	W&T	S/Wise	1 Side	W&T	S/Wise	1 Side	W&T	S/Wise
SIMPLE—First Color	75	100	125	150	175	225	300	350	450
Each Add'l Color	50	50	75						
AVERAGE—First Color	100	125	150	200	225	300	350	400	550
Each Add'l Color	75	100	125						
DIFFICULT—First Color	125	150	175	225	250	350	400	450	650
Each Add'l Color	100	125	150						

SPOILAGE PERCENTAGE PER EACH PRESS RUN

One Color Work			Two Color Work			Four Color Work		
1 Side	W&T	S/Wise	1 Side	W&T	S/Wise	1 Side	W&T	S/Wise
2.2	4.4	4.4	2.8	5.6	5.6	3.8	7.6	7.6

Above figures are for average job. Increase above percentages by 25% for difficult work.

LETTERPRESS SPOILAGE SCHEDULE

(Single Color Presses)

Sheets	One Color Printed 2 Sides	Each Additional Color Printed Two Sides	One Color Printed 1 Side	Each Additional Color Printed One Side
200	70	56	52	40
500	80	65	60	50
1,000	110	90	100	80
2,500	250	200	200	150
5,000	350	300	250	200
10,000	600	500	400	300
25,000 up	5%	4%	3%	2%

FINISHING SPOILAGE:

Be sure to allow for finishing spoilage — cut, fold, stitch or trim.

FIG. 11-24   Paper spoilage allowance schedule for offset and letterpress operations. (Courtesy Printing Industries Association of Southern California.)

SPOILAGE ALLOWANCE

In cutting paper for a printing job (Fig. 11-23), it is necessary to add a few extra sheets as a *spoilage allowance*. The additional sheets are meant for press and bindery setups. Spoilage allowance also makes up for sheets damaged as the job is being produced. Each printer determines a realistic spoilage allowance percentage. This figure is based on the complexity of the job, number of press runs, and binding and finishing operations required. A typical spoilage allowance schedule is shown in Fig. 11-24. Figure 11-25 shows a chart useful in determining common paper formulas.

HELPFUL PAPER FORMULAS

Basic Weight: The weight of one ream (500 sheets) of basic size.

Equivalent Weight: The weight of one ream (500 sheets) of a size larger or smaller than the basic size.

How to Find the Equivalent Weight:

$$Formula: \quad \frac{\text{Sheet Area of Desired Size} \times \text{Basic Weight}}{\text{Sheet Area of Basic Size}} = \text{Equivalent Weight}$$

Example: What is the weight of a 32-lb. ledger paper in size 28 x 34?
Solution: Filling in the known factors in the formula, the following equation is obtained:

$$\frac{952 \ (28 \times 34) \times 32}{374 \ (17 \times 22)} = 81.4$$

Thus, 28 x 34 — 81 lb. is equal to 17 x 22 — 32 lb., or one ream of the 32-lb. paper, in size 28 x 34, weighs 81 lbs.

How to Specify Paper:
An order for paper should contain this information: Quantity, brand name, color, finish, size and weight.
Thus: 15 reams, (Brand Name), Ivory, Laid, 17 x 22-40M.

How to Find the Weight of an Odd Number of Sheets:

$$Formula: \quad \frac{\text{Twice the Ream Weight} \times \text{Number of Sheets}}{1000} = \text{Total Weight}$$

Example: What is the weight of 1475 sheets of 17 x 22 — 28-lb. stock?
Solution: Filling in the formula —

$$\frac{56 \ (2 \times 28) \times 1475}{1000} = 82.6 \text{ lbs.}$$

How to Figure Pieces Per Sheet:
Formula: Place the dimensions of the piece under the dimensions of the sheet, then divide vertically and diagonally.
Example: How many 5 x 8 cards can be cut from a 25½ x 30½ sheet?

Divide vertically	—	then diagonally
25½ x 30½		25½ x 30½
5 x 8		5 x 8
5 x 3 = 15 out		6 x 3 = 18 out

ZELLERBACH PAPER COMPANY

FIG. 11-25 This chart is a handy reference when determining common paper formulas. (Courtesy Zellerbach Paper Co.)

PAPER CUTTING

There are two basic types of paper cutters used to cut and trim paper to size. One is operated by means of a simple hand lever (Fig. 11-26), and the other is electrically powered (Fig. 11-27). Sophisticated paper cutters, such as the one shown in Fig. 11-28, have built-in computers for programming a cycle of paper cuts or trims. The cutter automatically shifts to the required dimension after each cut in the cycle.

With both types of cutters, paper is placed on the cutting table and positioned for the desired size of cut or trim. The paper is held firmly in position with a clamp as the blade makes the cut (Fig. 11-29).

HINTS FOR SELECTING PAPER

Paper may be purchased through the printer or ordered from a paper house. Paper houses do not manufacture paper. They stock papers made by several different manufacturers. Paper samples and prices are available to all clients. When selecting paper for a particular printed piece, the following factors should be considered:

• Select paper that will be compatible with the printing process and ink to be used. Think about durability, permanence, foldability, and exposure to various weather conditions.

• Price is extremely important. Expensive paper is not always necessary. Intended use is usually the key to determining quality and price category.

• Paper that is heavier than necessary will lead to high mailing costs. A number of lightweight papers are available which have good opacity and exceptional printability qualities.

• The paper surface and finish should be selected on the basis of the printing process to be used and the aesthetic qualities desired. Rough-textured paper gives a different feel and appearance than a smooth-textured paper.

• Paper is available in many different sizes. The printed piece size and the maximum press sheet size should be considered for maximum efficiency and minimum waste.

• Colored paper can add to the aesthetics of a printed piece. It may also add cost. Paper and ink color combinations should be studied carefully. Color is a psychological factor that every designer must understand thoroughly.

• Paper grain direction is most important when planning folded pieces. Paper tears and folds most easily with the grain. The grain direction may affect color registration and folding and binding operations.

FIG. 11-26 Hand-lever paper cutter. (Courtesy Challenge Machinery Co.)

FIG. 11-27 Electrically powered paper cutter. (Courtesy Challenge Machinery Co.)

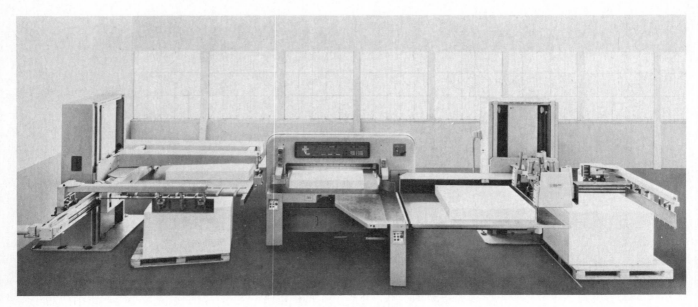

FIG. 11-28   Fully automated paper cutter. (Courtesy Heidelberg Eastern, Inc.)

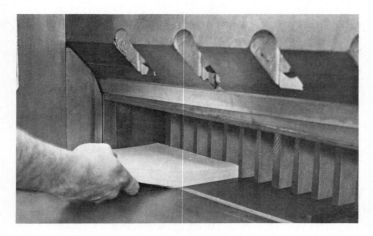

FIG. 11-29   Paper is held firmly in the cutter with a heavy clamp during the cutting cycle. (Courtesy Stephen B. Simms, photographer.)

12

BINDING AND FINISHING

The final processing of a printed job most often includes binding and finishing operations. The equipment used to perform these operations is usually automatic. Most web presses are equipped to handle some or all finishing operations as the job is printed. However, many printed jobs that run on large sheets must be processed through various binding and finishing operations.

Most printing jobs require binding and finishing operations before delivery to the client. The equipment used for these operations is usually automated. Binding and finishing operations are areas in which strict attention to detail is required. A mistake in this production stage can lead to a costly rerun of the job.

BINDING OPERATIONS

When a printed job is designed as a magazine, book, catalog, or booklet, various methods of fastening or *binding* are used. The more familiar binding methods include: (1) mechanical; (2) loose-leaf; (3) wire; (4) sewn soft-cover; (5) sewn case-bound; (6) perfect; and (7) padding.

Mechanical

The *mechanical* binding method is very popular for fastening books, catalogs, manuals, and other similar volumes. Mechanical binding requires punching holes in the paper so that metal or plastic wire or strips can be threaded through the holes. Two common

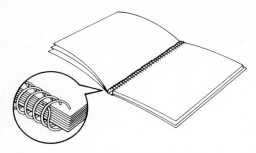

FIG. 12-1   Spiral binding. (Courtesy A.B. Dick Co.)

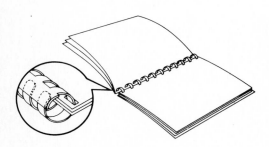

FIG. 12-2   Plastic binding. (Courtesy A.B. Dick Co.)

FIG. 12-3   Ring bindings are made of plastic and metal. (Courtesy A.B. Dick Co.)

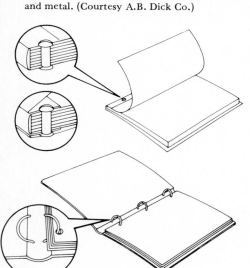

methods of mechanical binding include spiral (Fig. 12-1) and plastic (Fig. 12-2). Mechanical binding allows pages to lie perfectly flat. Adequate margin allowance must be provided for the holes.

Loose-Leaf

Pages that are bound together with removable rings or posts are called *loose-leaf* binding. With *ring* binding (Fig. 12-3), pages may be opened flat, and pages may either be removed or inserted. Since holes must be punched for this type of binding, adequate clearance along the binding edges is necessary.

Wire stitching

The *wire stitching* method of fastening sheets together is divided into *saddle-wire* and *side-wire* stitching. The saddle-wire method consists of wires or staples inserted on the fold line of the pages (Fig. 12-4). In the side-wire method, staples are inserted close to the fold and clinched at the back (Fig. 12-5). Pages of a side-wire stitched book cannot be opened flat. This type of fastening requires extra allowance on the margins for the staples. Stitching equipment ranges from manual units (Fig. 12-6) to the automatic variety as shown in Figs. 12-7 and 12-8.

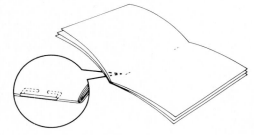

FIG. 12-4   Saddle-wire stitching. (Courtesy A.B. Dick Co.)

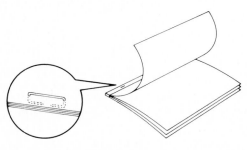

FIG. 12-5   Side-wire stitching. (Courtesy A.B. Dick Co.)

FIG. 12-6   Manually operated stitcher. (Courtesy Michael Business Machines.)

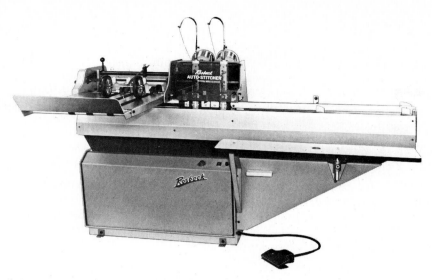

FIG. 12-7   Automatic stitcher. (Courtesy F.P. Rosback Co.)

FIG. 12-8   Automatic stitcher with three-knife book-trimmer attachment. (Courtesy F.P. Rosback Co.)

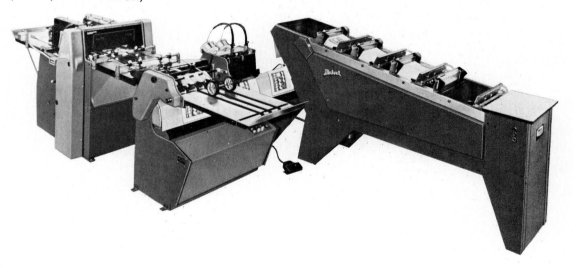

Sewn Soft-Cover

Sewn bindings with *soft covers* will withstand hard use for a limited time. Strong thread is sewn through the binding edge of each sheet and securely holds all sheets in place between the covers of a book. Technical information is often bound in this manner because the book usually passes through many hands during its brief but valuable life.

Sewn Case-bound

Books with hard covers are sewn when extremely hard use and long wear are expected. *Sewn case-bound* books (Fig. 12-9) are assembled in signatures, which are then sewn together with strong thread. The thickness of the signatures forms a wide "spine" to which the cover is attached. Sewn case-binding is the most expensive method, but it provides the best durability.

FIG. 12-9   Sewn case-bound books are assembled in signatures that are sewn together. (Courtesy A.B. Dick Co.)

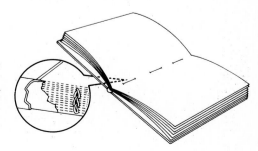

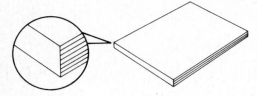

FIG. 12–10 Perfect binding. (Courtesy A.B. Dick Co.)

Perfect

Telephone directories, pocket-size books, magazines, and mail-order catalogs are examples of *perfect* binding (Fig. 12–10). The pages are held together with flexible adhesive. Books bound in this way lie flat when open and are less expensive to bind than if sewn. Perfect binding is fast and economical and results in attractive printed products.

Padding

Tablets, notebooks, and memo pads are familiar items that are bound by *padding* (Fig. 12–11). This method of binding utilizes a flexible coating of cement applied to one edge of the pile of printed or blank sheets. When dry, the "pads" are individually separated and trimmed to final size on a paper cutter.

FIG. 12–11 The simplest form of adhesive binding, called *padding*, is found on the edge of the common notepad. (Courtesy Stephen B. Simms, photographer.)

FINISHING OPERATIONS

Most printed jobs have as a final step in production some form of *finishing* operation. This might only be the packaging of the product for final delivery. Finishing operations include: (1) cutting and trimming; (2) folding; (3) punching; (4) drilling; (5) gathering; (6) collating; (7) jogging; (8) scoring; (9) perforating; (10) die-cutting; and (11) hot stamping.

Cutting and Trimming

After pages for magazines, books, and pamphlets are printed, they are *cut* and *trimmed*. The printed sheets are cut so that they can be folded into signatures. The signatures are bound together and the trimming is done after the binding. Paper cutters range from the single-knife hydraulic type to the fully automatic three-knife book trimmer (Fig. 12–12).

In the majority of printing, it is common practice to print or repeat the same image on a large sheet of paper. This method saves time on the press. For example, if a job requires 100,000 pieces, it

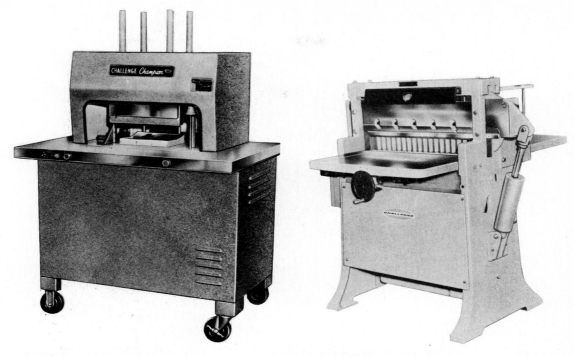

FIG. 12-12 Automatic three-knife book trimmer. (Courtesy Challenge Machinery Co.)

FIG. 12-13 Single-knife paper cutter. (Courtesy Challenge Machinery Co.)

might be run eight to a page and the press run reduced to 12,500. Sheets that are printed in this way usually end up being cut apart and trimmed to final size. This is usually done on a single-knife paper cutter (Fig. 12–13).

Folding

Signature sheets, booklets, flyers, and programs require *folding*. This operation is accomplished on automatic folding machines. Some are of the light-duty kind (Figs. 12–14 and 12–15), and others are

FIG. 12-14 Challenge Foldmaster 12 Auto-folder. (Courtesy Challenge Machinery Co.)

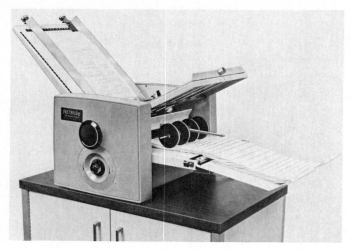

FIG. 12-15 Michael Fastfold 17 paper folder. (Courtesy Michael Business Machines.)

FIG. 12-16 Baumfolder 726 Model 4442 paper folder. (Courtesy Baumfolder Corp.)

FIG. 12-17 Baumfolder 700 Series paper folder. (Courtesy Baumfolder Corp.)

of the heavy-duty variety (Figs. 12-16 and 12-17). Folders produce the fold by forcing the paper between metal rollers. Most machine folding involves sheets printed as signatures. The signature sheets are fed through the folder and come out folded with the pages (folios) in the correct numbered order. Some of these machines are capable of stitching and trimming all in one operation (Fig. 12-18).

TYPES OF FOLDS In designing a printed piece, the different types of folds and the limitations of mechanical folding should be carefully considered. The various types of common folds are illustrated in Fig. 12-19.

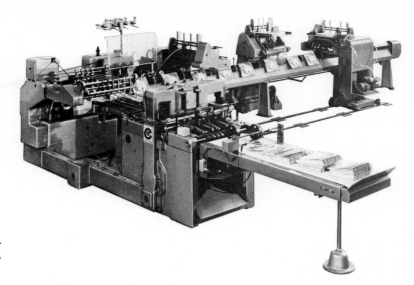

FIG. 12-18 Consolidated Jetstream 225 capable of stitching and trimming in one operation. (Courtesy Consolidated International Corp.)

STYLES OF FOLDS

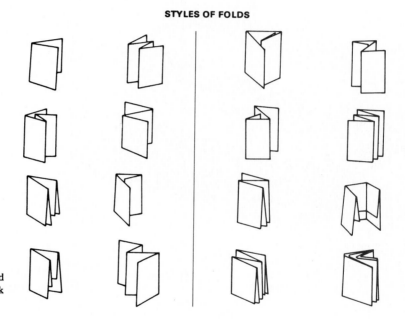

FIG. 12-19 These are typical folds produced by folding machines. (Courtesy A.B. Dick Co.)

Four-page Folder. The four-page folder is the simplest type. It can be used for price lists, programs, bill stuffers, and instruction sheets.

Six-page Folder. This folder is made with two parallel folds—either regular or accordion. It is used for envelope stuffers, letters, circulars, brochures, etc.

Eight-page Folder. There are three types of eight-page folders. The first makes one parallel and one right-angle fold, also called a *French fold,* when printing is on one side of the paper. The second type makes two parallel folds. The third type makes a three-parallel accordion fold and is used for ease of opening.

Twelve-page Folder. There are two ways to fold a twelve-page folder: (1) regular; or (2) accordion. These are often used as a four-page letter, with the two right-angle folds folding lettersize to fit a mailing envelope.

Sixteen-page Folder. A sixteen-page folder can be folded with one parallel and two right-angle folds or with three parallel folds.

The latter is used for easy-to-open transportation schedules. It can also be bound into a sixteen-page booklet.

Punching

Machines for *punching* are used for cutting rectangular or specially shaped holes in paper to accommodate plastic and spiral binding. Figure 12-20 shows a punching-inserting machine used to cut rectangular holes in printed sheets and to insert plastic binding in the punched sheets. The prongs on the top of the machine spread the plastic material, allowing the punched sheets to be placed in proper position. When released, the binding material curls and completes the operation.

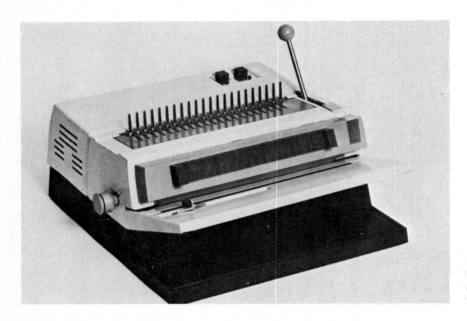

FIG. 12-20 Plastic binding punching-inserting machine used to punch a series of rectangular holes and insert plastic ring binding. (Courtesy GBC Corp.)

Drilling

Some printed materials require holes for use in ring binders. This is a process known as *drilling*. Machines for drilling vary in size and capacity from the single-drill model (Figs. 12-21 and 12-22) to the multiple-drill variety (Figs. 12-23 and 12-24). Most paper drilling machines are equipped with special attachments that can be used for drilling different shapes. The paper drill bit is hollow and allows the paper chips to escape to a rear compartment.

Gathering

Assembling individual sheets or signatures (large sheets folded to form pages) in the correct sequence is called *gathering*. This operation is done by placing piles of signatures or pages in order along the edge of a table. One sheet or signature at a time is picked up from each pile and assembled in proper sequence. Automatic gathering machines are used extensively in high-volume work (Fig. 12-25). Desk-top semiautomatic machines are used whenever a small volume of work is required (Fig. 12-26).

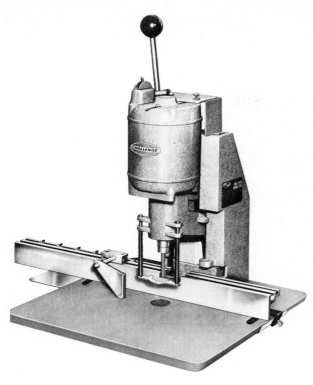

FIG. 12-21 Single-hole table-top paper drilling machine. (Courtesy Challenge Machinery Co.)

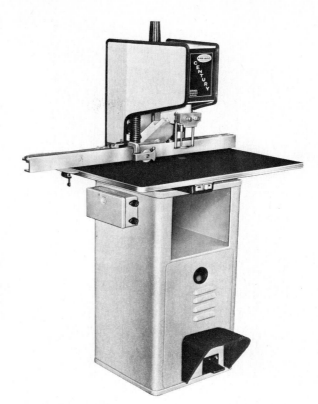

FIG. 12-22 Single-hole pedestal paper drilling machine. (Courtesy Challenge Machinery Co.)

FIG. 12-23 Three-hole paper drilling machine. (Courtesy Challenge Machinery Co.)

FIG. 12-24 Five-hole paper drilling machine. (Courtesy Challenge Machinery Co.)

FIG. 12-25 Automatic gathering machine used for high-volume work. (Courtesy A.B. Dick Co.)

FIG. 12-26 Table-top gathering machine that is operated manually. (Courtesy Challenge Machinery Co.)

Collating

The term *collating* is often confused with the term gathering. Collating is an operation performed for the purpose of checking to see that the correct number of signatures has been gathered. Collating codes are printed in different positions on the binding fold of signatures. After the magazine or book has been folded and gathered, a pattern is visible on the spine. Errors are quickly detected and easily corrected.

Jogging

Jogging is the term applied to straightening sheets of paper that have been delivered from the press. An automatic jogging machine is usually equipped with a two-sided slanting table (Fig. 12-27) that vibrates, thus straightening a pile of sheets in a matter of seconds. Many different models of joggers are available (Fig. 12-28).

Scoring

Placing a crease in a sheet of thick paper or cardboard to aid in folding is referred to as *scoring*. The crease produces an embossed or raised ridge on the sheet. The fold is made with the ridge on the inside of the sheet in order to prevent stretching. The width of the crease is varied according to the thickness of the paper (Fig. 12-29). A thicker paper requires a thicker crease, which gives a wider groove to help make a cleaner fold. Scoring is usually done on automatic equipment.

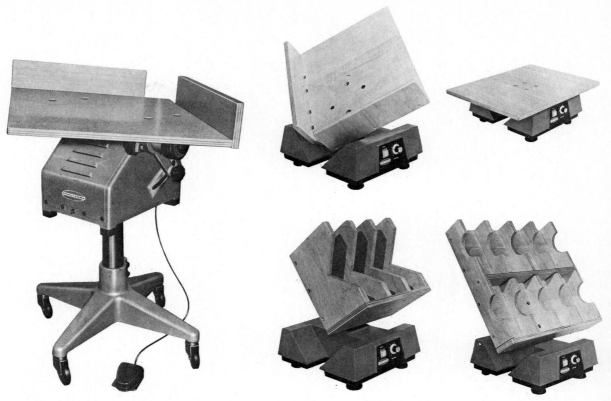

FIG. 12-27   Automatic jogging machine. (Courtesy Challenge Machinery Co.)

FIG. 12-28   Jogging machines are available in many styles and sizes. (Courtesy Challenge Machinery Co.)

FIG. 12-29   Scoring paper and cardboard aids in folding thicker sheets without difficulty. (Courtesy A.B. Dick Co.)

FIG. 12-30   Perforating allows printed pieces to be separated easily, such as with ticket stubs. (Courtesy A.B. Dick Co.)

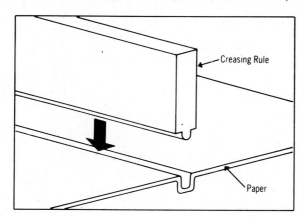

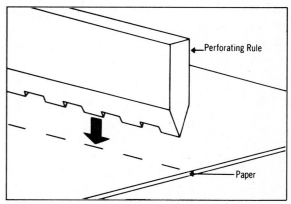

Perforating

Some printed jobs require that part of the job be removable—for example, a ticket stub. This operation is referred to as *perforating* (Fig. 12-30). In the process, a series of very short slits or holes is cut in the paper leaving only a small "bridge" of paper remaining intact. The perforated sheet is then easily pulled apart. Perforating can be done on both offset and letterpress printing presses.

Die-Cutting

Any irregular shape or design that cannot be cut with a straight cut is done by *die-cutting* (Fig. 12–31). Since there is no standard design used in this operation, each metal die is custom-made to match the requirements of the job. The die consists of a metal cutting edge that matches the outline shape of the job. The die is mounted on a wooden dieboard with the cutting edge up, similar to a cookie cutter. Die-cutting presses are similar to letterpress printing presses. Most boxes, cartons, and point-of-purchase items are die-cut.

(A)

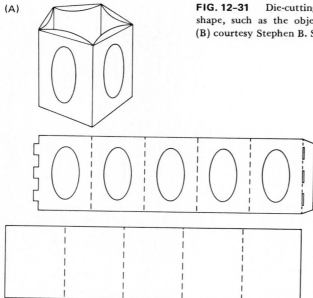

FIG. 12–31 Die-cutting is performed on any printed piece having an irregular shape, such as the objects shown here. [(A) courtesy Hammermill Paper Co.; (B) courtesy Stephen B. Simms, photographer.]

(B)

Hot Stamping

Gold, silver, or colored images of type or illustrations are frequently placed on covers of books, business letterheads, and certificates. Hot stamping is a letterpress process that uses relief images and heat. Gold, silver, or colored foil is positioned between the type or illustration and the surface to be printed. Through the use of pressure and heat a permanent image is formed. Hand-operated machines for a small volume of work are available (Figs. 12–32 and 12–33). Heavy-duty automatic equipment is used for large-volume work.

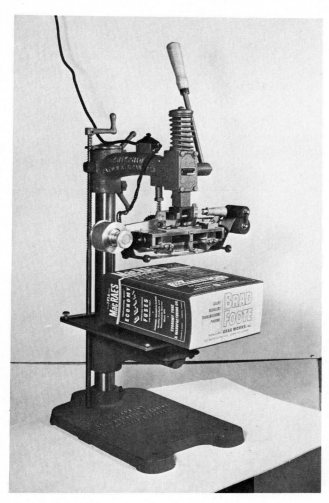 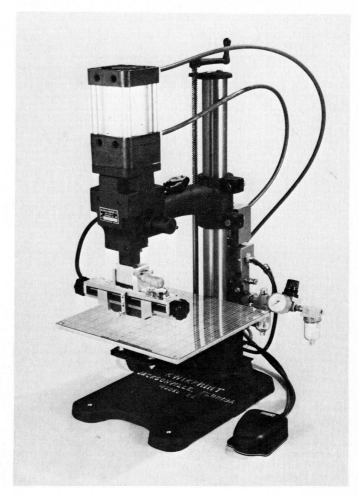

FIG. 12-32   Hand-operated hot-stamp machine. (Courtesy Halvorford Kwikprint Co.)

FIG. 12-33   Air-operated semi-automatic hot-stamp machine. (Courtesy Halvorford Kwikprint Co.)

chapter 13

PRINTING INKS

The manufacture of printing inks requires many skills and technologies. Ink is basically a chemical compound, different types of which have specific physical properties. Ink is manufactured from a variety of natural and synthetic materials. It is made in modern, efficient plants that use the latest in automated and computer-directed machinery. Essentially, printing inks are colored coatings graphically applied to a surface by one of the printing processes. Inks are broadly classified by the printing process used: letterpress, offset lithography, gravure, and screen process. This chapter covers the ingredients of ink, how ink is manufactured, and the ink characteristics of each printing process.

The almost unbelievable variety of printing applications within the graphic arts requires different types of printing inks suited to the several printing processes. Each ink manufacturer has specific formulas for making different inks. In general, however, the ingredients used in manufacturing printing inks fall into three major classifications which include: (1) vehicles; (2) pigments; and (3) additives.

INGREDIENTS

Vehicles

Vehicles consist of petroleum oils, rosin oils, linseed oil, litho varnish, cottonseed oil, castor oil, soybean oil, and others. The vehicle forms the basic ingredient of printing ink. The function of the vehicle is to act as a carrier for the pigment and as a binder to affix the pigment to the printed surface. The nature of the vehicle determines to a large measure the body, length, tack, and drying characteristics of the ink.

BODY The consistency, stiffness, or softness of an ink relates to its *body*. Ink consistencies vary from being very stiff or thick

190

to being very soft or thin. Letterpress inks are very thick in comparison to gravure inks, which are extremely thin.

LENGTH The property of an ink referred to as *length* has to do with the ink's ability to flow. Inks can be *short* or *long*. Short inks have the consistency of butter and have poor flow properties. Short inks can pile up on the rollers, plate, and blanket on some offset presses. Long inks flow well but have a tendency to form a "mist" on high-speed presses.

TACK The stickiness of an ink is called *tack*. It relates to the force required to "split" an ink film between two surfaces. Tack is important in the offset printing process. In offset printing there must be correct transfer of ink from ink rollers to the plate and then from the rubber blanket to the paper. Tack is also important in determining whether or not the ink will pick or lift particles from the surface of the paper.

HINTS ON PRINTING PROCESS
INK-DRYING CHARACTERISTICS

LETTERPRESS

- Designed to print from raised (relief) surfaces.
- Letterpress inks are usually of moderate body and tack.
- Most letterpress inks dry by oxidation, penetration, evaporation, or a combination of any one of these.

OFFSET LITHOGRAPHY

- Designed to print from a plane (flat) surface.
- Offset inks are usually of moderate body.
- Offset inks are generally very strong in color value to compensate for the lesser amount applied on the press.
- Offset inks are formulated to run in the presence of water.
- Most offset inks dry by a combination of oxidation and penetration.

GRAVURE

- Designed to print by being pulled from the engraved (recessed) wells in the cylinder or plate.
- Gravure inks are very thin in body, which means that they are almost liquid.
- Gravure inks dry primarily by solvent evaporation.

SCREEN PROCESS

- Designed to print by application through a screen (fabric or metal) mesh.
- Screen process inks are extremely thick (comparable to the consistency of paint).
- Screen process inks dry primarily through the evaporation of the solvent in the ink.

DRYING Printing inks dry by several different methods. Inks printed on soft absorbent papers dry by the *absorption* of the vehicle into the paper. Inks printed on hard surface papers normally dry by *oxidation*. Oxidation consists, essentially, of the absorption of oxygen by drying oils. Most inks dry by a combination of the two drying mechanisms.

Pigments

The color in an ink is called the *pigment*. It is primarily the pigment that is seen when one examines printed matter. Black pigments are prepared from furnace black and thermal black. These pigments are produced from oil and natural gas, respectively. The various other ink pigments are produced from inorganic and organic mineral compounds.

Black pigments are primarily carbon, which is produced by burning gas or oil. Some common black pigments include furnace black, lampblack, and channel black.

White pigments are either opaque or transparent. Pigment ingredients used include zinc sulfide, zinc oxide, and titanium dioxide. Inks considered to be opaque whites are mixing whites and cover whites. Transparent whites permit light to pass through the pigment so that the color below the ink can be seen. Transparent white pigments are manufactured from clays, magnesium carbonate, aluminum hydrate, and calcium carbonate.

Additives

Special ingredients called *additives* are often added to inks for specific purposes. These ingredients include driers, waxes, lubricants, reducing oils, and gums. Some additives are incorporated in the ink during manufacture. Additives can also be added to the finished ink to modify it for special conditions on the printing press.

MANUFACTURE OF INK

Depending on the requirements of the particular ink, the manufacture of ink involves careful formulation (Fig. 13-1). Almost all inks are made in batches. Basically, ink manufacture involves the operations of mixing, milling, and packaging.

Mixing

Introducing pigment to the vehicle is the first step in the manufacture of ink and is known as *mixing*. The vehicle is broken down and thoroughly mixed with the pigment. The mixing step is done in batch containers or tubs by means of large mixing blades (Fig. 13-2). The speed of the blades can be regulated depending on the nature of the ink and pigment being introduced into the vehicle.

Milling

Many printing inks cannot be reduced to their final production specifications by simple mixing. In these cases, *milling* (sometimes called grinding) is necessary in order to thoroughly disperse the

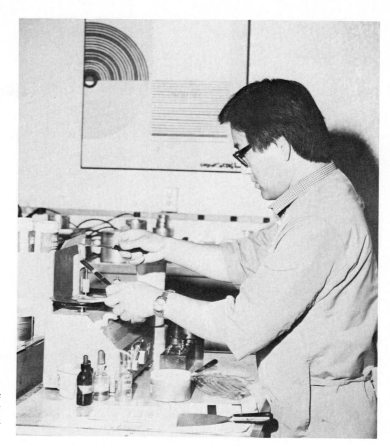

FIG. 13-1 The first step in ink manufacture is the careful formulation of all necessary ingredients. (Courtesy General Printing Ink Co.)

FIG. 13-2 Batch container is used to mix ingredients. (Courtesy General Printing Ink Co.)

FIG. 13-3 After mixing the ingredients, milling is done in a large metal container called a *mill*. (Courtesy General Printing Ink Co.)

pigment into the vehicle. A mill (Fig. 13-3) is used for the purpose. These machines consist of several steel rollers that revolve in opposite directions. The speed of the mill, the temperature of the rollers, and the pressure between the rollers determine grinding efficiency.

Packaging

Ink is *packaged* in several ways (Fig. 13-4). These packaging devices include cartridges, cans, drums, and bulk tanker-trucks. Ink is often formulated (mixed) specifically to fit individual customer paper and press requirements. Checking quality control and color consistency and carrying out product research are continuous functions of the ink chemists and technologists (Fig. 13-5).

FIG. 13–4 Various kinds of containers are used for the packaging of inks. (Courtesy General Printing Ink Co.)

FIG. 13–5 Chemists and technologists are responsible for ink quality control, color consistency, and product research. (Courtesy General Printing Ink Co.)

GLOSSARY
OF TERMS

Airbrushing. A method of placing smooth tint surfaces on a photograph or wash drawing.

Ascender. The portion of the vertical stroke that extends above a letter, for example, b, d, f, h, and k.

Author's Alteration (AA). Correction made by the author on a proof sheet.

Benday. A method of laying a pressure-sensitive material (dots, lines, or other textures) on a paste-up to obtain various tones and shadings.

Black Letter. A general term used to describe a Gothic or Old English type design.

Blanket. Sheet of rubber-coated fabric placed on the offset cylinder to receive ink from the plate and offset it to the sheet on the impression cylinder.

Bleed. An illustration that extends to one or more edges of a printed page.

Blueline. A photographic print of blue color made by exposing sensitized paper to a negative in contact.

Body Type. Type used for the main body of a printed job.

Bold Face. Heavy face type, in contrast to light face type. Used for emphasis, captions, subheadings, etc.

Bond Paper. A broad term used to describe stationery used for letterheads, forms, and general business purposes.

Book Paper. A class of paper used for books, catalogs, periodicals, booklets, and general advertising literature.

Broadside. A large, specially folded printed sheet.

Brochure. A pamphlet bound in the form of a booklet.

Brownprint. A photographic print of brown color made by exposing sensitized paper to a negative in contact.

Camera-ready copy. Copy that is ready to be photographed without further alteration.

Caps and Small Caps. Two sizes of capitals made on one size of type body, commonly used in most forms of Roman letters.

Caption. Descriptive matter about an illustration.

Case-bound Book. A book with a stiff cover. The cover is made separately and the sewn book is inserted into it.

Characters per Pica. Number of average characters that will fit in one pica.

Chinese White. White paint used to remove unwanted marks on finished copy.

Coated Paper. Paper that has a smooth glossy finish.

Cold Type. A trade term denoting the use of composition methods not involving hot-metal type.

Collate. In bookmaking, to examine gathered signatures to verify their order and number.

Composing Machine. Any of the three categories of typesetting equipment: (1) hot metal; (2) typewriter; or (3) photographic.

Composition. Setting of text copy into type either in hot metal or cold type or by photography.

Comprehensive. A detailed layout designed to show exactly how the job will look when printed.

Computerized Typesetting. Refers to perforated or magnetic tape or discs used to drive a computer which in turn produces photographic type on paper or film.

Condensed Type. Narrow or slender type faces.

Contact Screen. A photographically made halftone screen having a dot structure of graded density and usually used in vacuum contact with the film.

Continuous Tone. Tonal gradation without use of halftone dots.

Copy. Any material furnished by the customer (typewritten manuscripts, pictures, artwork, etc.) to be used in the production of printing.

Copyfitting. Calculating the proper size of type and width of line to fit the copy into a given area of space.

Crop. To cut down in size or eliminate unwanted areas of a photograph or other artwork.

Descender. The portion of the vertical stroke that extends below the main portion of a letter—for example, p, q, and y.

Die Cutting. Process of cutting openings or unusual shapes in paper and paperboard; examples of end results are egg cartons and counter displays.

Differential Spacing. Individual character widths required in quality typography.

Dirty Proof. Proof that contains many errors.

Display Type. Larger or heavier type than that used for body text. Used to attract attention.

Drilling. Piercing of paper with a rotating hollow drill to make round binder holes.

Dropout Halftone. A halftone having no halftone screen dots in the highlights and usually made in the form of a silhouette.

Dummy. Accurate preview of proposed booklet, folder, etc., cut to size and bound with illustrations sketched or actually pasted in place and with all copy indicated.

Duotone. Two-color halftone reproduction made from a continuous tone original and requiring two halftone negatives. One plate is usually printed in dark ink and the other in a lighter ink.

Em. The square of a type body. So named because in early fonts (and sometimes in modern fonts) the letter M was usually cast on a square body.

En. One-half the width of an em.

Enamel Paper. Coated paper that has a high-gloss surface.

Face. Printing surface of a type; the particular design of a font of type.

Family. A number of series of related type designs that have characteristics in common.

Felt Side. The correct side of paper for one-side printing.

Flat. One or more pages or other image units in the form of negatives or positives arranged, positioned, and secured to a sheet for exposure in a vacuum frame to a press plate.

Flush Left. Lines of type set even at the left margin.

Flush Right. Lines of type set even at the right margin.

Folio. Page number.

Font. Complete assortment of all the different characters of a particular size and style of type.

Foot Margin. White space below the type at bottom of the page.

Foot of the Job. Bottom or end of the job or page of type.

Format. The size, style, shape, printing requirements, etc., of any magazine, catalog, book, or printed piece.

Galley Proof. Proof taken of type matter while it is still in a galley.

Ganging. Process whereby various pieces of not necessarily related art copy are combined so that the camera operator can shoot them all on one negative. Also, the combining of a number of unrelated jobs for a single press run.

Gather. To assemble folded signatures of a book in consecutive order.

Grain. Roughened or irregular surface of an offset printing plate. Also, direction of grain in paper.

Gravure. A process of printing in which the sunken-image plate is generally run on a direct rotary press.

Gripper Bite. The amount of paper that extends beneath the press gripper. Sometimes called gripper margin.

Hairline. Thin stroke on a type character.

Halftone. A photomechanical printing surface and impression therefrom in which detail and tone values are represented by a series of evenly spaced dots of varying size and shape. The dot areas vary in direct proportion to the intensity of the tones they represent.

Halftone Tint. A solid area of an image transformed into a gray tone of any desired density by stripping in a piece of film leaving uniform dot density.

Highlights. The lightest or whitest parts in a photograph represented in a halftone reproduction by the smallest dots or the absence of all dots.

Imposition. The proper placement of page forms according to the press layout so that pages will print in the correct sequence in the signature when folded.

Italic. A style or form of letter that generally slants to the right.

Jog. To align sheets of paper.

Justify. To make a line of text copy fit both left and right margins exactly.

Kern. That part of a letter of type that projects beyond the metal body on which it is cast such as the head and tail of some italic letters; "*f*" is an example. Also, to selectively adjust unit spacing between characters.

Key. To identify copy as it appears in a dummy by means of symbols, usually letters. Insertions are sometimes "keyed" in like manner.

Keylining. Technique used in copy preparation to handle copy for simple color separations or for indicating reverses or outline of backgrounds. The purpose is to provide copy for the camera that does not need excessive opaquing of photographic negatives or positives.

Key Plate. In color printing, the printing plate that is used as a guide for the register of other colors. It normally contains the most detail.

Layout. Plan of a job showing margins, headings, spacing, type specifications, pictures, etc.

Leaders. Row of dots or dashes on a type base, commonly used in programs and reports.

Leading. Additional space between lines of type.

Legend. Descriptive matter below an illustration.

Letterpress. Printing process utilizing plates, type, or forms wherein the image area is raised and when inked is applied directly to the paper.

Letter Spacing. Lateral spacing between each letter of a word.

Ligature. Two characters joined in one body or key, such as fi, fl, ffl, ffi, etc.

Light Face. Type used most commonly in composition of text or bookwork.

Line Copy. Copy that consists of only solid blacks and whites, such as type and line drawings.

Line Gauge. Printer's rule used for measuring purposes.

Line Spacing. Number of points between lines or number of lines per inch.

Logotype. Name of a product or company in a special design used as a trademark in advertising.

Make-up. Assembling of type, plates, or negatives into complete pages.

Margins. White space at sides and top and bottom of copy.

Markup. To write up instructions, as on a dummy or manuscript copy.

Measure. Width of type matter in picas.

Mechanical. Also known as a paste-up. An assemblage of all copy elements into a unit for photographic plate-making (copy ready for the camera). Referred to as camera-ready copy.

Middletones. Tonal range between highlights and shadows of a photograph and represented in a halftone reproduction by middle-size dots, usually 40% to 50% as measured with a densitometer.

Moiré. Undesirable patterns resulting when reproductions are made from halftone negatives. Caused by conflict between the ruling of the halftone screen and the dots or lines of the original.

Mortising. Cutting out areas in a plate or in cold-type artwork so that type can be inserted.

Negative. A photographic image of the original on paper, film, or glass in reverse from that of the original copy.

Nonpareil. A unit of measure equaling 6 points (one-half of a pica).

Offset Lithography. Printing process that utilizes a flat plate and oil-base ink. Water rolled on the plate moistens the nonprinting area and repels the ink so that it adheres only to the image area.

Oldstyle Roman. General classification of type derived from early Dutch, Venetian, and English designs. Caslon, Garamond, and Cloister are examples.

Optical Center. Point where the eye normally strikes the page—approximately two-fifths of the way down and slightly to the left of center.

Overprinting. Double printing; printing on an area that already has been printed.

Pagination. Number and arrangement of pages.

Parallel Fold. A second fold in a sheet parallel to the first fold.

Paste-up. Assembling on one page the art, display, and text copy ready for photographing.

Perfect Binding. A method of holding pages of a book together without stitching or sewing. The backbones of the gathered books are ground off leaving a rough surface of intermingled fibers to which adhesive is applied. The books are usually finished with a wraparound cover.

Perforate. To punch a series of small holes in a row in a material to facilitate tearing.

Pica. The standard for measuring type—approximately one-sixth of an inch, or 6 picas to 1 inch.

Plastic Binding. A solid back comb rolled to make a cylinder of any thickness. Slots are punched along the binding side of the book, and the plastic comb is inserted through the slots.

Point. Unit of measurement (72 points equal 1 inch).

Positive. A photographic image on paper film or glass which exactly corresponds to the original subject in all details.

Process Printing. Printing from a series of two or more plates in halftone to produce other colors and shades. Usually in four-color process—magenta, cyan, yellow, and black.

Progressive Proofs. In color process printing, a set of proofs showing each color separately and in combination.

Proof. Sample of copy and/or layout made at various stages of production of a printing job. Proofs are either checked internally or sent to the customer for corrections or approval.

Proofread. The act of reading and correcting copy internally at the earliest stage of production to ensure accuracy.

Quad. Type space used for blanking out lines of type. Usual sizes include en, em, 2 ems, and 3 ems.

Ragged Copy. Line of copy set with uneven left- or right-hand margins. Often used in advertising copy.

Ream. Five hundred sheets of paper.

Register. Exact correspondence of the position of pages or other printed matter on both sides of a sheet or in its relation to other matter already ruled or printed on the same side of the sheet. In photo reproduction and color printing, the correct relative position of two or more colors so that no color is out of its proper position.

Register Marks. Small crosses, guides, or patterns placed on originals before reproduction to facilitate registration of plates and printing therefrom.

Right-Angle Fold. A second fold that is at a right angle to the first fold.

Roman. Serifed type in which the upright strokes are vertical as distinguished from italic in which the uprights are slanted.

Rotogravure. Intaglio (below surface) printing process (*see* gravure).

Runaround. Copy arrangement that allows for positioning pictures, diagrams, etc., within columns of type.

Running Head. Headline at the top of the page in a book.

Saddle Stitch. Wire staples driven through the back-fold of a booklet and clinched in the middle enabling the booklet to open out flat.

Sans Serif. A type face lacking serifs.

Scoring. Creasing paper or cover stock mechanically to facilitate folding without breaking or cracking at the fold. Scoring is most effective when done with the grain of the paper.

Screen Process Printing. Printing process that utilizes a screen of silk or other fine mesh material stretched on a frame across which a squeegee is drawn to force ink through the open, or image, areas of the screen.

Self-Cover. Cover printed on the same stock as text pages.

Serif. A projection at the top or bottom of a letter.

Setoff. *See* Offset Lithography.

Shadow. The darkest parts in a photograph; represented in a halftone reproduction by the largest openings.

Side Stitch. Wire staples driven through sheets or signatures of a pamphlet or book on the cover side close to the inside margin.

Signature. A section of a book, ordinarily obtained by folding a single sheet into 8, 12, 16, or more pages.

Silhouette. A halftone from which the screen surrounding any part of the image has been cut or otherwise removed. The operation of painting out the background of a negative to produce a white background on the final print.

Small Caps. Capital letters that are smaller than the regular capital letters. They are used as subheads, running heads, etc.

Solid Matter (Set Solid). Lines of type leaving no extra space between them.

Spiral Binding. Book binding with wires in spiral form inserted through holes punched along the binding side of the book.

Triangle. Plastic triangle used to produce vertical or uniformly slanting lines, usually 45° and 30°/60°.

Trim. Paper trimmed off a printed piece to square the edges or remove bleed. Excess paper allowed around a printed piece for bleed. Actual operation of cutting off bleeds or folds with a three-knife trimmer.

Trimmed Size. Final size of a printed piece after all bleeds and folds have been cut off.

T-square. T-shaped, precision straight edge used to square copy or edges of paper with the edge of a drawing board or table.

Typography. The art of type selection that involves style, arrangement, and appearance of the printed page.

Velox®. Eastman Kodak's trade name for a screened photographic print used in the preparation of paste-ups. Since it is line art, it can be photographed along with line copy and thus saves stripping costs.

Vignette. A halftone with a background gradually fading away and blending into the surface of the paper.

Watermark. Mark, name, or design made into the sheet of paper by the dandy roll during the process of paper manufacture.

Web Offset. Lithographic press in which paper is fed from a roll, or web.

Widow. A short line ending a paragraph at the top of a page.

Wire Side. Underside of a sheet of paper as it comes off the papermaking machine. The side of the sheet that touches the screen.

With the Grain. Paper folded parallel to the grain of the paper.

Work and Turn. A printing imposition, where the form contains the material to be printed on both sides of the sheet. The entire form first prints on one side of the sheet for half the number of impressions desired; then the sheet is turned over sideways from left to right, and the run is completed on the reverse side.

Wrong Font. A letter of type that does not correspond to the type face being set.

PASTE-UP ASSIGNMENTS

FOR GRAPHIC ARTS PRODUCTION

assignment 1

POINT SYSTEM

INFORMATION

Knowledge of the printer's point system is important in understanding and handling paste-up. This system of measurement is the accepted standard of communicating dimensions in the printing industry. This assignment will familiarize you with the point system as well as some of the methods and materials of paste-up.

MATERIALS REQUIRED

Paste-up tools
Print trimmer, scissors
Rubber cement
Masking tape and transparent tape
One piece of 10″ × 12″ black or red construction paper
One piece of 11″ × 14″ illustration board
One piece of 11″ × 15″ tissue overlay paper
One piece of 11″ × 16″ cover flap paper

PROCEDURE

1. Fasten the illustration board squarely and smoothly to the table work surface with the 11″ dimension running horizontally. Place the T-square over the board, holding it firmly against the left-hand edge of the table, and line up the lower edge of the board so that it is parallel with the upper edge of the T-square approximately 3″ from the left and bottom of the table. Tape the upper-left corner of the board to the table with a piece of masking tape (approximately 1″ long); then tape the upper right-hand corner. Draw the board smoothly and tightly to the bottom, and tape both the left-hand and right-hand corners with masking tape.

2. Using a nonreproducing blue pencil or pen, outline a paper area of 9″ × 12″ and an image area of 8″ × 10″ on the board.

3. Using the print trimmer and a line gauge, trim the squares of construction paper to the exact dimension specified in the rough layout.

4. Using rubber cement, adhere the pieces down in the positions shown in the layout, checking carefully the relationships of space around each piece.

5. Using a drawing pen or ruling pen, ink in all crop and center marks ½″ long with thin, black lines.

6. Attach a piece of tissue overlay paper to the paste-up by taping it with transparent tape on the reverse side at the top. Fold over the extra 1″ at the top of the paste-up.

7. Attach a piece of colored text paper (cover flap) to the paste-up by taping it with masking tape on the reverse side at the top. Fold over the extra 2″ at the top, and cut back at a 30-degree angle on both sides.

8. Write your name on the front of the Evaluation Check List sheet, and rubber cement the sheet to the back of the paste-up.

9. Turn in assignment for evaluation.

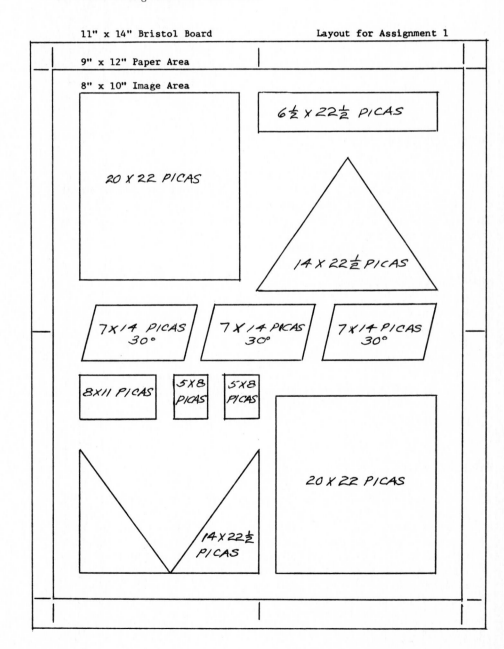

Name_____

PROJECT EVALUATION CHECK LIST
ASSIGNMENT 1: POINT SYSTEM

This check list is designed to assist you in identifying the specific points upon which this assignment will be evaluated. Your instructor will indicate by the use of a check mark those areas requiring additional attention.

PASTE-UP PLANNING

_____ 11″ X 14″ illustration board
_____ 9″ X 12″ paper area (blue pencil)
_____ 8″ X 10″ image area (blue pencil)

PASTE-UP PREPARATION

_____ Elements trimmed smoothly
_____ Elements trimmed to correct dimensions
_____ Elements positioned according to rough layout
_____ Accurate alignment of elements
_____ Uniform application of adhesive and burnished
_____ Crop and center marks in black ink approximately ½″ long
_____ Protective tissue overlay and cover flap attached

FINAL EVALUATION _____

assignment **2**

LETTERHEAD, ENVELOPE, AND BUSINESS CARD

INFORMATION

Now that you have become acquainted with the printer's point system of measurement, this assignment will assist you in sharpening the skills you will need to become competent in paste-up preparation.

A basic stationery package for any organization consists of a letterhead, envelope, and business card. This assignment has been designed around a furnished layout. In addition, you will add your name to the business card to give it a personal touch.

Normally, the letterhead, envelope, and business card use progressively smaller type sizes. The letterhead (see rough layout) incorporates the largest type, the matching envelope uses smaller type, and the business card uses even smaller type. It is important that the type styles be harmonious with the nature of the business firm. No more than two to three type styles should be used in the design. Sometimes line art or halftones are used in the design, but these should be appropriate to the occasion.

MATERIALS REQUIRED

Paste-up tools
Print trimmer and scissors
Masking tape and transparent tape
Rubber cement and/or waxer
Two pieces of 11″ × 14″ illustration board
Two pieces of 11″ × 15″ tissue overlay paper
Two pieces of 11″ × 16″ cover flap paper

PROCEDURE (Letterhead)

1. Fasten one of the pieces of illustration board squarely and smoothly to the table work surface with the 11″ dimension running horizontally.
2. Using a nonreproducing blue pencil or pen, start with the letterhead by outlining a paper area of $8\frac{1}{2}$″ × 11″.
3. Wax the back of the reproduction proofs. Cut out the elements you will need for the letterhead. Cut all elements square and clean, leaving approximately $\frac{1}{16}$″ white space on all sides.
4. Align the elements on the paste-up board, and mark them with blue pencil for quick and easy repositioning. Light-blue guidelines on the board will also help in positioning the elements. Check layout for positioning.
5. Carefully reposition the elements, and align them with the alignment marks. Check the alignment with a T-square. Cover the elements with a clean piece of white paper, and burnish in place.
6. Ink in crop and center marks in black ink with thin lines approximately $\frac{1}{2}$″ long.
7. Remove any excess wax. Use a cotton wipe for this purpose.
8. Attach a piece of tissue overlay paper to the illustration board by taping it with transparent tape on the reverse side at the top. Fold over the extra 1″ at the top of the paste-up.
9. Attach a piece of colored text paper (cover flap) to the illustration board by taping it with masking tape on the reverse side at the top. Fold over the extra 2″ at the top, and cut back at a 30–degree angle on both sides.
10. Use a blue pencil to mark the paste-up at the bottom for width (see rough layout) of $8\frac{1}{2}$″.

PROCEDURE (Envelope and Business Card)

1. Fasten the second piece of illustration board squarely and smoothly to the table work surface with the 11″ dimension running horizontally.
2. Using a nonreproducing blue pencil or pen, center a 2″ × $3\frac{1}{2}$″ paper size area above the horizontal center line for the business card and a $4\frac{1}{4}$″ × 9″ area below for the envelope. Make sure the card and envelope are about 2″ apart. Ink in all crop and center marks.
3. Examine the rough layout and locate the needed copy elements. Cut each element from the reproduction proofs, and place in position on the paste-up board. Light-blue guidelines will assist in this operation. Use the small type supplied on the reproduction proof to personalize the business card with your name.
4. Using a T-square, reposition the elements, and then burnish in place.
5. Follow the same procedure in aligning elements for the envelope. Do not include the telephone number on the envelope. Copy for the envelope should include:

GBC General Binding Corporation
  O&M Machinery
  2030 W. McNab Road
  Ft. Lauderdale, FL 33309

6. Remove any excess wax. Use a cotton wipe for this purpose.
7. Attach a piece of tissue overlay paper to the illustration board by taping it with transparent tape on the reverse side at the top. Fold the extra 1″ over at the top of the paste-up.
8. Attach a piece of colored text paper (cover flap) to the illustration board by taping it with masking tape on the reverse side at the top. Fold the extra 2″ over at the top, and cut back at a 30–degree angle on both sides.
9. Use a blue pencil to mark the paste-up at the bottom for the $3\frac{1}{2}$″ business card and 9″ envelope.

10. Write your name on the front of the Evaluation Check List sheet, and rubber cement the sheet to the back of the letterhead paste-up. Place the paste-ups in a Manila envelope to keep the assignment intact.
11. Turn in assignment for evaluation.

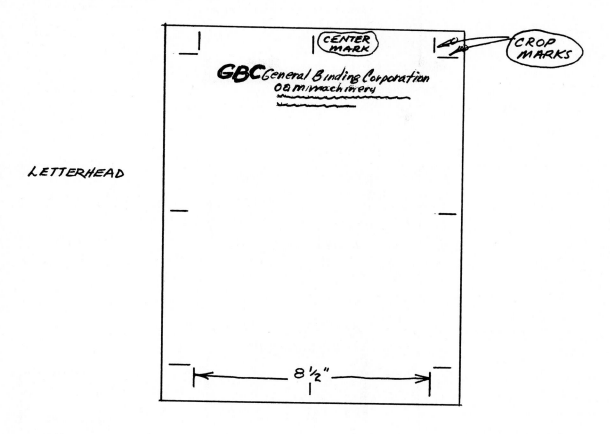

LETTERHEAD

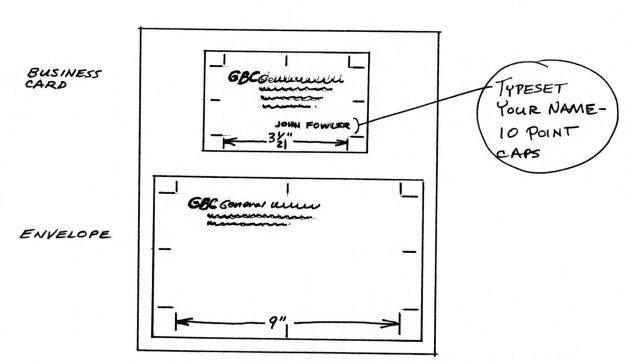

BUSINESS CARD

ENVELOPE

ENVELOPE STYLES

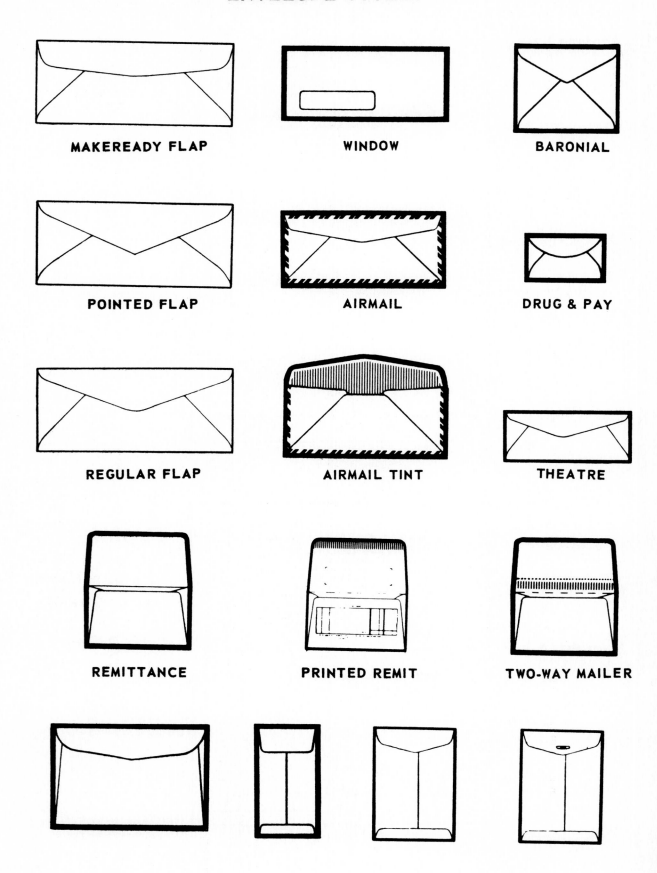

MAKEREADY FLAP   WINDOW   BARONIAL

POINTED FLAP   AIRMAIL   DRUG & PAY

REGULAR FLAP   AIRMAIL TINT   THEATRE

REMITTANCE   PRINTED REMIT   TWO-WAY MAILER

REPRO - Letterhead, Envelope,
and Business Card

General Binding Corporation
O & M Machinery

General Binding Corporation
O & M Machinery

General Binding Corporation
O & M Machinery

GBC

General Binding Corporation
O & M Machinery

GBC

General Binding Corporation
O & M Machinery

GBC

General Binding Corporation
O & M Machinery

GBC

General Binding Corporation
O & M Machinery

GBC

General Binding Corporation
O & M Machinery

GBC

2030 W. McNAB ROAD, FT. LAUDERDALE, FL 33309
PHONE: 305-971-1350

GBC

2030 W. McNAB ROAD, FT. LAUDERDALE, FL 33309
PHONE: 305-971-1350

GBC

2030 W. McNAB ROAD, FT. LAUDERDALE, FL. 33309
PHONE: 305-971-1350

2030 W. McNAB ROAD, FT. LAUDERDALE, FL. 33309
PHONE: 305-971-1350

2030 W. McNAB ROAD, FT. LAUDERDALE, FL. 33309
PHONE: 305-971-1350

2030 W. McNAB ROAD, FT. LAUDERDALE, FL. 33309
PHONE: 305-971-1350

2030 W. McNAB ROAD, FT. LAUDERDALE, FL. 33309
PHONE: 305-971-1350

2030 W. McNAB ROAD, FT. LAUDERDALE, FL. 33309
PHONE: 305-971-1350

REPRO - Letterhead, Envelope, and Business Card

A A A A A A B B B C C C D D D E E E E E E F F F G G G H H H I I I I I I J J K K L L L L L

A A A A A A B B B C C C D D D E E E E E E F F F G G G H H H I I I I I I J J K K L L L L L

A A A A A A B B B C C C D D D E E E E E E F F F G G G H H H I I I I I I J J K K L L L L L

A A A A A A B B B C C C D D D E E E E E E F F F G G G H H H I I I I I I J J K K L L L L L

A A A A A A B B B C C C D D D E E E E E E F F F G G G H H H I I I I I I J J K K L L L L L

A A A A A A B B B C C C D D D E E E E E E F F F G G G H H H I I I I I I J J K K L L L L L

A A A A A A B B B C C C D D D E E E E E E F F F G G G H H H I I I I I I J J K K L L L L L

A A A A A A B B B C C C D D D E E E E E E F F F G G G H H H I I I I I I J J K K L L L L L

A A A A A A B B B C C C D D D E E E E E E F F F G G G H H H I I I I I I J J K K L L L L L

A A A A A A B B B C C C D D D E E E E E E F F F G G G H H H I I I I I I J J K K L L L L L

A A A A A A B B B C C C D D D E E E E E E F F F G G G H H H I I I I I I J J K K L L L L L

M N N N O O O O O P P P Q Q R R R S S S T T T U U U U U V W W W X X Y Y Y Z Z

M N N N O O O O O P P P Q Q R R R S S S T T T U U U U U V W W W W X X Y Y Y Z Z

M N N N O O O O O P P P Q Q R R R S S S T T T U U U U U V W W W W X X Y Y Y Z Z

M N N N O O O O O P P P Q Q R R R S S S T T T U U U U U V W W W W X X Y Y Y Z Z

M N N N O O O O O P P P Q Q R R R S S S T T T U U U U U V W W W W X X Y Y Y Z Z

M N N N O O O O O P P P Q Q R R R S S S T T T U U U U U V W W W W X X Y Y Y Z Z

M N N N O O O O O P P P Q Q R R R S S S T T T U U U U U V W W W W X X Y Y Y Z Z

M N N N O O O O O P P P Q Q R R R S S S T T T U U U U U V W W W W X X Y Y Y Z Z

M N N N O O O O O P P P Q Q R R R S S S T T T U U U U U V W W W W X X Y Y Y Z Z

M N N N O O O O O P P P Q Q R R R S S S T T T U U U U U V W W W W X X Y Y Y Z Z

1 1 1 2 2 3 3 4 4 5 5 6 6 7 7 8 8 9 9 0 0 0 0 0 0 & & ? ? ? ! ! ! $ $ $ ¢ ¢ ;;;;;;;;; :::::: //////

1 1 1 2 2 3 3 4 4 5 5 6 6 7 7 8 8 9 9 0 0 0 0 0 0 & & ? ? ? ! ! ! $ $ $ ¢ ¢ ;;;;;;;;; :::::: //////

REPRO - Letterhead, Envelope, and Business Card

a a a b b c c d d e e e e f g h h i i i i j k l l m n n o o o p q r r s s t t t u u u u v w w x x y y z z

a a a b b c c d d e e e e f g h h i i i i j k l l m n n o o o p q r r s s t t t u u u u v w w x x y y z z

a a a b b c c d d e e e e f g h h i i i i j k l l m n n o o o p q r r s s t t t u u u u v w w x x y y z z

a a a b b c c d d e e e e f g h h i i i i j k l l m n n o o o p q r r s s t t t u u u u v w w x x y y z z

a a a b b c c d d e e e e f g h h i i i i j k l l m n n o o o p q r r s s t t t u u u u v w w x x y y z z

a a a b b c c d d e e e e f g h h i i i i j k l l m n n o o o p q r r s s t t t u u u u v w w x x y y z z

a a a b b c c d d e e e e f g h h i i i i j k l l m n n o o o p q r r s s t t t u u u u v w w x x y y z z

a a a b b c c d d e e e e f g h h i i i i j k l l m n n o o o p q r r s s t t t u u u u v w w x x y y z z

a a a b b c c d d e e e e f g h h i i i i j k l l m n n o o o p q r r s s t t t u u u u v w w x x y y z z

a a a b b c c d d e e e e f g h h i i i i j k l l m n n o o o p q r r s s t t t u u u u v w w x x y y z z

a a a b b c c d d e e e e f g h h i i i i j k l l m n n o o o p q r r s s t t t u u u u v w w x x y y z z

a a a b b c c d d e e e e f g h h i i i i j k l l m n n o o o p q r r s s t t t u u u u v w w x x y y z z

a a a b b c c d d e e e e f g h h i i i i j k l l m n n o o o p q r r s s t t t u u u u v w w x x y y z z

a a a b b c c d d e e e e f g h h i i i i j k l l m n n o o o p q r r s s t t t u u u u v w w x x y y z z

a a a b b c c d d e e e e f g h h i i i i j k l l m n n o o o p q r r s s t t t u u u u v w w x x y y z z

a a a b b c c d d e e e e f g h h i i i i j k l l m n n o o o p q r r s s t t t u u u u v w w x x y y z z

a a a b b c c d d e e e e f g h h i i i i j k l l m n n o o o p q r r s s t t t u u u u v w w x x y y z z

a a a b b c c d d e e e e f g h h i i i i j k l l m n n o o o p q r r s s t t t u u u u v w w x x y y z z

a a a b b c c d d e e e e f g h h i i i i j k l l m n n o o o p q r r s s t t t u u u u v w w x x y y z z

a a a b b c c d d e e e e f g h h i i i i j k l l m n n o o o p q r r s s t t t u u u u v w w x x y y z z

1 1 1 2 2 3 3 4 4 5 5 6 6 7 7 8 8 9 9 0 0 0 0 0 0 & & ? ? ? ! ! ! $ $ $ ¢ ¢ ;;;;;;;;;; :::: (( )) - - - //////

1 1 1 2 2 3 3 4 4 5 5 6 6 7 7 8 8 9 9 0 0 0 0 0 0 & & ? ? ? ! ! ! $ $ $ ¢ ¢ ;;;;;;;;;; :::: (( )) - - - //////

Name_____

**PROJECT EVALUATION CHECK LIST
ASSIGNMENT 2:
LETTERHEAD, ENVELOPE, AND BUSINESS CARD**

This check list is designed to assist you in identifying the specific points upon which this assignment will be evaluated. Your instructor will indicate by the use of a check mark those areas requiring additional attention.

PASTE-UP PLANNING (letterhead)

_____ 11" × 14" illustration board
_____ 8½" × 11" paper area (blue pencil)
_____ Appropriate image area margins

PASTE-UP PLANNING (envelope and business card)

_____ 11" × 14" illustration board
_____ 4¼" × 9" and 2" × 3½" paper size areas
_____ Appropriate image area margins

PASTE-UP PREPARATION

_____ Elements trimmed smoothly
_____ Elements trimmed to correct dimensions
_____ Elements positioned according to the rough layouts
_____ Accurate alignment of elements
_____ Transfer type and artwork level and applied correctly
_____ Uniform application of adhesive and burnished
_____ Crop and center marks in black ink approximately ½" long
_____ Protective tissue overlay and cover flap attached to paste-ups
_____ Overall cleanliness of paste-ups

FINAL EVALUATION _____

POSTER

INFORMATION

Posters are a unique form of graphic communications intended for display on bulletin boards and other prominent places. Posters are produced in many shapes and sizes and often include reply cards for interested persons to obtain additional information about the product, service, or opportunities advertised. Posters are usually printed on heavy cardboard to withstand handling and abuse from weathering. This assignment incorporates a poster with return address reply card for recruiting Peace Corps volunteers.

One of the most difficult things to learn in paste-up is the proper utilization of available space. It is sometimes troubling to judge the amount of space required for a given amount of copy. Try to become aware of copy requirements and space available so that you learn to make minor spacing adjustments while grouping material into logical units.

MATERIALS REQUIRED

Paste-up tools
Print trimmer and scissors
Rubber cement and/or waxer
Masking tape and transparent tape
Adhesive border tapes
One piece of 14″ × 20″ illustration board
One piece of 6″ × 12″ illustration board
One piece of 15″ × 20″ tissue overlay
One piece of 16″ × 20″ cover flap paper
One piece of 7″ × 12″ tissue overlay
One piece of 8″ × 12″ cover flap paper

PROCEDURE

1. Fasten the illustration board squarely and smoothly to the table work surface with the 20″ dimension running horizontally.
2. Using a nonreproducing blue pencil or pen, outline a paper area of 11″ × 17″ and an image area of 61 × 97 picas.
3. Following the layout, rule in the appropriate guidelines for the box and border areas in light-blue pencil or pen. Indicate the perforation line as shown on the layout. Write PERFORATE on the paste-up in blue. The information card is 3¾″ × 8½″, including ½″ at the top for perforation and stapling.

   Note: The Vista and Peace Corps information card on the right side of the poster is pasted in as one-piece copy. It will be separated by the camera department to form a separate printing run. The information cards will be stapled to the poster in the position indicated. The address side (reverse) of the card will be assembled on a separate paste-up later in this assignment.

4. Use adhesive tapes for the box and border areas. The point size is indicated on the layout.
5. Wax the proofs, and cut out the necessary elements as needed. Be sure the type and artwork are positioned according to the layout. Lay the elements in position lightly for position check.
6. When you are satisfied that all elements are positioned and spaced correctly, burnish the paste-up elements carefully.
7. Ink in crop and center marks with fine black lines approximately ½″ long.
8. Attach a piece of tissue overlay paper to the illustration board by taping it with transparent tape on the reverse side at the top. Fold over the extra 1″ at the top of the paste-up.
9. Attach a piece of colored text paper (cover flap) to the illustration board by taping it with masking tape on the reverse side at the top. Fold over the extra 2″ at the top, and cut back at a 30–degree angle on both sides.
10. Fasten the second piece of illustration board squarely and smoothly to the table work surface with the 10″ dimension running horizontally.
11. This paste-up consists of the reverse side of the Peace Corps return information card. Outline a paper area of 3¾″ × 10″ in light-blue pencil or pen.
12. Cut out the necessary elements from the waxed proof. Position the elements according to the rough layout, and burnish. Indicate the perforation line in blue pencil, and write PERFORATE in blue pencil as shown on the layout.
13. Attach a tissue overlay and cover flap to the illustration board.
14. Write your name on the front of the Evaluation Check List sheet, and rubber cement the sheet to the back of the large paste-up. Place the paste-ups in a Manila envelope.
15. Turn in assignment for evaluation.

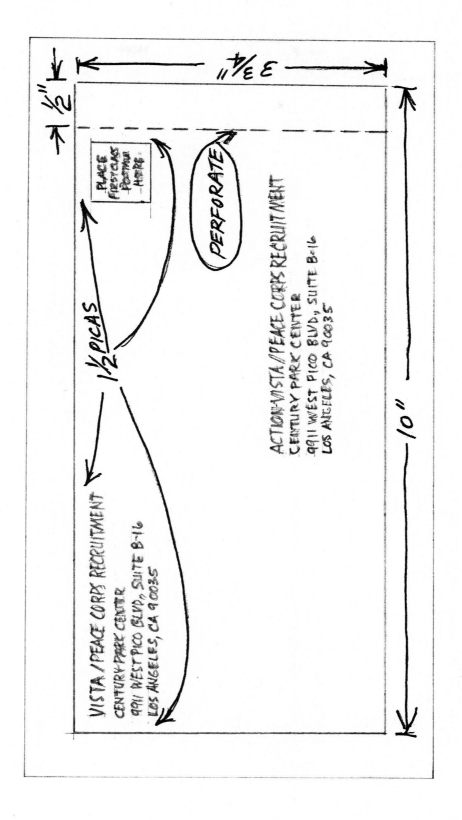

221

222

VISTA and PEACE CORPS INFORMATION CARD

Please complete and mail this postage paid card if you are interested in further information about opportunities.

☐ VISTA   ☐ PEACE CORPS

Date _____

Name _____

Address _____

City _____ State _____ Zip _____

Telephone Number [ ][ ][ ] [ ][ ][ ]▨[ ][ ][ ]
                  Area Code

Availability Date _____/_____
                     month   year

Marital Status ☐ married ☐ single

Date of Birth _____/_____/_____
               day   month   year

Please check the box which best describes your skill area.

☐ Agriculture   ☐ Fisheries
☐ Architecture   ☐ Forestry
☐ Business/Econ/Acc't   ☐ Home Economics
☐ Comm Development   ☐ Industrial Arts
☐ Consumer Affairs   ☐ Legal Services
☐ Education   ☐ Math/Science
☐ Environment   ☐ Trades

Please check the highest education level attained

☐ High School
☐ Associate Arts
☐ Bachelors
☐ Masters
☐ Doctorate

☐ Other _____

Number of Years Practical Experience in skill area:

[   ]

FIELD OF SPECIALIZATION WITHIN SKILL AREA

_____
_____
_____

Privacy Act Notice: Recipients are advised that providing the information herein requested is voluntary and if furnished will be used only to determine interest in ACTION programs and will not be disclosed outside ACTION (Auth.: 22 U.S.C. 2501 and 42 U.S.C. 4951 et seq.).

There's a reward out for VISTA and Peace Corps volunteers. It's the personal satisfaction that comes from knowing that what you are doing works to help others. Americans want a bigger voice in community decisions here at home. As a VISTA volunteer, you can show them how to get it. Help identify issues that daily confront the poor and elderly. Then, work in the building of a strong community organization which responds to those needs. You'll find the same satisfaction overseas in the Peace Corps. There are over 6,000 Peace Corps teachers, engineers, nurses, tradespeople and others who want to share this feeling of accomplishment with you. A college degree or several years of experience can qualify you for most assignments in over 60 developing countries of Asia, Africa, Latin America and the Pacific. You should also be a citizen, over 20 years of age, single or married with no dependents. Two years overseas with Peace Corps or one year here at home in VISTA. Maybe more information can help you make a choice. Complete and mail us a card. It's a start.

Volunteers In Service To America

VISTA/PEACE CORPS RECRUITMENT
CENTURY PARK CENTER
9911 WEST PICO BLVD., SUITE B-16
LOS ANGELES, CA 90035

REPRO – Poster

The toughest job you'll ever love . . .

ACTION-VISTA/PEACE CORPS RECRUITMENT
CENTURY PARK CENTER
9911 WEST PICO BLVD., SUITE B-16
LOS ANGELES, CA 90035

```
PLACE
FIRST CLASS
POSTAGE
HERE
```

VISTA/PEACE CORPS RECRUITING OFFICES

This is a list of the area offices where you can reach VISTA/PEACE CORPS representatives.

NORTHERN CALIFORNIA
VISTA/PEACE CORPS RECRUITING OFFICE
1375 Sutter Street
2nd Floor
San Francisco, CA 94109
(415) 556-8400

SOUTHERN CALIFORNIA
VISTA/PEACE CORPS RECRUITING OFFICE
Century Park Center
9911 West Pico Blvd.
Suite B-16
Los Angeles, CA 90035
(213) 824-7742

ARIZONA
VISTA/PEACE CORPS RECRUITING OFFICE
522 North Central Avenue
Phoenix, Arizona 85004
(602) 261-6621

HAWAII
VISTA/PEACE CORPS RECRUITING OFFICE
Federal Building
Room 6326
300 Ala Moana Boulevard
P.O. Box 50024
Honolulu, Hawaii 96850
(808) 546-2178

PACIFIC NORTHWEST
VISTA/PEACE CORPS RECRUITING OFFICES

SEATTLE, WASHINGTON
1601 Second Avenue
10th Floor
Seattle, Washington 98101
(206) 442-5490

PORTLAND, OREGON
1220 S.W. Morrison
Portland, Oregon 97205
(503) 423-2411

Name_____

PROJECT EVALUATION CHECK LIST
ASSIGNMENT 3: POSTER

This check list is designed to assist you in identifying the specific points upon which this assignment will be evaluated. Your instructor will indicate by the use of a check mark those areas requiring additional attention.

PASTE-UP PLANNING

_____ 14" X 20" illustration board
_____ 11" X 17" paper area (blue pencil)
_____ 61 X 97 pica image area (blue pencil)
_____ 6" X 12" illustration board
_____ 3¾" X 8½" paper area (blue pencil)

PASTE-UP PREPARATION

_____ Elements trimmed smoothly
_____ Elements trimmed to correct dimensions
_____ Elements positioned according to rough layout
_____ Accurate alignment of elements
_____ Correct point size border; square corners; aligned and applied correctly
_____ Border corners cut smoothly with no overlap
_____ Crop and center marks in black ink approximately ½" long
_____ Uniform application of adhesive and burnished
_____ Protective tissue overlays and cover flaps attached
_____ Perforation noted on paste-up in blue pencil

FINAL EVALUATION _____

assignment 4

BUSINESS REPLY MAIL CARD

INFORMATION

Business forms printing is a large segment of the printing industry. This assignment is designed to help you develop the skill needed to paste up one of the many common business forms that are produced for firms of every description. In addition, you will be responsible for proofreading the job after the paste-up is completed.

In some cases, the paste-up artist rules the required lines in ink using a technical drawing pen. For other work, the rules are scribed on the film negative after the job has been photographed. Many business forms containing rules (horizontal and vertical) are set on phototypesetting equipment. The different ways of handling forms containing rules are usually a matter of preference within each printing firm.

MATERIALS REQUIRED

Paste-up tools
Print trimmer and scissors
Rubber cement and/or waxer
Masking tape and transparent tape
One piece of 9″ × 12″ illustration board
One piece of 9″ × 13″ tissue overlay paper
One piece of 9″ × 14″ cover flap paper

PROCEDURE

1. Fasten the illustration board squarely and smoothly to the table work surface with the 9″ dimension running horizontally. Tape the corners with masking tape.

2. Outline the two 4″ × 5¼″ paper size areas vertically, ½″ apart as shown in the rough layout. Use light-blue pencil.

3. Ink in crop and center marks approximately ½″ long.

4. Wax the back of the reproduction proof. Using a stiff cutting board, cut out the copy elements as needed leaving approximately 1/16″ white space on all sides.

5. Position the elements on the paste-up board according to the rough layout. Mark them with blue pencil for quick and easy repositioning.

6. Carefully reposition the elements, and align them with the blue alignment marks. Use a T-square to check and align all elements. Cover the elements with a clean piece of white paper, and burnish in position. Check all lines once again for squareness with a T-square.

7. Remove any excess wax from the board and elements, and apply a tissue overlay. Attach the tissue overlay to the board by taping it with transparent tape on the reverse side at the top. Fold over the extra 1″ at the top of the paste-up.

8. Using a red pencil, proofread the copy on the paste-up carefully, and mark corrections on the tissue overlay only. Use the proofreaders marks provided in this assignment.

9. Attach a cover flap to the illustration board by taping it to the reverse side at the top with masking tape. Fold over the extra 2″ at the top, and cut back at a 30–degree angle on both sides.

10. Write your name on the front of the Evaluation Check List sheet, and rubber cement the sheet to the back of the paste-up.

11. Turn in assignment for evaluation.

Below are the principal marks used by the proofreader in marking a proof for correction by the Compositor, with a brief explanation of the use of each

Caps or ‗‗‗‗ Set in CAPITALS.

S.C. or ‗‗‗ Set in SMALL CAPS.

Ital. or ——— Set in *italic* type.

Bold or ⌒⌒⌒ Set in **bold face**

rom Set in roman type.

l.c. Set in lowercase.

(*w.f.*) Character is from wrong font.

(*tr*) Transpose.

℈ Take out.

℥ Turn over.

[or *flush* Move to left.

] or *flush* Move to right.

✕ Bad letter—change.

⊥ Push down space.

▭ Indent.

Put in space.

⌣ Close up.

⫽ or *Strai* Straighten.

(*Stet*) Leave as it is.

æ̂, f̂i, etc. Use logotype.

⊙ Period.

⋀̣ Comma.

⋁̓ Apostrophe.

❝ ❞ Quotation marks.

=/ Hyphen.

⊙ Colon.

;/ Semicolon.

├m̄┤ 1-em dash.

├2̄m┤ 2-em dash.

?/ Interrogation point.

!/ Exclamation mark.

⋀ Caret.

⌄ᵃ Superior character.

⌃ₐ Inferior character.

[/] Enclose in brackets.

(/) Enclose in parentheses.

ℬ Use short and.

⌗ New paragraph.

no ⌗ No paragraph; run in.

out—see copy Something left out of copy.

(? OK) Query to author.

CROP
MARKS

BUSINESS REPLY MAIL

CROP
MARKS

STEP AND REPEAT
FOR 8½" x 11"

ROOSEVELT MOTOR HOTEL

Name

Address

Arriving:

Rooms cancelled

Circle first

The number of rooms

CENTER MARK

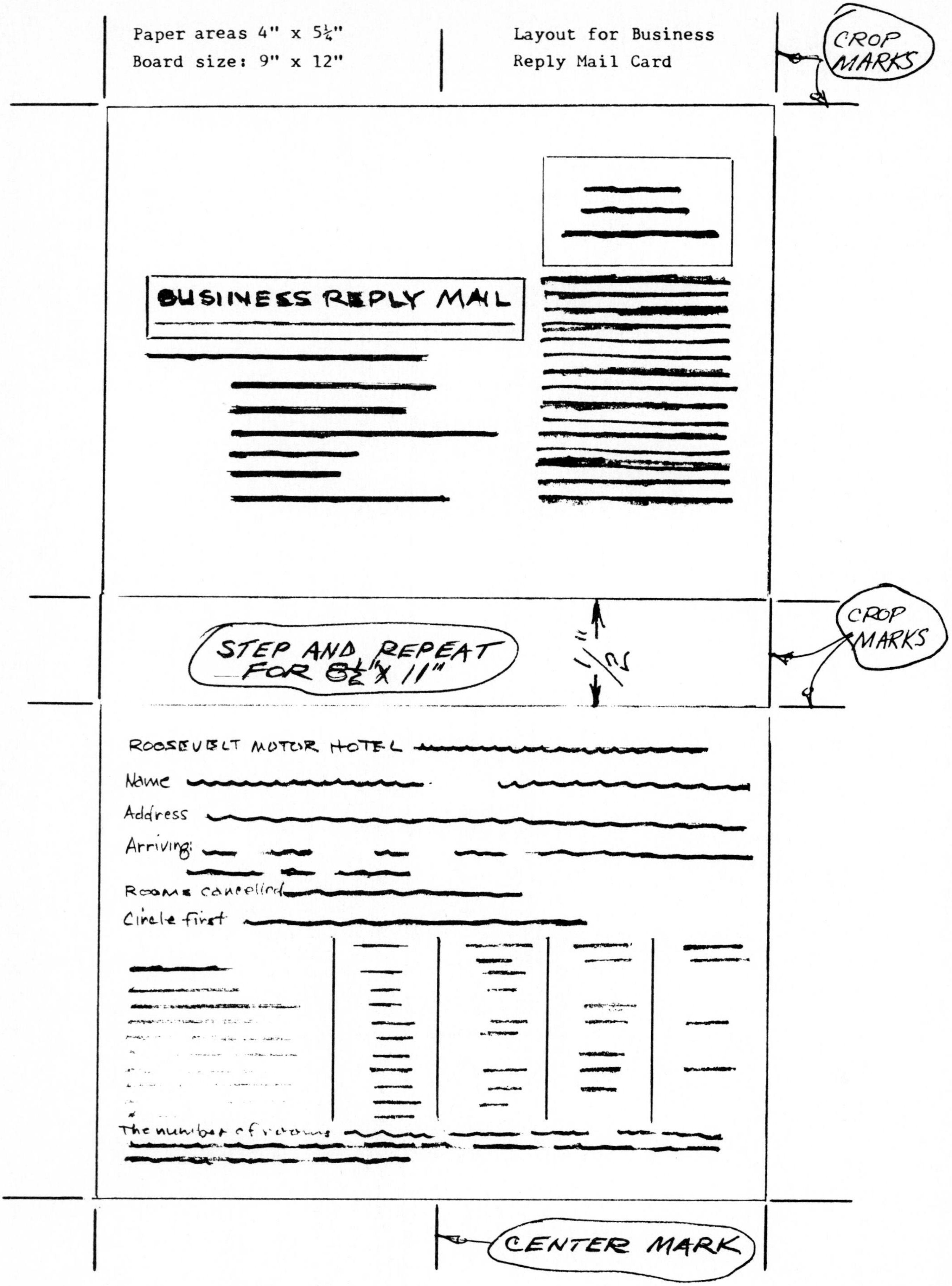

REPRO – Business Reply Mail Card

ROOSEVELT MOTOR HOTEL 200 First Avenue N.E. Cedar Rapids, Iowa 52407

Name _____ American Advertising Federation

Address _____

Arriving: Day   Date   Time: A.M.   P.M.   **How many nights?** _____

     By car   Yes   No

Rooms canceled at 6 P.M. unless prepaid or payment guaranteed.

Circle first, second and third choice accommodations desired.

	1 person	2 persons 1 bed	2 persons 2 beds	3 persons 2 beds
Kings Quarters (king bed)	$17	$26		
Bachelor Quarters (queen bed)	$16	$24		
Corner Suite Rooms (2 twins)	$15		$22	
Queen Rooms (queen & single)	$14	$20	$20	$24
Queen Rooms (queen bed)	$13	$18		
Twin Rooms (2 twin beds)	$12		$16	
Twin Rooms (double & single)	$12	$16	$16	$18
Good Rooms (double bed)	$11	$14		
Small Rooms (double bed)	$10	$12		
Small Rooms (single bed)	$ 9			

The number of rooms in each category is limited. We will try to room you as close as possible to what you have indicated, from what is **available at the time of your check in.** Priority is given to double and triple occupanies. Rates are subject to change.

POSTAGE WILL BE PAID BY —

Chuck Edwards
Ninth District Governor
American Advertising Federation
% Pepco Litho, Inc.
P. O. Box 489
Cedar Rapids, Iowa 52406

BUSINESS REPLY MAIL
No Postage Necessary if Mailed in the United States

FIRST CLASS
Permit No. 195
Cedar Rapids, Iowa

Name_____

PROJECT EVALUATION CHECK LIST
ASSIGNMENT 4: BUSINESS REPLY MAIL CARD

This check list is designed to assist you in identifying the specific points upon which this assignment will be evaluated. Your instructor will indicate by the use of a check mark those areas requiring additional attention.

PASTE-UP PLANNING

_____ 9″ × 12″ illustration board
_____ 4″ × 5¼″ paper size area (blue pencil)

PASTE-UP PREPARATION

_____ Elements trimmed smoothly
_____ Elements trimmed to correct dimensions
_____ Elements positioned according to rough layout
_____ Accurate alignment of elements
_____ Uniform application of adhesive and burnished
_____ Crop and center marks in black ink approximately ½″ long
_____ Protective tissue overlay and cover flap attached
_____ Proofreading complete on tissue overlay in red pencil/pen

FINAL EVALUATION _____

assignment **5**

DISPLAY ADVERTISEMENT

INFORMATION

Business firms often use newspapers, magazines, leaflets, flyers, and direct mail pieces as promotional advertising. These ads include text in boxes, bordered elements, illustrations, and large display prices. Paste-ups for these jobs require that a large amount of the copy and illustrations be placed in a relatively confined area. Sometimes it is best to work oversize and then reduce the copy for final printing.

Advertisements must be planned carefully, since each element is positioned to fit in a precise amount of space. Therefore, the layout artist prepares a rough pencil layout indicating the positions of all elements of copy.

The paste-up artist draws blue-pencil guidelines on the illustration board to locate each element of copy, including text matter, artwork, borders, boxes, etc. (see illustration below). Finally, the large display letters are adhered, copy is inserted into the boxes, and all other text matter is adhered.

The illustration below shows the relative positions of copy elements on a paste-up and how each piece fits into a predetermined space that has been penciled in with light-blue pencil or pen.

MATERIALS REQUIRED

Paste-up tools
Adhesive border tapes
Rubber cement and/or waxer
Masking tape and transparent tape
Print trimmer and scissors
One piece of 11″ × 14″ illustration board
One piece of 11″ × 15″ tissue overlay paper
One piece of 11″ × 16″ cover flap paper

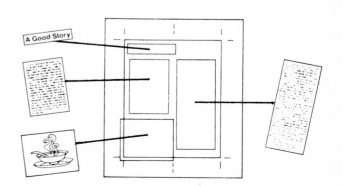

PROCEDURE

1. Examine and familiarize yourself with the rough layout.
2. Fasten the illustration board squarely and smoothly to the table work surface with the 11″ dimension running horizontally. Tape the corners with 1″ pieces of masking tape.
3. Using a nonreproducing blue pencil or pen, outline a 32 X 60 pica image area in the center of the board.
4. Following the layout, rule in the appropriate guidelines for all boxes, borders, rules, illustrations, type elements, etc.
5. Use adhesive border tapes for bordered boxes and the straight lines.
6. Wax the back of the reproduction proof, and place the proof on a stiff cutting board. Cut the elements out as needed with an X-acto® knife. Square the elements with a T-square as you cut them.
7. Position the elements on the paste-up board according to the rough layout. Check alignment with a T-square.
8. Cover the paste-up elements with a piece of white paper and burnish with a hand roller.
9. Do not ink in crop or center marks.
10. Attach a piece of tissue paper to the illustration board by taping it with transparent tape on the reverse side at the top. Fold over the extra 1″ at the top of the paste-up.
11. Attach a piece of colored text paper (cover flap) to the illustration board by taping it with masking tape on the reverse side at the top. Fold over the extra 2″ at the top, and cut back at a 30–degree angle on both sides.
12. Write your name on the front of the Evaluation Check List sheet, and rubber cement the sheet to the back of the paste-up.
13. Turn in assignment for evaluation.

PRESSURE-SENSITIVE TAPES

A variety of pressure-sensitive tapes are available that can be applied directly to artwork. The tapes come in many patterns (see illustration), including solid lines, broken lines, stripes, crosshatch patterns, etc. The tapes come in rolls of various widths, from under $\frac{1}{16}''$ to over $\frac{1}{2}''$. An adhesive coating on the back of the tape facilitates applying them to camera-ready copy.

These tapes can be used to prepare column charts, bar graphs, line charts, organization charts, plant and office layouts, newspaper and magazine advertisements, and a variety of other uses.

To use the tape, unwind the desired length, press it onto the illustration board, and burnish it into position on the artwork. Some tapes are available in plastic dispensers, which enable them to be applied directly to the artwork with a minimum of handling.

A light blue guideline should be drawn on the artwork to facilitate aligning the tape before burnishing it down into position. All tapes should be burnished to be sure they are permanently bonded to the paste-up. A blunt, smooth instrument does a satisfactory job. A roller made of plastic is ideal.

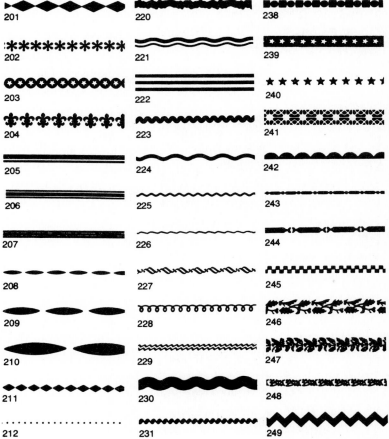

HOW TO CUT MITERED CORNERS

USING PRESSURE-SENSITIVE TAPES

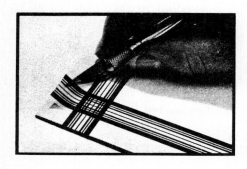

1. When applying the tape to the paste-up, overlap the ends as shown.

2. Lay a straightedge on the overlapped area, and cut it at a right angle.

3. Remove the excess material, and burnish the border into position.

32 X 60 PICAS BOX
They're As Fresh As A Day in Spring!
30 UNIVERS BOLD ITALIC C&L.C.
2 POINT RULE
2 POINT RULE
2 POINT BORDER
4 POINT BORDER
Special
24 POINT UNIVERS BOLD C&L.C.
WELL
14 POINT UNIVERS BOLD C&L.C.
00
30 POINT UNIVERS BOLD
12 POINT BODONI BOLD C&LC
NAME AUTOMATIC LAUNDRY
36 POINT GOTHIC CONDENSED CAPS

NAME AUTOMATIC LAUNDRY

They're As Fresh As A Day in Spring!

Special 25¢

. . . and you did it all yourself, quickly . . . economically, with our double capacity washers and dryers! There's always an attendant on hand to help! It's a smart way to wash your clothes. Come see!

We'll Do Your Wash for You!

(Clip out and rubber cement to back of paste-up)

Name_____

PROJECT EVALUATION CHECK LIST
ASSIGNMENT 5: DISPLAY ADVERTISEMENT

This check list is designed to assist you in identifying the specific points upon which this assignment will be evaluated. Your instructor will indicate by the use of a check mark those areas requiring additional attention.

PASTE-UP PLANNING

_____ 11" X 14" illustration board
_____ 32 X 60 pica image area (blue pencil)

PASTE-UP PREPARATION

_____ Elements trimmed smoothly
_____ Elements trimmed to correct dimensions
_____ Elements positioned according to rough layout
_____ Accurate alignment of elements
_____ Uniform application of adhesive and burnished
_____ Adhesive borders, rules, and boxes applied correctly
_____ Overall cleanliness of paste-up
_____ Protective tissue overlay and cover flap attached

FINAL EVALUATION_____

assignment 6

BUS
SCHEDULE

INFORMATION

Transportation schedules for bus, airline, and sea travel are common forms of graphic communication. Formats include brochures, pamphlets, posters, booklets, and books. These printed pieces usually include times of departure and arrival and maps to locate routes and stops.

In this assignment you will prepare a 16-page fold-out brochure for a rapid transit bus company. The assignment requires two paste-ups containing eight pages each.

MATERIALS REQUIRED

Paste-up tools
Print trimmer and scissors
Rubber cement and/or waxer
Masking tape and transparent tape
Two pieces of 15″ × 18″ illustration board
Two pieces of 16″ × 18″ tissue overlay paper
Two pieces of 17″ × 18″ cover flap paper

PROCEDURE

1. Fasten the illustration board squarely and smoothly to the table work surface with the 18″ dimension running horizontally.
2. Start with the cover side panels by outlining a paper area of 12″ × 14″. Use a nonreproducing blue pencil or pen.
3. Measure and divide the paper area into eight equal panels (see rough layout) with blue pencil or pen. Each panel should measure exactly 3½″ × 6″.

4. Draw light-blue head margin guidelines $2\frac{1}{2}$ picas from both sides of the 14″ horizontal center line. These lines will be used to align the type and artwork at the top of each panel. Type matter columns are approximately 18 picas in width and will be aligned within the panels.

5. Wax the proofs, and begin cutting elements as needed.

6. Using a T-square and triangle, position the elements (light pressure for position only), and make sure that the elements fit according to the rough layout. Note that the type is placed head-to-head along the 14″ dimension. This is necessary so that after the booklet is folded, pages will appear in the correct sequence.

7. When you are satisfied that all elements are positioned and spaced correctly, check alignment with the T-square, and burnish the paste-up elements carefully.

8. Ink in crop marks in black ink with thin lines approximately $\frac{1}{2}$″ long. Ink in the fold lines (see layout) at the top and bottom outside edges of the 12″ × 14″ paper area. Use black ink dashes approximately $\frac{1}{8}$″ long.

9. Attach a piece of tissue overlay paper to the illustration board by taping it with transparent tape on the reverse side at the top. Fold over the extra 1″ at the top of the paste-up.

10. Attach a piece of colored text paper (cover flap) to the illustration board by taping it with masking tape on the reverse side at the top. Fold over the extra 2″ at the top, and cut back at a 30–degree angle on both sides.

11. Fasten the second piece of illustration board squarely and smoothly to the table work surface with the 18″ dimension running horizontally.

12. Proceed with the reverse (map side) of the folder using the same procedure as outlined previously. The dimensions are the same. Note that a 4–point rule is required around the map. The border measures 60 × 67 picas. Be sure that the adhesive tape border material is applied squarely. Corners must be mitered and cut square to avoid overruns. The map is centered within the box created by the border tape.

13. The remaining two pages contain schedules (301 and 302), which are positioned foot-to-head, not head-to-head as on the other side of the folder.

14. When the second paste-up is completed, attach a tissue overlay and cover flap.

15. Write your name on the front of the Evaluation Check List sheet, and rubber cement the sheet to the back of one paste-up.

16. Turn in assignment for evaluation.

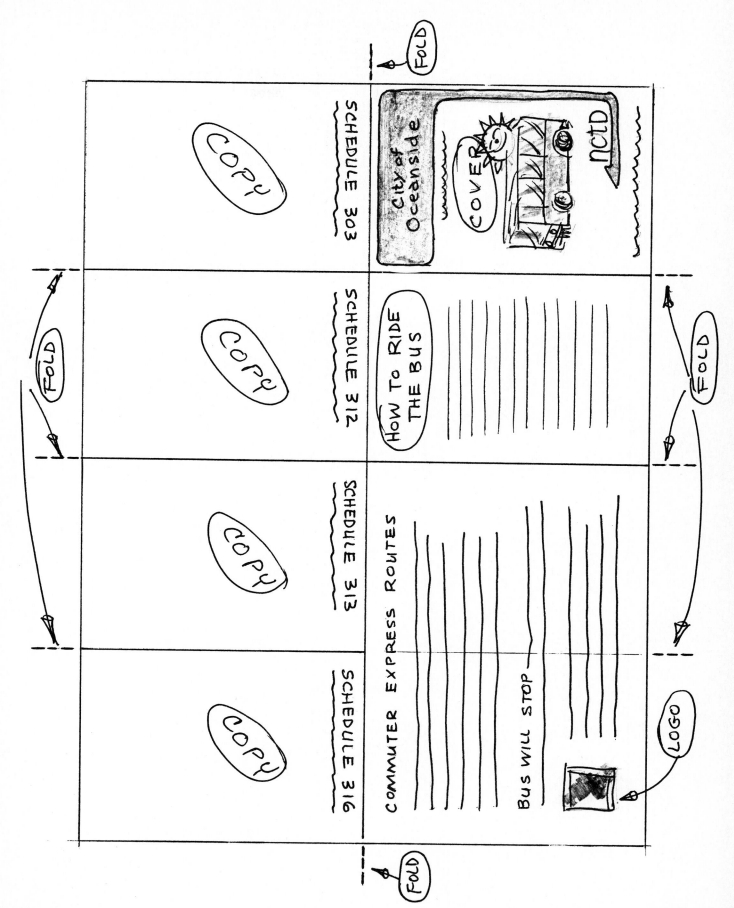

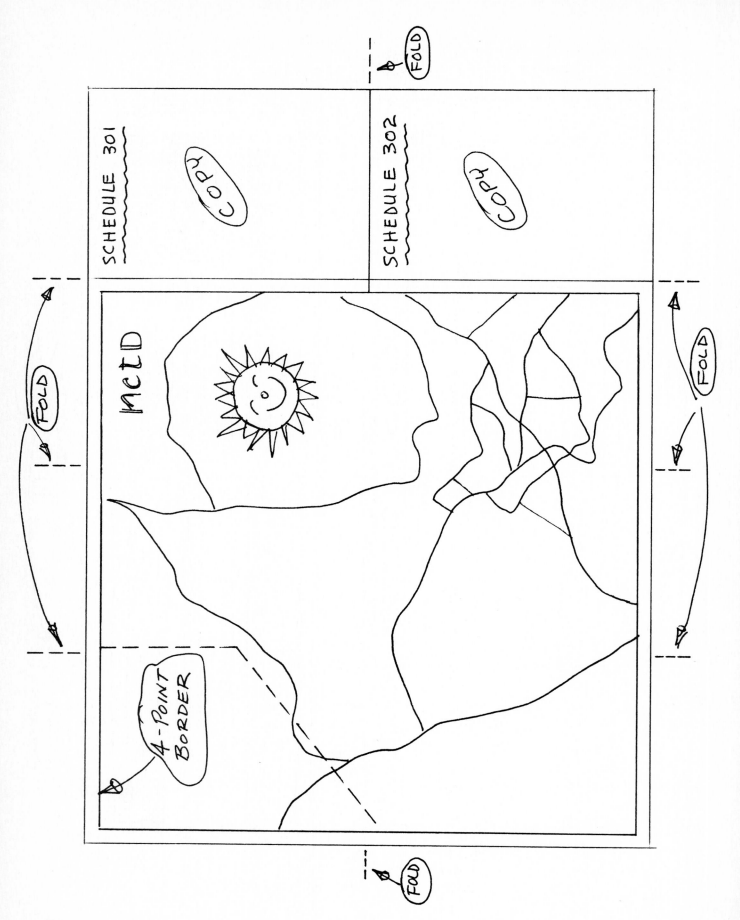

Effective February 25, 1980

City of
Oceanside

Map 1

NCTD

NORTH COUNTY TRANSIT DISTRICT

Commuter Express Routes:
Escondido to downtown San Diego (commuter hours only) 340
Escondido to Sorrento Valley (commuter hours only) 390
Coastal cities to downtown San Diego (commuter hours only)370
Operating between Escondido and Oceanside (all day) 320

Bus will stop at bus stops and at a wave from you on safe corner areas — no wave stops in downtowns, shopping centers or heavily used streets.

For NCTD and San Diego Transit information call:
From Escondido, San Marcos & Valley Center 484-2550
From Del Mar, Solana Beach and Rancho Santa Fe (toll free) 1-484-2550
From Oceanside, Carlsbad, Vista, Fallbrook,
San Dieguito and Camp Pendleton 438-2550
Se habla Español

ROUTE

301 Oceanside Del Mar

Minutes Past Hour

Departs From	South Bound	North Bound	South Bound	North Bound
Third & Tremont (T)	:00	:60	:30	:30 (arrival)
Mission & Hill (T)	:02	:58	:32	:28
Oceanside Blvd & Hill (T)	:05	:55	:35	:25
Vista Way & Hill	:08	:52	:38	:22
Grand & Washington (T)	:15	:45	:45	:15
101 & La Costa Downs	:25	:35	:55	:05
101 & Leucadia	:30	:23	:00	:53
1st & E St	:35	:20	:05	:50
Birmingham & San Elijo	:45	:15	:15	:45
101 & Lomas Santa Fe	:53	:07	:23	:37
101 & Via De La Valle	:55	:03	:25	:33
15th & Camino Del Mar (T)	:60	:00	—	—
Flowerhill Center (T)	—	—	:30	:30 (arrival)

(Southbound columns "Read Down" ↓, Northbound columns "Read Up" ↑)

First bus leaves: Oceanside at 5:00 am Del Mar at 6:00 am
Flower Hill 6:30 a.m.
Washington & Grand 6:15 am Northbound
Last bus leaves: Oceanside 7:30 p.m. Del Mar 8:00 p.m.
Flower Hill 8:30 p.m.

Service seven days a week.

Work Trips into Stillman's From Oceanside: 6:30 am
From Del Mar: 3:00 pm only

ROUTE

302 Oceanside Escondido

To: Escondido

Departs From	Minutes Past Hour	
3rd & Tremont (T)	:15	:45
Mission & Hill (T)	:17	:47
Plaza Camino Real	:35	:05
MiraCosta College	:41	:11
Waring & Thunder	:45	:15
Broadway Shopping Center (T)	:00	:30
Palomar College	:15	:45
Mission & Pico (T)	:17	:47
Grand & Maple (T)	:30	:00
Escondido Village Mall (T)	:37	:07 (arr.)

To: Oceanside

Departs From		
Escondido Village Mall (T)	:45	:15
Grand & Maple (T)	:50	:20
Mission & Pico (T)	:05	:35
Palomar College	:07	:37
Broadway Shopping Center (T)	:30	:00
Waring & Thunder	:35	:05
MiraCosta College	:39	:09
Plaza Camino Real (T)	:55	:25
Mission & Hill (T)	:08	:38
3rd & Tremont (T)	:10	:40 (arr.)

Service 7 days a week

1st bus leaves either 3rd & Tremont or the Escondido
Village Mall at 5:15 am and every ½ hr. thereafter

Last bus leaves either 3rd & Tremont or the Escondido
Village Mall at 9:45 pm.

ROUTE

316 Oceana Francine Villas Plaza Camino Real

FROM PLAZA CAMINO REAL:

Departs From	Minutes Past Hour	
Plaza Camino Real (T)	:30	:00
Oceana		:10
Oceanside Blvd. & Hill St. (T)	:41	:16
Mission & Horne (T)	:00	:30
San Raphael & Capistrano	:07	
Francine Villas	:12	
San Raphael & Capistrano	:17	
Loretta & Zeiss		:38
Mission & Horne (T)	:30	:00

TO PLAZA CAMINO REAL

Mission & Horne (T)	:30	:00
Oceanside Blvd. & Hill St. (T)	:35	:05
Oceana		:15
Gemco		:25
Plaza Camino Real (T)	:00	:30

First bus leaves Plaza Camino Real at 6:00 A.M.
Last bus leaves Plaza Camino Real at 9:00 P.M.
First bus leaves Mission & Horne to Plaza Camino Real at 6:30 A.M.
Last bus leaves Mission & Horne to Plaza Camino Real at 8:30 P.M.
First bus leaves Mission & Horne to Francine Villas at 6:00 A.M.
Last bus leaves Mission & Horne to Francine Villas at 9:00 P.M.

Hourly Service to Oceana :10 to Mission & Horne
:15 to Plaza Camino Real
Hourly Service to Francine Villas :00 from Mission & Horne
Hourly Service to Loretta & Zeiss :30 from Mission & Horne

Limited SUNDAY SERVICE start 10:00 am from Mission
and Horne to Plaza Camino Real . 1½ hours between buses.
Service terminates at Mission and Horne at 7:00 P.M.

HOW TO RIDE THE BUS

If you are unfamiliar with the schedule, call 438-2550. Ask that a schedule be mailed or request one from the driver.

Be sure the driver knows that you want to board the bus.

As you board the bus, be ready to deposit exact fare in coin, or show a pass. Drivers do not carry change.

When approaching your destination, please pull the cord or press yellow strip in time for a smooth stop.

FARES

35¢, (15¢ for seniors and handicapped), will take you most everywhere in North County.

Higher fares to Ramona and outer Camp Pendleton

EXACT FARE IN COIN IS REQUIRED.

Econopass is only $10.00 a month. Studentpass for youth up to full time college students is $8.00 a month. Helperpass for seniors and handicapped is $5.00 a month.

Passes are good for unlimited rides except Route 305 (outer Camp Pendleton), Route 307 (Ramona), and Express Routes

Passes are available at many outlets. For information on where to buy a pass and where the buses go, call 438-2550.

TRANSFERS

Transfers are free. Just request a transfer upon boarding the bus. Transfers are used to complete a trip and are not valid for a return trip. They also must be used within two hours.

If you plan to transfer to a higher fare route please pay full fare to destination and inform driver of your destination. The driver will then validate your transfer for ultimate destination.

FOR INFORMATION:

NORTH COUNTY TRANSIT DISTRICT

438-2550 Se habla Espanol.

REPRO –
Bus Schedule

ROUTE 312
Plaza Camino Real
South Oceanside
Mission Avenue
Oceanside Harbor

Departs from:	Minutes Past Hour
Plaza Camino Real (T)	:00
Ridgeway & California	:06
California & Stewart	:11
Cassidy & Hill (T)	:14
Pacific & 3rd	:21
Harbor Dr. & Pacific	:25
Mission & Hill (T)	:30
Mission & Canyon	:38
Oceanside Blvd. & Crouch (T)	:40
Laurel & Fire Mountain	:45
Plaza Camino Real (arrival) (T)	:52

Plaza Camino Real (T)	:30
Laurel & Fire Mtn.	:38
Oceanside Blvd. & Crouch (T)	:43
Canyon & Mission	:45
Mission & Hill (T)	:51
Harbor Dr. & Pacific	:57
Pacific & 3rd	:00
Cassidy & Hill (T)	:07
California & Stewart	:10
Ridgeway & California	:16
Plaza Camino Real (arrival) (T)	:22

First bus leaves Plaza Camino Real at 6:00 a.m. and every 30 minutes thereafter.

Last bus leaves Plaza Camino Real at 8:30 p.m.

Monday thru Saturday Service
See supplemental schedule for Sunday service.

ROUTE 303
Camp Pendleton
Oceanside
Commissary
Hospital
Mainside

To: Main Gate

Departs From:	Minutes Past Hour
Mission & Hill (T)	:00
Main Gate	:05
22 Area (T)	:20
33 Area	:30
Hospital	:40
11 Area — Main Exchange	:50
San Luis Rey Gate	:57
Guadacanal & Mission	:10
Mission & Hill (T)	:15 (arrival)

To: Rear Gate

Departs From:	
3rd & Hill	:30
Guadacanal & Mission	:35
San Luis Rey Gate	:47
11 Area — Main Exchange	:55
Hospital	:05
33 Area	:15
22 Area (T)	:30
Main Gate	:40
Mission & Hill (T)	:45 (arrival)

Service 5:00am thru 5:00 am
Service 7 days a week.

Service to 22 Area and Industrial Center
6:00 am to 6:00 pm Mon. thru Fri.

ROUTE 313
Mesa Margarita
Hermosa Homes
Downtown Oceanside

To: San Luis Rey - Mesa Margarita - Hermosa Homes

Departs From:	Minutes Past Hour	
Mission Avenue & Hill Street (T)	:05	:35
Oceanside Industrial Center	:17	:47
Los Arbolitos & Fireside Dr.	:28	:58
East Parker & Vandergrift (T)	:44	:14
Mission Avenue & Francesca Dr.	:52	:22
El Camino High School	:55	:25
Mission & Canyon	:07	:37
Mission & Hill (T)	(arrival) :10	:40

To: Hermosa Homes - Mesa Margarita - San Luis Rey

Departs From:		
Mission Avenue & Hill St. (T)	:20	:50
El Camino High School	:34	:04
Mission Avenue & Francesca Dr.	:43	:13
East Parker & Vandegrift (T)	:53	:23
Los Arbolitos & Fireside Dr.	:05	:35
Oceanside Industrial Center	:15	:45
Mission & Canyon	:20	:50
Mission & Hill (T)	(arrival) :23	:53

1st bus leaves E. Parker & Vandegrift 6:21 am
1st bus leaves Mission & Hill 5:50 am
Last bus leaves Mission & Hill at 8:35 pm

Monday thru Saturday Service
See supplemental schedule for Sunday service.

255

REPRO – Bus Schedule
(Combine with map on p. 259.)

REPRO – Bus Schedule
(Combine with map on p. 257.)

(Clip out and rubber cement to back of paste-up)

Name_____

PROJECT EVALUATION CHECK LIST
ASSIGNMENT 6: BUS SCHEDULE

This check list is designed to assist you in identifying the specific points upon which this assignment will be evaluated. Your instructor will indicate by the use of a check mark those areas requiring additional attention.

PASTE-UP PLANNING

_____ Two 15" X 18" illustration boards
_____ 12" X 14" paper size area (blue pencil)

PASTE-UP PREPARATION (cover side)

_____ Elements trimmed smoothly
_____ Elements trimmed to correct dimensions
_____ Elements positioned according to rough layout
_____ Accurate alignment of elements
_____ Accurate alignment and application of head margin elements
_____ Crop, center, and fold marks in black ink
_____ Uniform application of adhesive and burnished
_____ Protective tissue overlay and cover flap attached

PASTE-UP PREPARATION (inside)

_____ Elements trimmed smoothly
_____ Elements trimmed to correct dimensions
_____ Elements positioned according to rough layout
_____ Accurate alignment of elements
_____ Accurate alignment and application of adhesive border tape; corners mitered square
_____ Crop, center, and fold marks in black ink
_____ Uniform application of adhesive and burnished
_____ Protective tissue overlay and cover flap attached

FINAL EVALUATION _____

assignment 7

DIRECT MAIL ADVERTISEMENT

INFORMATION

Businesses of all kinds use direct mail advertising to promote their products. Most of this type of printing utilizes the offset printing process. Advertising agencies and printing firms are called upon to produce the multitude of direct mail advertising that finds its way into the homes of millions of people in this country.

In some cases, business firms maintain a staff of layout and paste-up artists to produce the camera-ready copy as well as final printing. These are known as "in-plant" operators. Business firms such as Boeing Aircraft, IBM, Ford Motor Company, and many others maintain in-plant operations.

MATERIALS REQUIRED

Paste-up tools
Adhesive screen tint material
Print trimmer and scissors
Rubber cement and/or waxer
Masking tape and transparent tape
One piece of 11" × 14" illustration board
One piece of 11" × 15" tissue overlay paper
One piece of 11" × 16" cover flap paper

PROCEDURE

1. Examine and familiarize yourself with the rough layout.
2. Fasten the illustration board squarely and smoothly to the table work surface with the 11" dimension running horizontally.

3. Using a nonreproducing blue pencil or pen, outline the paper size and the trim size as shown on the rough layout. Draw in any guide marks that may be helpful when starting to make up the paste-up.

4. Using adhesive border tape, position the 2–point rules, making certain that the top and right sides of the rules extend into the trim area at least $\frac{1}{4}''$.

5. Wax the back of the reproduction proof, and place the proof on a stiff piece of cutting board. Cut out the elements as needed with an X-acto® knife. Do not adhere the line that reads "The NEW in" until later. Square all elements with a T-square.

6. When cutting out the line that reads "The NEW in" be sure to leave enough paper around it so that it will be larger than the screen tint area. It must bleed at least $\frac{1}{8}''$ on the left side.

7. Place "The NEW in" line in its correct position.

8. Use a 55–line, 20% adhesive screen tint to create the screened effect in the paste-up copy. Draw an outline in light-blue pencil on the paste-up to indicate the exact dimensions of the screen tint area.

9. Cut a piece of adhesive screen tint material slightly larger than the dimension drawn. Use the X-acto® knife to cut the material. Best results are obtained if a steel straight edge or T-square is used when cutting a straight line.

10. Place the screen tint material directly over the area you have marked on the paste-up; allow the edges to overlap the blue guidelines. Smooth out the material very lightly.

11. With the aid of a steel straight edge, trim the screen tint material to the exact size required.

12. Place a piece of clean white paper over the screen tint material, and using a burnishing roller, force out all of the air bubbles that may be trapped between the screen tint material and the illustration board. If air bubbles remain, they will show on the finished printed piece and give the screened area a mottled effect.

13. Cover the paste-up with a piece of white paper, and burnish the remaining elements with a hand roller.

14. Ink in all crop, trim, and center marks with thin, black lines approximately $\frac{1}{2}''$ long.

15. Attach a piece of tissue paper to the illustration board by taping it with transparent tape on the reverse side at the top. Fold over the extra $1''$ at the top of the paste-up.

16. Attach a piece of colored text paper (cover flap) to the illustration board by taping it with masking tape on the reverse side at the top. Fold over the extra $2''$ at the top, and cut back at a 30–degree angle on both sides.

17. Write your name on the front of the Evaluation Check List sheet, and rubber cement the sheet to the back of the paste-up.

18. Turn in assignment for evaluation.

CUTTING BENDAY (TINT) SCREEN MATERIAL

1. Cut lightly around the entire area of benday film material.

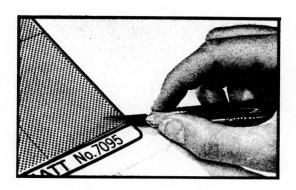

2. Turn the X-acto® knife so that the blade is parallel to the surface of the sheet, and slide the knifepoint under the corner of the film.

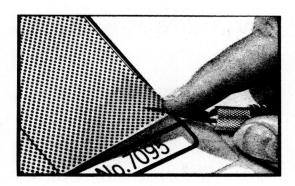

3. Place your finger over the corner where you have inserted the knifepoint, and lift the shading film off of the backing sheet.

BENDAY (TINT) SCREEN MATERIAL

Benday (tint) screen material is widely used in cold-type copy preparation as a shading medium, background, and other design effects. This material is manufactured in a variety of *densities* (percentage of area covered by dots) and a variety of *rulings* (number of lines of dots per inch). A screen tint of any given density can be obtained in a variety of rulings. Examples of benday (tint) screen densities and rulings are shown below.

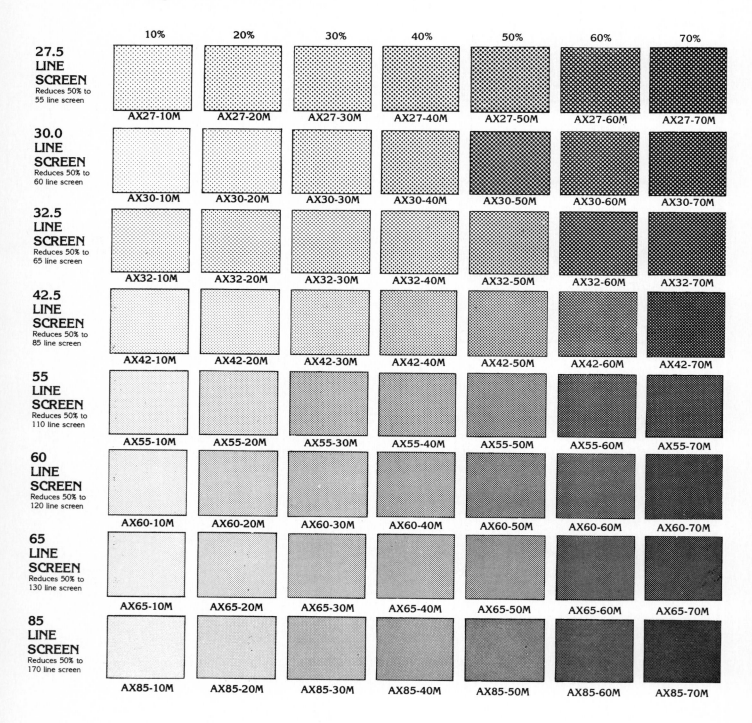

	10%	20%	30%	40%	50%	60%	70%
27.5 LINE SCREEN Reduces 50% to 55 line screen	AX27-10M	AX27-20M	AX27-30M	AX27-40M	AX27-50M	AX27-60M	AX27-70M
30.0 LINE SCREEN Reduces 50% to 60 line screen	AX30-10M	AX30-20M	AX30-30M	AX30-40M	AX30-50M	AX30-60M	AX30-70M
32.5 LINE SCREEN Reduces 50% to 65 line screen	AX32-10M	AX32-20M	AX32-30M	AX32-40M	AX32-50M	AX32-60M	AX32-70M
42.5 LINE SCREEN Reduces 50% to 85 line screen	AX42-10M	AX42-20M	AX42-30M	AX42-40M	AX42-50M	AX42-60M	AX42-70M
55 LINE SCREEN Reduces 50% to 110 line screen	AX55-10M	AX55-20M	AX55-30M	AX55-40M	AX55-50M	AX55-60M	AX55-70M
60 LINE SCREEN Reduces 50% to 120 line screen	AX60-10M	AX60-20M	AX60-30M	AX60-40M	AX60-50M	AX60-60M	AX60-70M
65 LINE SCREEN Reduces 50% to 130 line screen	AX65-10M	AX65-20M	AX65-30M	AX65-40M	AX65-50M	AX65-60M	AX65-70M
85 LINE SCREEN Reduces 50% to 170 line screen	AX85-10M	AX85-20M	AX85-30M	AX85-40M	AX85-50M	AX85-60M	AX85-70M

ASSIGNMENT 7

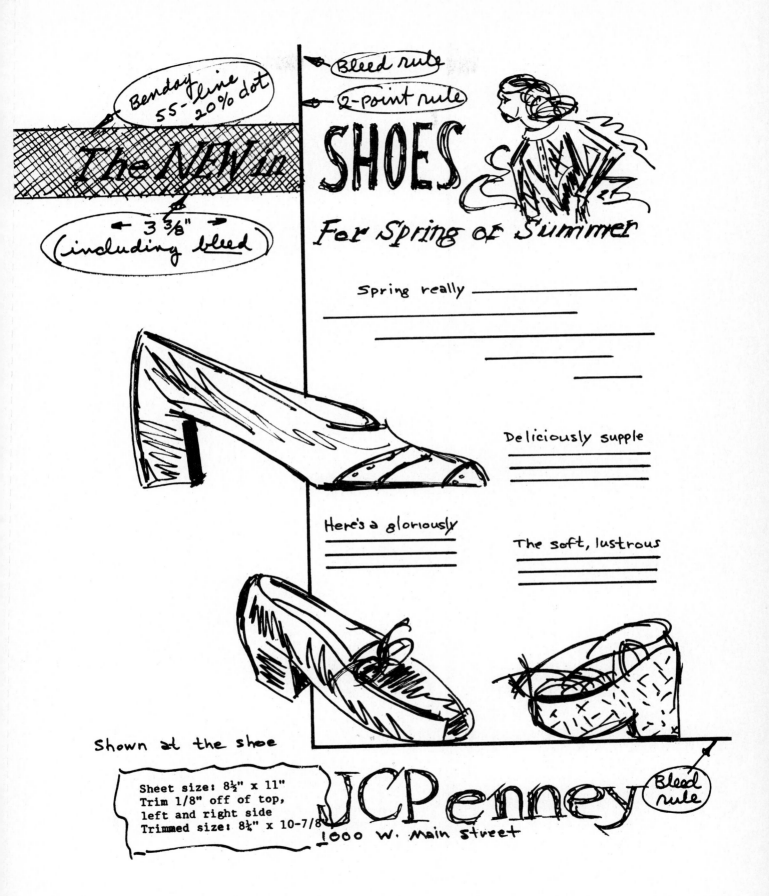

Benday line
55-line 20% dot

The NEW in

← 3 3/8" →
(including bleed

Bleed rule
2-point rule

SHOES
For Spring or Summer

Spring really _____
_____
_____
_____

Deliciously supple
_____
_____

Here's a gloriously
_____
_____

The soft, lustrous
_____
_____

Shown at the shoe

Sheet size: 8½" x 11"
Trim 1/8" off of top,
left and right side
Trimmed size: 8¼" x 10-7/8"

JCPenney
1000 W. Main street

Bleed rule

267

(Clip out and rubber cement to back of paste-up)

Name_____

PROJECT EVALUATION CHECK LIST
ASSIGNMENT 7: DIRECT MAIL ADVERTISEMENT

This check list is designed to assist you in identifying the specific points upon which this assignment will be evaluated. Your instructor will indicate by the use of a check mark those areas requiring additional attention.

PASTE-UP PLANNING

_____ 11″ × 14″ illustration board
_____ 8½″ × 11″ paper area (blue pencil)
_____ 8¼″ × 10⅞″ trim size (blue pencil)

PASTE-UP PREPARATION

_____ Elements trimmed smoothly
_____ Elements trimmed to correct dimensions
_____ Elements positioned according to rough layout
_____ Accurate alignment of elements
_____ Uniform application of adhesive and burnished
_____ 2–point rule adhered accurately
_____ 2–point rule bleeds top and right side approximately ¼″
_____ Benday tint screen applied correctly
_____ Shoes positioned correctly and butted against 2–point rules
_____ Crop marks in black ink approximately ½″ long
_____ Trim marks in black ink approximately ½″ long
_____ Center marks in black ink approximately ½″ long
_____ Overall cleanliness of paste-up
_____ Protective tissue overlay and cover flap attached

*FINAL EVALUATION*_____

AIRLINE FLIGHT SCHEDULE

INFORMATION

Direct advertising is printed communication that is given directly to someone either in person or through the mail. Brochures and folders are two principle forms of direct advertising literature.

The printed piece must be an aid in selling goods or informing people about services offered. The rules of good layout and design are very important if the printed piece is to attract attention, create interest, and get the message to the reader.

Brochures usually consist of more than one page. These are sometimes called panels. Folding is required, and depending on the number of pages or panels, intricate fold patterns are frequently necessary. Fold lines are indicated on the paste-up with a dashed line in ink. Some brochures are designed to be "self-mailers" and leave space for the address and stamp on one outside page. Brochures are also designed to be mailed in envelopes or to be inserted in a counter display rack.

MATERIALS REQUIRED

Paste-up tools
Print trimmer and scissors
Rubber cement and/or waxer
Masking tape and transparent tape
Adhesive border tape
One piece of 11″ × 14″ illustration board
One piece of 12″ × 14″ tissue overlay paper
One piece of 13″ × 14″ cover flap paper

PROCEDURE

1. Fasten the illustration board squarely and smoothly to the table work surface with the 14″ dimension running horizontally.

2. Using a nonreproducing blue pencil or pen, outline a paper area of 8½″ × 11″ and an image area of 45 × 63 picas.

3. Following the rough layout, rule in the appropriate guidelines for all boxes, artwork, and display and text type in light-blue pencil or pen. Indicate fold lines with ⅛″-long dashes in black ink (see layout). Write FOLD on the paste-up in blue pencil.

4. Ink in crop and center marks with thin, black lines approximately ½″ long.

5. Use 1-point adhesive border tape for the cover page box. Be sure the width of the box is exactly the same as the artwork (see the rough layout).

6. Wax the proof, and cut out necessary elements as needed.

7. Lay the individual elements in position lightly to check position and fit. Do not burnish until all elements are in position.

8. When you are sure that the individual panel elements correspond to the rough layout, check final alignment with a T-square, and burnish the elements.

9. Attach a piece of tissue overlay paper to the illustration board by taping it with transparent tape on the reverse side at the top. Fold over the extra 1″ at the top of the paste-up.

10. Attach a piece of colored text paper (cover flap) to the illustration board by taping it with masking tape on the reverse side at the top. Fold over the extra 2″ at the top, and cut back at a 30-degree angle on both sides.

11. Write your name on the front of the Evaluation Check List sheet, and rubber cement the sheet to the back of the paste-up.

12. Turn in assignment for evaluation.

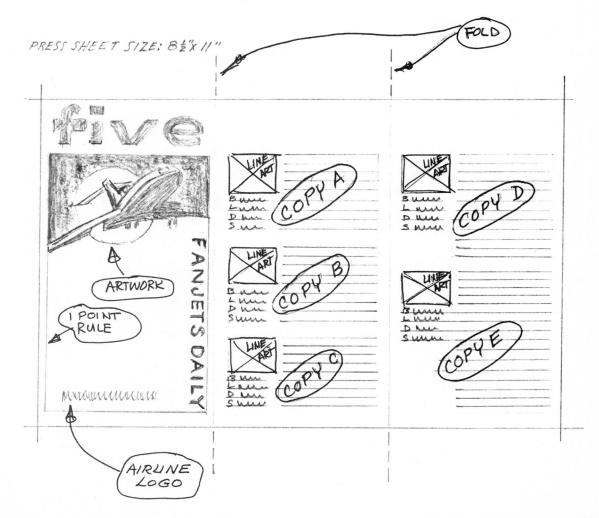

COPY A

FROM
BURBANK (PDT)
Passenger   Air Freight
213-246-7181   213-845-7816
Airport: B-Burbank/Glendale/Pasadena

To: CALGARY (MDT)				
B 7 25a	3 00p	422/WA773	B S	DEN

To: CASPER (MDT)				
B 3 00p	8 57p	42/55	S	DEN

To: CHICAGO (CDT)
Airports: O-O'Hare M-Midway

B 7 25a O 5 36p	422/82$	B S	DEN
B 3 00p O 10 08p	42/88	S D	DEN

COPY B

FROM
CASPER (MDT)
Passenger   Air Freight
307-577-0670   307-266-4213

To: ALBUQUERQUE (MDT)

7 45a	10 10a	22/257	S	DEN
5 32p	8 50p	205/247	S	DEN

To: ANCHORAGE (ADT)

5 32p	11 13p	★ 205/989	S D	DEN

Service Via CO-WA Interchange

To: AUSTIN (CDT)

7 45a	4 05p	22/21/54	S L	DEN/
				ELP

COPY C

FROM
FORT LAUDERDALE (EDT)
Passenger   Air Freight
305-525-4126   305-761-1860

To: ALBUQUERQUE (MDT)

8 42a	4 30p	403/445	B S	DEN

To: AUSTIN (CDT)

8 42a	12 08p	403/65	B	MIA

To: BURBANK (PDT)
Airport: B-Burbank/Glendale/Pasadena

8 42a B	2 00p	403/37	B L	DEN

COPY D

FROM
LOS ANGELES (PDT)
Passenger   Air Freight
213-772-6000   213-776-2421
Airports: L-Los Angeles Int'l O-Ontario

To: ALBUQUERQUE (MDT)

L 12 35a	7 58a	254/91$	S	ELP

To: AUCKLAND, NEW ZEALAND (GMT + 12)

L 10 55a	10 25p+1	★ 1	257	L D	2
	Dis Oct. 25				
L 7 35p	7 50a+2	★ 1	135	D B	1
	Eff Oct. 26				

COPY E

FROM
ONTARIO (PDT)
Passenger   Air Freight
714-988-6541   714-983-8412
Airport: O-Ontario

To: CALGARY (MDT)				
O 7 10a	3 00p	86/WA773	B S	DEN

To: CASPER (MDT)

O 11 45a	4 57p	300/23	L	DEN
O 3 10p	8 57p	426/55	S	DEN

To: CHICAGO (CDT)
Airports: O-O'Hare M-Midway

O 7 10a O 2 00p	86/24	B L	DEN
O 11 45a O 6 36p	300/40	L D	DEN
O 3 10p O 10 08p	426/88	S D	DEN

To: COLORADO SPRINGS (MDT)

O 7 10a	11 20a	86/219	B	DEN
O 11 45a	5 05p	300/29	L	DEN
O 3 10p	8 05p	426/415	S	DEN

To: DENVER (MDT)

O 7 10a	10 10a	86	B	O
O 11 45a	2 45p	300	L	O
O 3 10p	6 10p	426	S	O
O 9 09p	2 00a+1	205/18$		LAX

To: EL PASO/JUAREZ (MDT)

O 9 09p	3 18a+1	205/254$		LAX

To: FORT LAUDERDALE (EDT)

O 11 45a	9 57p	300/402	L D	DEN

five
FANJETS DAILY
TWA

REPRO - Airline Flight Schedule

B—Breakfast
L—Lunch
D—Dinner
S—Snack
$—Lower Fares Applicable
▲—Higher Fare Routing Applies

B—Breakfast
L—Lunch
D—Dinner
S—Snack
$—Lower Fares Applicable
▲—Higher Fare Routing Applies

B—Breakfast
L—Lunch
D—Dinner
S—Snack
$—Lower Fares Applicable
▲—Higher Fare Routing Applies

B—Breakfast
L—Lunch
D—Dinner
S—Snack
$—Lower Fares Applicable
▲—Higher Fare Routing Applies

B—Breakfast
L—Lunch
D—Dinner
S—Snack
$—Lower Fares Applicable
▲—Higher Fare Routing Applies

(Clip out and rubber cement to back of paste-up)

Name_____

PROJECT EVALUATION CHECK LIST
ASSIGNMENT 8: AIRLINE FLIGHT SCHEDULE

This check list is designed to assist you in identifying the specific points upon which this assignment will be evaluated. Your instructor will indicate by the use of a check mark those areas requiring additional attention.

PASTE-UP PLANNING

_____ 11" X 14" illustration board
_____ 8½" X 11" paper area (blue pencil)
_____ 45 X 63 pica image area (blue pencil)

PASTE-UP PREPARATION

_____ Elements trimmed smoothly
_____ Elements trimmed to correct dimensions
_____ Elements positioned according to rough layout
_____ Accurate alignment of elements
_____ Adhesive border tape applied correctly
_____ Adhesive border tape corners cut smooth and square with no overruns
_____ Uniform application of adhesive and burnished
_____ Crop and center marks in black ink approximately ½" long
_____ Fold marks (indicated with ⅛" dashes in black ink) positioned at fold lines outside paper size area at top and bottom
_____ Protective tissue overlay and cover flap attached

FINAL EVALUATION _____

assignment ⑨

PACIFIC TELEPHONE BROCHURE

INFORMATION

Brochures are used extensively in advertising by a variety of firms desiring to make the public aware of their services. Since hundreds of design options are possible, the designer is limited only by imagination and/or budget. The number of pages, the kinds of folds, the number of colors, the size, and whether or not the brochure should be stapled are only a few of the creative decisions necessary.

One important consideration in designing a brochure is distribution. If distribution is by mail, will the brochure be a self-mailer, or will it be stuffed into an envelope? If an envelope is to be used, what size will be needed? The designer should always check with current post office regulations to avoid costly mistakes and loss of time.

MATERIALS REQUIRED

Paste-up tools
Print trimmer and scissors
Rubber cement and/or waxer
Masking tape and transparent tape
One piece of 11″ × 22″ illustration board
One piece of 11″ × 23″ tissue overlay paper
One piece of 11″ × 24″ cover flap paper

PROCEDURE

1. Examine and familiarize yourself with the rough layout.
2. Fasten the illustration board squarely and smoothly to the table work surface with the 11″ dimension running horizontally.

3. Following the rough layout, use a nonreproducing blue pencil or pen to outline an 8″ × 9″ paper size area (9″ dimension running vertically) in the top half of the 11″ × 22″ board.
4. Do the same for the bottom half of the board.
5. Following the rough layout, draw light-blue guide marks to indicate the positions for center marks, fold lines, illustrations, and all type elements.
6. Wax the back of the reproduction proofs, and place on a cutting board next to the work area. Cut out elements as needed with an X-acto® knife. Square all elements on the paste-up with a T-square and triangle. Note where pieces of artwork "bleed," and make the necessary allowances. Bleed allowance will be ⅛″.
7. Cover the paste-up with a piece of white paper, and burnish elements with a hand roller.
8. Check all elements for final alignment with a T-square and triangle.
9. Ink in all crop, center, and fold marks. Ink in ⅛″–long fold marks at the top and bottom just outside the paper size area (see rough layout).
10. Attach a piece of tissue paper to the board by taping it with transparent tape on the reverse side at the top. Fold over the extra 1″ at the top of the paste-up.
11. Attach a piece of colored text paper (cover flap) to the illustration board by taping it with masking tape on the reverse side at the top. Fold over the extra 2″ at the top, and cut back at a 30–degree angle on both sides.
12. Write your name on the front of the Evaluation Check List sheet, and rubber cement the sheet to the back of the paste-up.
13. Turn in assignment for evaluation.

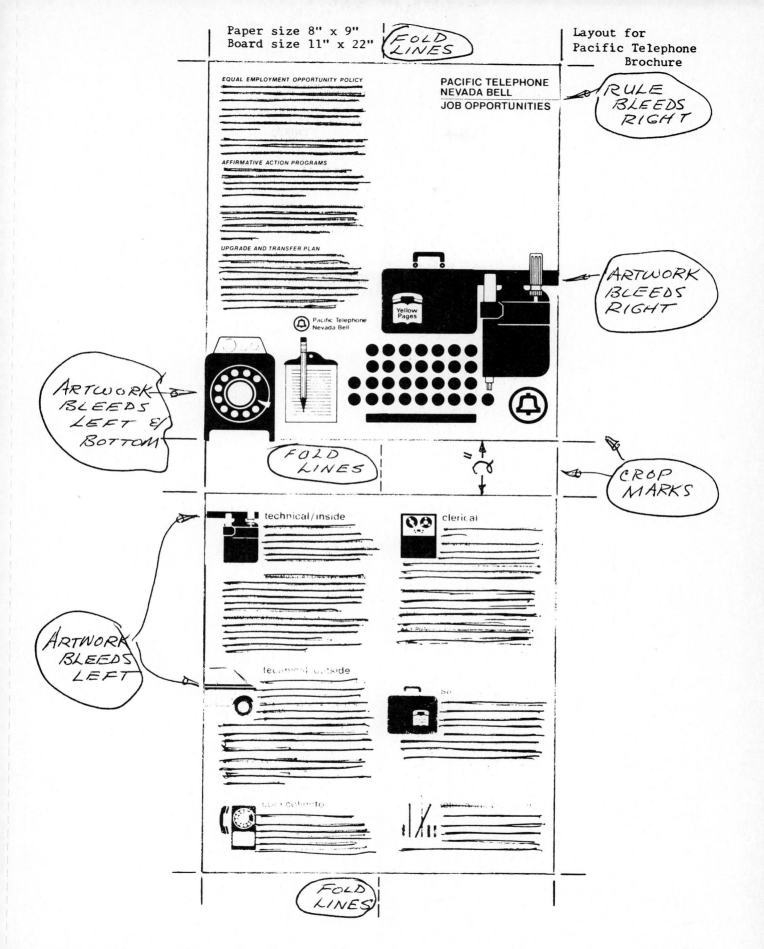

Paper size 8" x 9"
Board size 11" x 22"

FOLD LINES

Layout for
Pacific Telephone
Brochure

RULE BLEEDS RIGHT

EQUAL EMPLOYMENT OPPORTUNITY POLICY

PACIFIC TELEPHONE
NEVADA BELL
JOB OPPORTUNITIES

AFFIRMATIVE ACTION PROGRAMS

UPGRADE AND TRANSFER PLAN

ARTWORK BLEEDS RIGHT

Yellow Pages

Pacific Telephone
Nevada Bell

ARTWORK BLEEDS LEFT & BOTTOM

FOLD LINES

CROP MARKS

technical/inside

clerical

ARTWORK BLEEDS LEFT

technical outside

FOLD LINES

283

PACIFIC TELEPHONE
NEVADA BELL
JOB OPPORTUNITIES

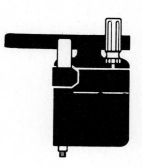

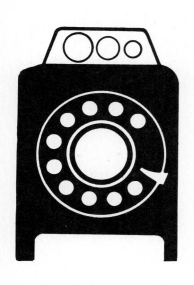

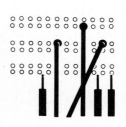

technical/outside

These jobs involve working outdoors in all kinds of weather, climbing poles and driving motor vehicles.

STATION INSTALLATION TECHNICIAN Installs and connects many types of telephone equipment ranging from single telephones to complex switching systems in customers' homes and business offices.

SPLICING TECHNICIAN Joins cables together and solders connections in manholes, along pole lines and in cable vaults in buildings.

OUTSIDE PLANT TECHNICIAN Rearranges and removes telephone poles, lays underground cable and strings overhead wires. Also operates heavy equipment.

COMMUNICATIONS TECHNICIAN Repairs and maintains telephone switching equipment. Locates trouble by inspecting and testing equipment and analyzing test data and trouble reports. Some past technical work experience or training is generally needed for this job.

COMMUNICATIONS TECHNICIAN-TOLL Repairs and does preventive maintenance of microwave, television, teletype and data equipment. Seeks out and corrects various electronic problems. Some past technical work experience or training is generally needed for this job.

telephone operating

These jobs involve a variety of hours. Operators may be required to work various shifts (day, evening, night, or split shift), Saturdays, Sundays and holidays. They sit at their own position wearing a headset all day.

Pacific Telephone
Nevada Bell

sales

DIRECTORY SALES Visits business firms to discuss their telephone directory advertising. Prepares and presents advertising programs that will be beneficial to the customers. Also writes and coordinates orders. Works out-of-town three to six months a year. Another sales job involves selling telephone directory advertising by telephone.

coin collector

Collects receptacles of money deposited in public telephones, inspects coin telephone booths and equipment and keeps reports and records. Drives a company motor vehicle and travels over a wide area.

clerical

There is a wide variety of clerical jobs.

GENERAL OFFICE CLERK Posts and summarizes data, maintains records, sorts, files, processes customers' payments and answers telephones. Some jobs may involve typing or the operation of office machines, comptometers, calculators and tabulating equipment.

TYPIST Types letters, reports, forms and other correspondence. May also type and process customers' orders for service.

STENOGRAPHER Takes dictation and transcribes correspondence and reports.

KEY PUNCH OPERATOR Records information about payrolls, inventories, material costs and production figures on tabulating cards.

EQUAL EMPLOYMENT OPPORTUNITY POLICY It is our policy as an equal opportunity employer, to select and assign individuals without regard to race, color, religion, national origin, sex or age.

It is also our policy to provide equal employment opportunity to qualified individuals who are handicapped, disabled veterans or veterans of the Vietnam-era.

We seek to treat each person as an individual and provide opportunity for each employee to develop his or her own talents and advance in the business.

AFFIRMATIVE ACTION PROGRAMS Our Company's Affirmative Action Programs provide the procedures to make equal opportunity a reality. They contain plans for recruiting, hiring, and developing the abilities of all employees so that our objectives can be met.

Annual targets are set which are designed to bring the ethnic/sex profile of each job classification into an appropriate relationship with that of the relevant source pool. We are totally committed to the good faith efforts required to attain these targets.

UPGRADE AND TRANSFER PLAN The Upgrade and Transfer Plan for Pacific Telephone and Nevada Bell provides all non-management employees an equal opportunity to compete for nonmanagement job openings. After working for a specified period of time, an employee may submit a transfer request for any nonmanagement job he or she desires. Selections for job openings are based on length of service and qualifications as specified in the Plan.

technical/inside

FRAME ATTENDANT Connects, changes or disconnects customer telephone lines that are located in central office equipment rooms. Also prepares records and reports. Works with hand tools and testing equipment.

(Clip out and rubber cement to back of paste-up)

Name_____

PROJECT EVALUATION CHECK LIST
ASSIGNMENT 9: PACIFIC TELEPHONE BROCHURE

This check list is designed to assist you in identifying the specific points upon which this assignment will be evaluated. Your instructor will indicate by the use of a check mark those areas requiring additional attention.

PASTE-UP PLANNING

_____ 11" X 22" illustration board
_____ 8" X 9" paper area (blue pencil)

PASTE-UP PREPARATION

_____ Elements trimmed smoothly
_____ Elements trimmed to correct dimensions
_____ Elements positioned according to rough layout
_____ Accurate alignment of elements
_____ Uniform application of adhesive and burnished
_____ Crop and center marks in black ink approximately ½" long
_____ Fold marks (indicated by ⅛" dashes in black ink) positioned at fold lines outside paper size area top and bottom
_____ Bleed allowance ⅛"
_____ Protective tissue overlay and cover flap attached

*FINAL EVALUATION*_____

10

NEWSLETTER MAKE-UP

INFORMATION

Continuous tone photographs are not suitable for inclusion with line material on the same paste-up. They require an additional step on the camera to transform the continuous tones into areas of black and white. The result is a halftone negative. It is, therefore, necessary to separate all camera copy into two groups: line and halftone.

All continuous tone copy should be "keyed" to the line material by using capital letters A, B, C, etc., placed on the paste-up where the photos are to appear (see rough layout for this assignment) and also on the back of the photos.

In addition, the paste-up must contain windows to accommodate the halftone negatives. This is done by placing pieces of red masking film on the line paste-up in the exact positions that the photos will eventually occupy [see (A) on p. 292]. This material will reproduce as clear window openings on the line negative. The halftone negatives are then stripped in behind the window openings of the line negative to produce the effect seen in (B) (p. 292).

This assignment requires that you assemble a newsletter form and handle windows for the halftones. The body or text matter is contained on the reproduction proof. The rough layout shows approximate positions for the various page elements.

MATERIALS REQUIRED

Paste-up tools
Amberlith® film material
Rubber cement and/or waxer
Masking tape and transparent tape
One piece of 11″ × 14″ illustration board
One piece of 11″ × 15″ tissue overlay paper
One piece of 11″ × 16″ cover flap paper

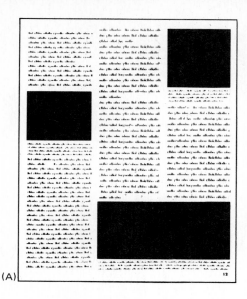

(A)

(B)

PROCEDURE

1. Examine and familiarize yourself with the newsletter rough layout.
2. Fasten the illustration board squarely and smoothly to the table work surface with the 11″ dimension running horizontally.
3. Using a light-blue pencil, outline a paper area of 8½″ × 11″ and an image area of 45 × 60 picas. Be sure that the illustration board is square on the table before attempting to draw guidelines.
4. Divide the image area into three 14–pica columns, allowing 1½ picas space between columns (see rough layout).
5. Carefully trim three pieces of Amberlith® film material to the sizes indicated on the layout. These will be rubber cemented into the positions shown.
6. Wax the back of the reproduction proof containing the text matter. Cut and position (light pressure for position check only) the text areas as shown in the rough layout. Note that the photos have captions that are set slightly apart from the text matter. The single-column text matter is 14 picas wide, and the double column matter is 29½ picas wide. Use your blue pencil to mark approximate positions for pictures and text matter. Alignment of the columns must be flush at top and bottom. Since the columns of type on the reproduction proof have irregular spacing between some paragraphs, be sure to adjust paragraph spacing on the paste-up so that it is equal.
7. When you are satisfied that the positioning of elements is correct, "key" the windows as shown with blue pencil on the illustration board. Cement the windows in position emulsion side up by "spot welding" at the corners and center. Do not cover the entire surface of the film material with rubber cement, because this material is often lifted from one job and used on another job.
8. Align all material with a T-square. Be sure that the columns align at top and bottom. Space between paragraphs must also appear equal.
9. Cover the paste-up elements with a piece of clean white paper, and burnish with a roller.
10. Ink in all crop and center marks with thin, black lines approximately ½″ long.
11. Attach a piece of tissue overlay paper to the illustration board by taping it with tape on the reverse side at the top. Fold over the extra 1″ at the top of the paste-up.
12. Attach a piece of colored text paper (cover flap) to the illustration board by taping it with masking tape on the reverse side at the top. Fold over the extra 2″ at the top, and cut back at a 30–degree angle on both sides.
13. Write your name on the front of the Evaluation Check List sheet, and rubber cement the sheet to the back of the paste-up.
14. Turn in assignment for evaluation.

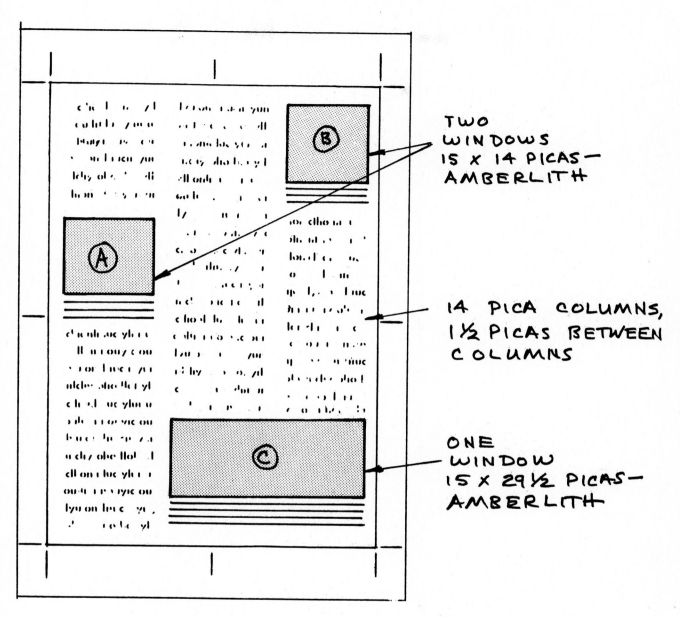

TWO
WINDOWS
15 X 14 PICAS—
AMBERLITH

14 PICA COLUMNS,
1½ PICAS BETWEEN
COLUMNS

ONE
WINDOW
15 X 29½ PICAS—
AMBERLITH

8½ X 11 PAPER AREA
45 X 60 PICA IMAGE AREA

Ingrid Skinner (left) and Wendy Goodrich are among the increasing numbers of women taking courses in the Department of Industrial Studies. They are shown learning woodworking skills in a Tools for the Artist course, led by Professor Fred Zahrt. This issue of Keynotes features articles and photographs about women in industrial education.

Cal State Los Angeles graduate Don Miller earned a Bachelor of Science degree in Printing Management.

Dr. Phillips was cited for his thirty-five years in education including twelve years at Cal State Los Angeles.

The primary objective of the Printing Management program at California State University, Los Angeles is to prepare men and women to assume positions of leadership in the printing industry. Although considerable emphasis is given to the area of manipulative skills involved in printing, the underlying objective is to provide the prospective printing management student with a solid foundation in the areas of industrial psychology, administration, finance, sales, production control, estimating, and other related manager-oriented subjects.

Upon completion of the prescribed four-year sequence, students are granted a Bachelor of Science degree representing a total of 192 quarter units, which includes coursework in business, graphic arts and general education. To assist students in supplementing their educations, financial assistance is available in the form of graphic arts scholarships and industry internships.

Under the proposed graphic arts/printing management course structure, students will be afforded an opportunity to gain an understanding of all the various techniques of the printing industry, including layout and design, composition, photomechanics, presswork, bindery and the cost estimation and production control of such work. The training, as in the past, will be broad in scope with emphasis on a wide background of operations and skills. In addition, students will be given an opportunity to become involved as production controllers, supervisors, estimators, and sales people in a "production laboratory" sequence of courses. There will also be opportunity for students to gain additional "hands-on" experience in any one of several machine areas under study.

The standardized test tells a superintendent, roughly, how well his students are doing within the national norm, or

within the school system. Because entrance to colleges is competitive the educators insist they need these tests. Another argument for their continued use is that these tests also give the U.S. education community a sense of whether there is a continuity and continuum in learning results across the U.S.

But one of the sharpest criticisms of the standardized tests is that they discriminate against minorities. Almost all black educators are using these tests and telling black parents that their children must make their way, in "standard brand" U.S. society.

More and more, however, criterion-referenced tests are being used to test the acquisition of the very specific skills and knowledge demanded of youngsters today.

The program was judged by Honda officials as so successful that advanced courses are being planned for next summer in Los Angeles and Honda training centers throughout the United States.

Where do managers come from today? Generally speaking, the larger industrial establishments in the United States prefer to select their supervisors, planners, and other executives from the ranks. In so doing they encourage or even subsidize these individuals to take additional coursework at colleges and universities. In addition, the manager-trainee is subjected to a thorough in-plant management training and development program including industrial psychology, administration, finances, sales and other subjects the firm wants the new executive to add as a foundation of expertise. The larger the company, the more elaborate the educational program.

During the last twenty years the Southern California automotive industry has sponsored summer workshops for industrial education teachers at the General Motors and Ford training centers located in Los Angeles.

In conjunction with the summer workshop programs, Ray Fausel, professor of automotive technology at California State University, Los Angeles accepted an offer by American Honda Corp. last March to develop a training program for automotive teachers who are interested in expanding their current programs to include motorcycle repair and maintenance.

Professor Fausel developed an introductory course organized to include course outlines, training aids and laboratory activities. This included four one-week programs and involved twelve teachers who were instructed at the Honda factory school in Gardena, California. The teachers were taught basic motorcycle set-ups, two and four-stroke engine repair, tune-up, transmissions, electrical systems, fuel systems, brakes and chassis repair.

To help meet the management personnel needs of the Los Angeles area printing industry—one of the fastest growing and most diversified in the world—the Graphic Arts/Printing Management program at California State University, Los Angeles is currently in the process of revising its course structure to more adequately reflect the contemporary needs, desires and technology of the printing industry in Los Angeles.

A group of California State University, Los Angeles Students that have been involved with a project for the Jet Propulsion Laboratory, will be invited guests for the viewing of the first Jupiter close-encounter pictures from the Voyager spacecraft in early March. The students are among a group that accompanied Professor Cortland Doan on a JPL sponsored trip to Cape Canaveral during the Summer of 1977 when the first Voyager was launched.

(Clip out and rubber cement to back of paste-up)

Name_____

PROJECT EVALUATION CHECK LIST
ASSIGNMENT 10: NEWSLETTER MAKE-UP

This check list is designed to assist you in indentifying the specific points upon which this assignment will be evaluated. Your instructor will indicate by the use of a check mark those areas requiring additional attention.

PASTE-UP PLANNING

_____ 11″ × 14″ illustration board
_____ 8½″ × 11″ paper area (blue pencil)
_____ 45 × 60 pica image area (blue pencil)

PASTE-UP PREPARATION

_____ Elements trimmed smoothly
_____ Elements trimmed to correct dimensions
_____ Elements positioned according to rough layout
_____ Accurate alignment of elements
_____ Amberlith® cut square and smooth
_____ Amberlith® applied and adhered correctly, emulsion up
_____ Windows "keyed" for the halftones
_____ Uniform application of adhesives and burnished
_____ Text material applied correctly, flush top and bottom of columns
_____ Crop marks in black ink approximately ½″ long
_____ Center marks in black ink approximately ½″ long
_____ Overall cleanliness of paste-up
_____ Protective tissue overlay and cover flap attached

FINAL EVALUATION _____

assignment 11

SIMPLE NEWSPAPER DISPLAY ADVERTISEMENT

INFORMATION

Every day millions of people seek special sales and discounts by scanning the ads in newspapers. Some of the larger advertisers maintain their own staff of artists. In most cases, however, the task of designing and paste-up is assumed by the newspaper staff. The entire process, from design to final printing, is often completed in less than one week.

This assignment will test your ability to visualize the finished advertisement and make it visually appealing while drawing information from several sources. Plan and organize this assignment carefully.

MATERIALS REQUIRED

Paste-up tools
Print trimmer and scissors
Masking tape and transparent tape
Rubber cement and/or waxer
Adhesive border tapes (2-, 3-, and 4-point)
One piece of 14″ × 24″ illustration board
One piece of 14″ × 25″ tissue overlay paper
One piece of 14″ × 26″ cover flap paper

PROCEDURE

1. Fasten the illustration board squarely and smoothly to the table work surface with the 14″ dimension running horizontally.
2. Following the rough layout, use a nonreproducing blue pencil or pen to outline an image area of 64 × 120 picas. Crop and center marks are not necessary. Draw guidelines for the type and art elements.

3. Carefully position and adhere a 3-point border 64 × 120 picas. Be sure that the final dimensions are accurate; measure to the outside edges of the border. Miter all four corners, being careful not to leave a thin white line or overrun.

4. Wax the reproduction proofs, and cut the individual elements; use a stiff cutting board for this purpose. Note that 2-point and 4-point rules are required as you progress further into the job. Position the elements according to the rough layout, and adhere the elements.

5. Follow the rough layout carefully when positioning the copy elements. Be sure that the rule is adhered straight and square with clean-cropped corners.

6. Double check your work. Make sure that the correct copy is in the corresponding areas on the paste-up. Cover the paste-up elements with a clean piece of white paper, and burnish in place with a roller.

7. Attach a piece of tissue overlay paper to the illustration board by taping it with transparent tape on the reverse side at the top. Fold over the extra 1″ at the top of the paste-up.

8. Attach a piece of colored text paper (cover flap) to the illustration board by taping it with masking tape on the reverse side at the top. Fold over the extra 2″ at the top, and cut back at a 30-degree angle on both sides.

9. Write your name on the front of the Evaluation Check List sheet, and rubber cement the sheet to the back of the paste-up.

10. Turn in assignment for evaluation.

Bullock's

SPORT COATS
Solids colors and a fine variety of patterns. $35

SUITS
Lightweight worsteds and double-knit polyesters styled in plain fabrics & patterns. $98

PRE-EASTER

301

Sale!

Men . . . it's your time to cash-in on the finest buys in suits and sport coats during our special Pre-Easter Sale. Come early . . . these will sell fast !

TOP COATS

Smartly luxurious in styling and feel. Button and belted front in new check patterns. **$50**

303

(Clip out and rubber cement to back of paste-up)

PROJECT EVALUATION CHECK LIST
ASSIGNMENT 11: SIMPLE NEWSPAPER DISPLAY ADVERTISEMENT

This check list is designed to assist you in identifying the specific points upon which this assignment will be evaluated. Your instructor will indicate by the use of a check mark those areas requiring additional attention.

PASTE-UP PLANNING

_____ 14" X 24" illustration board
_____ 4" X 5¼" paper size area (blue pencil)

PASTE-UP PREPARATION

_____ Elements trimmed smoothly
_____ Elements trimmed to correct dimensions
_____ Elements positioned according to rough layout
_____ Accurate alignment of adhesive rules (square and cropped corners)
_____ Accurate alignment of type and art elements
_____ Uniform application of adhesive and burnished
_____ Protective tissue overlay and cover flap attached

FINAL EVALUATION _____

COMPLEX NEWSPAPER DISPLAY ADVERTISEMENT

INFORMATION

These two newspaper display advertisements will further test your ability to visualize the finished advertisement by carefully utilizing a limited amount of space to arrange image elements. The two ads are coordinates (men's and women's fashions) being offered by the same apparel shop. Make-up is similar, and the ads will run on facing pages of a daily newspaper, giving a symmetrical appearance and creating interest.

MATERIALS REQUIRED

Paste-up tools
Print trimmer and scissors
Rubber cement and/or waxer
Masking tape and transparent tape
Adhesive border tape (Oxford—3-point/1-point combination)
Two pieces of 12″ × 18″ illustration board
Two pieces of 12″ × 19″ tissue overlay paper
Two pieces of 12″ × 20″ cover flap paper

PROCEDURE

1. Fasten one of the pieces of illustration board squarely and smoothly to the table work surface with the 12″ dimension running horizontally.
2. Using a nonreproducing blue pencil or pen, outline a paper area of 10½″ × 14″ and an image area of 59 × 83 picas on the board.
3. Following the rough layout (women's), rule in the appropriate guidelines in light-blue pencil or pen for the border, illustrations, and display and text type. Note that several pieces of artwork extend over the edge of the border to the paper area lines.

4. Obtain a roll of Oxford border tape (3–point/1–point combination) and carefully lay the tape along the edge of the image area lines. Be sure that the corners are joined squarely and that they do not overrun.

5. Wax the proof, and cut the elements as needed.

6. Position elements (light pressure for position only), and make sure that the elements fit according to the rough layout.

7. When you are satisfied that all elements are positioned and spaced correctly, burnish the paste-up elements carefully.

8. Crop or center marks are not required for these paste-ups since they will be converted into PMT prints and inserted in the newspaper page along with other ads and news articles.

9. Attach a piece of tissue overlay paper to the illustration board by taping it with transparent tape on the reverse side at the top. Fold over the extra 1″ at the top of the paste-up.

10. Attach a piece of text paper (cover flap) to the illustration board by taping it with masking tape on the reverse side at the top. Fold over the extra 2″ at the top, and cut back at a 30–degree angle on both sides.

11. Fasten the second piece of illustration board squarely and smoothly to the table work surface with the 12″ dimension running horizontally.

12. Using the same procedure as outlined previously, proceed with the second advertisement. The dimensions are the same.

13. Once the second paste-up is completed, attach a tissue overlay and cover flap.

14. Write your name on the front of the Evaluation Check List sheet, and rubber cement the sheet to the back of one paste-up.

15. Turn in assignment for evaluation.

OXFORD BORDER:
3 PT. / 1 PT.

Spring Daisy S

Blouses
15.99

Blouse Clearance
1/3 - 1/2 off

Knit Tops
9.99

Cardigans
31.99

V-Necks
19.99

Wrap Skirts
13.99

Pants
15.99

Alex Colman
9.99 - 11.99

Jackets
1/3 - 1/2 off

Blouses
1/3 - 1/2 off

Pants
1/3 - 1/2 off

Skirts
1/3 - 1/2 off

RILEYS

LOGO

OXFORD BORDER: 3 PT. / 1 PT.
Spring Daisy Sale
He'll look like a million and love the savings!
Sport Shirts 8.99-10.99
Casual Slacks 14.99
Dress Shirts 9.99-11.99
Knit Shirts 13.99-15.99
Golf Shirt 8.99
Walk Shorts 9.99
Golf Sweaters 18.99
pajamas 9.99-13.99
Sweatshirts 11.99
Polar Boots 7.99
LOGO
RILEYS

Blouses
15.99
Styled in both short and long sleeves for today's easy dressing. 6-16. Reg. to 18.00. DT MB AT

Blouse Clearance
1/3-1/2 Off
Poly sheers, wovens and blends from regular stock. 6-18. Reg. 20.00-30.00. DT MB AT

Knit Tops
9.99
Soft and cuddly Designer Knits in new shades for spring. Long sleeves in mock and turtle neck styles. Sizes 34-42. Reg. to 17.00. DT MB AT

Cardigans
31.99
Pretty spring colors in LeRoy's favorite styling. S-M-L-XL. Reg. 46.00. DT MB AT

V-Necks
19.99
Long sleeve pullover in lightweight polyester. New shades for spring. S-M-L-XL. Reg. 30.00. DT MB AT

Wrap Skirts
13.99
A back wrap in casual calcutta cloth. Soft colors. 6-20. Values to 20.00. DT MB AT

Pants
15.99
Pull-on calcutta in beautiful new shades of spring. 6-20. Reg. to 20.00. DT MB AT

Misses Sportswear... picked from regular stock for the Daisy Sale

Alex Colman
9.99-11.99
Classically tailored tops and pants that move the way you do. Soft blouses and tee's in poly ribs and boucles. Reg. to 20.00. DT MB AT

Jackets
1/3-1/2 Off
Assorted long and short sleeve styles. 8-18. Reg. to 33.00. DT MB AT

Blouses
1/3-1/2 Off
Assorted stripes, plaids and solid interlocks in long and short sleeve styles. 8-18. Reg. to 33.00. DT MB AT

Pants
1/3-1/2 Off
Choose pull-ons or zip-front styles. 8-18. Reg. to 28.00. DT MB AT

Skirts
1/3-1/2 Off
A-line and straight styles. 8-18. Reg. to 25.00. DT MB AT

RILEYS

Golf Shirt
8.99
Classic styling by Munsingwear in a rainbow of spring colors. Reg. 13.00. DT US MB AT

Walk Shorts
9.99
2 front bush pockets in dacron/cotton poplin by Harris. Reg. 15.00-18.00. DT US MB AT

Sweatshirts
11.99
Zip-front draw string hood with two hand-warmer pockets. Reg. 14.50. DT US MB AT

Golf Sweaters
18.99
Orlon link on link stitch with ribbed cuffs and bottom; machine washable. Reg. 25.00. DT MB AT

Pajamas
9.99-13.99
Popular coat styling for added comfort. Selected styles from regular stock. Reg. to 19.50. DT MB AT

Polar Boots
7.99
Nylon cushioned boot in solid colors. Reg. 10.00. DT US MB AT

Sport Shirts
8.99-10.99
Crisp colors for spring in plaids and solids. Values to 20.00. DT US MB AT

Casual Slacks
14.99
Poly double knit slack for comfort and long wearing by Haggar. Reg. 20.00. DT US MB AT

Dress Shirts
9.99-11.99
Tightly woven in polyester and cotton short sleeved shirts from Arrow. Assorted solids and patterns. Reg. 13.00-16.00. DT US MB AT

Knit Shirts
13.99-15.99
Collar and placket styling in bright bold stripes for spring by famous makers. Reg. to 22.50. DT US MB AT

He'll look like a million and love the savings!

RILEYS

Spring Daisy Sale

(Clip out and rubber cement to back of paste-up)

Name_____

PROJECT EVALUATION CHECK LIST
ASSIGNMENT 12: COMPLEX NEWSPAPER DISPLAY ADVERTISEMENT

This check list is designed to assist you in identifying the specific points upon which this assignment will be evaluated. Your instructor will indicate by the use of a check mark those areas requiring additional attention.

PASTE-UP PLANNING

_____ Two 12″ × 18″ illustration boards
_____ 10½″ × 14″ paper area (blue pencil)
_____ 59 × 83 pica image area (blue pencil)

PASTE-UP PREPARATION (women's fashion ad)

_____ Elements trimmed smoothly
_____ Elements trimmed to correct dimensions
_____ Elements positioned according to rough layout
_____ Accurate alignment of adhesive border; square and cropped corners
_____ Accurate alignment of type and art elements; artwork extends over border where applicable
_____ Uniform application of adhesive and burnished
_____ Protective tissue overlay and cover flap attached

PASTE-UP PREPARATION (men's fashion ad)

_____ Elements trimmed smoothly
_____ Elements trimmed to correct dimensions
_____ Elements positioned according to rough layout
_____ Accurate alignment of adhesive border; square and cropped corners
_____ Accurate alignment of type and art elements; artwork extends over border where applicable
_____ Uniform application of adhesive and burnished
_____ Protective tissue overlay and cover flap attached

FINAL EVALUATION _____

13

SUPERMARKET DISPLAY ADVERTISEMENT

INFORMATION

Supermarkets use newspapers for promotional advertising. The advertisements usually occupy a full page or more and contain illustrations, text matter in boxes, and large display prices. Most of the copy is tightly spaced, and careful layout is essential.

Before beginning the paste-up, study the layout carefully. Blue-pencil guidelines should be drawn on the illustration board to locate each piece of copy, boxes, and borders.

MATERIALS REQUIRED

Paste-up tools
Print trimmer and scissors
Rubber cement and/or waxer
Adhesive border tapes
Masking tape and transparent tape
One piece of 16″ × 26″ illustration board
One piece of 16″ × 27″ tissue overlay paper
One piece of 16″ × 28″ cover flap paper

PROCEDURE

1. Fasten the illustration board squarely and smoothly to the table work surface with the 16″ dimension running horizontally.
2. Using a nonreproducing blue pencil or pen, outline a paper area of 13¾″ × 23″ and an image area of 77 × 127 picas.
3. Following the rough layout, rule in the appropriate guidelines for all boxes, borders, rules, etc., in light-blue pencil or pen.
4. Use adhesive border tapes for all rules and boxes; note point sizes on rough layout.

5. Wax proofs, and cut out necessary elements as needed.

6. Crop and center marks are not required on this paste-up.

7. Using a T-square and triangle, position the elements (light pressure for position only), and make sure that the elements fit according to the rough layout. Care must be taken at this stage since space allocation for the various elements is very tight.

8. When you are satisfied that all elements are positioned and spaced correctly, check alignment with the T-square once again, and burnish the paste-up elements carefully.

9. Attach a piece of tissue overlay paper to the board by taping it with transparent tape on the reverse side at the top. Fold over the extra 1″ at the top of the paste-up.

10. Attach a piece of text paper (cover flap) to the board by taping it with masking tape on the reverse side at the top. Fold over the extra 2″ at the top, and cut back at a 30–degree angle on both sides.

11. Write your name on the front of the Evaluation Check List sheet, and rubber cement the sheet to the back of the paste-up.

12. Turn in assignment for evaluation.

Washington State Apple Sale!

Extra Fancy Red or Golden • Controlled Atmosphere

Delicious Apples .... Lb. **59¢**

Albertson's White or Yellow

Bathroom Tissue .... 4 Pack **78¢**

Kitchen Sliced or French Cut

Green Giant Green Beans .... 16-Oz. **3 $1 For**

Anthony's

Macaroni & Cheese .... 7.25-Oz. **4 $1 For**

Janet Lee

Wheat Or White Bread .... 16-Oz **3 $1 For**

Wilson's Certified Regular

Sliced Bacon .... 1-Lb. **88¢**

Wilson's Certified Eastern Grain-Fed Pork

Whole Pork Loins
17-20 Pound Average
Cut & Wrapped Free in 1 Pkg. .... Lb. **98¢**

Wilson's Certified Pork Loin

Loin Pork Chops Center Cut .... Lb. **$1⁴⁸**

Wilson's Certified Pork Loin

Sirloin Pork Chops .... Lb **$1²⁸**

Price Effective Thursday, May 1 thru Wednesday, May 7, 1980

De Ville Designer Collection

Stoneware **79¢**
This Week's Feature:
Coffee Cup .... Ea.
With Every $5 Purchase

AVAILABILITY
Each of these advertised items is required to be readily available for sale at or below the advertised price in each Albertson's store, except as specifically noted in this ad.

RAIN CHECK
We strive to have on hand sufficient stock of advertised merchandise. If for any reason we are out of stock a RAIN CHECK will be issued enabling you to buy the item at the advertised price as soon as it becomes available.

CORNER OF BASELINE & ARCHIBALD RANCHO CUCAMONGA

Fryer Parts Sale
Southern • With Ribs Attached
Fryer Breasts .... Lb. **98¢**
Southern Fryer
Drumsticks or Thighs .... Lb. **88¢**
Southern
Fryer Livers .... Lb. **68¢**

Bananas
Cinco de Mayo **48¢** Lb.

Beef Tripe
Beef Feet
Pure Lard

323

Save 7¢

Save 26¢

Save 32¢

Save 17¢

2 ply soft **bathroom tissue**

Green Giant *Kitchen Sliced* Green Beans

Anthony's Macaroni 'n Cheese Dinner

FOOD SALE

Albertsons®

QUALITY PRODUCE

WILSON/AMANA PORK-A-RAMA

LOW GROCERY PRICES

We just can't wait to save you money.

Drop everything! Grab a basket and wheel down the aisles. Treat the family to super meals, super savings!

Most stores open 24 hours or 7 AM til midnight ● We gladly accept USDA Food Stamp Coupons ● Money Orders available up to $300 just 50¢ ● Express checkout stands always open.

Wilson's Certified Small-Size
Fresh Pork Spareribs .... **$1¹⁸** Lb.

Thomas E. Wilson
Boneless Hams Half .... **$2²⁸** Lb.

New Crop
Valencia Oranges .... **4 $1** Lbs.

Cinco de Mayo Sale

Crisp
Ortega Taco Shells ..... 4-Oz. **69¢**

Salsa Suprema, Victoria or
Salsa Ranchera La Victoria .... 12-Oz. **79¢**

Ortega
Diced Chilies .... 4-Oz. **49¢**

La Victoria Red or Green
Taco Sauce .... 12-Oz. **79¢**

**SLIM PRICE
SALAD
OIL** 48-OUNCE BOTTLE **169**

WHOLE
**SHOULDER
CLOD ROAST** TABLE KING BEEF 8-10 LBS. BONELESS CHUCK LB. **1⁷⁸**

**SLIM PRICE
BATHROOM
TISSUE** 4 ROLL PACKAGE **.69**

**BEEF
PORTERHOUSE
STEAKS** VALUE PAK LOIN CUT LB. **2⁶⁸**

**AIM
TOOTHPASTE
REGULAR** 8.2-OUNCE INCLUDES 24¢ OFF **.99**

**FRESHLY
GROUND
BEEF** BULK PACK DOES NOT EXCEED 30% FAT 3-LBS. OR MORE LB. **1¹⁹**

**SLIM PRICE
PEELED
TOMATOES** 28-OUNCE CAN **.37**

**SLIM PRICE
REAL
MAYONNAISE** 32-OUNCE JAR **.99**

**SLIM PRICE
SLICED
PEACHES** 29-OUNCE CAN **.53**

Looking For A Special Plant For That Special Someone? Check Our Produce Dept.!

327

REPRO – Supermarket Display Advertisement

Golden
Ripe

4 $1 Lbs.

(Clip out and rubber cement to back of paste-up)

Name_____

PROJECT EVALUATION CHECK LIST
ASSIGNMENT 13: SUPERMARKET DISPLAY ADVERTISEMENT

This check list is designed to assist you in identifying the specific points upon which this assignment will be evaluated. Your instructor will indicate by the use of a check mark those areas requiring additional attention.

PASTE-UP PLANNING

_____ 16" X 26" illustration board
_____ 13¾" X 23" paper area (blue pencil)
_____ 77 X 127 pica image area (blue pencil)

PASTE-UP PREPARATION

_____ Elements trimmed smoothly
_____ Elements trimmed to correct dimensions
_____ Elements positioned according to rough layout
_____ Image area width and depth correct
_____ Accurate alignment of elements
_____ Uniform application of adhesive and burnished
_____ Correct point size adhesive borders; applied smoothly, aligned, and corners mitered with no overruns
_____ Correct point size boxes; applied smoothly, aligned, and corners mitered with no overruns
_____ Protective tissue overlay and cover flap attached

FINAL EVALUATION_____

assignment 14

DAILY TAB-SIZE NEWSPAPER PAGE

INFORMATION

Many daily and most weekly newspapers are printed by the offset process. A paste-up is prepared for each page of the newspaper. Regular-size newspapers are approximately 13¾″ × 23″ in format; the popular smaller-size newspapers are approximately 11½″ × 14½″. The smaller-size format is referred to as *tabular size*.

Photographs are usually converted to PMT photo prints and pasted in position on the page along with type and other artwork. This procedure saves a step in the preparation of a page negative, since the PMT photo prints are photographed along with the other elements on the page. A halftone negative is not required.

MATERIALS REQUIRED

Paste-up tools
Print trimmer and scissors
Rubber cement and/or waxer
Masking tape and transparent tape
Adhesive border tapes
One piece of 14″ × 18″ illustration board
One piece of 14″ × 19″ tissue overlay paper
One piece of 14″ × 20″ cover flap paper

PROCEDURE

1. Fasten the illustration board squarely and smoothly to the table work surface with the 14″ dimension running horizontally.
2. Using a nonreproducing blue pencil or pen, outline a paper area of 11½″ × 14½″ and an image area of 63 × 83 picas on the board.

3. Following the layout, rule in the appropriate guidelines for all halftones, artwork, boxes, borders, text matter, and advertisements in light-blue pencil or pen. Care must be taken to see that all elements fit properly and that columns of type are aligned at the top and bottom of the page area.

4. Wax the proofs, and cut the elements as needed.

5. Position the elements (light pressure for position only), and make sure that all elements fit according to the rough layout.

6. Measure the halftone to be positioned at the top of the page. Lay a 1–point rule box at the top of the page, leaving a $\frac{1}{2}$ pica margin on all four inside margins. This will act as a frame for the halftone.

7. Measure and check the smaller halftone, artwork, headline, and advertisements for proper space allowance. The name of the newspaper, dateline, page number, and page catchline should also be checked for proper fit and space allowance. (*Note:* Image width and depth must be exactly 63 × 83 picas).

8. Corner and center marks are not required for this paste-up.

9. After making a final check for position and alignment, burnish all elements.

10. Attach a piece of tissue overlay paper to the board by taping it with transparent tape on the reverse side at the top. Fold over the extra 1″ at the top of the paste-up.

11. Attach a piece of colored text paper (cover flap) to the board by taping it with masking tape on the reverse side at the top. Fold over the extra 2″ at the top, and cut back at a 30–degree angle on both sides.

12. Write your name on the front of the Evaluation Check List sheet, and rubber cement the sheet to the back of the paste-up.

13. Turn in assignment for evaluation.

The country-Western trend goes on — with music

● **Les Petites Fugues** is a sensitive and muted film (except during an explicit sex scene that clashes harshly with the rest of the picture) about an old man living and working on a French farm that is in the throes of modernization. Faced with changing conditions around him, this gentle old codger cheerfully retreats into his own fantasy life — acting out his whimsies with the aid of a motorbike, an instant camera, and a few friends who do their best to be sympathetic toward his "little escapes." It's a leisurely film, directed by Yves Yersin, that speaks in a whisper more often than a shout and doesn't hesitate to soar spiritedly away from the occasionally sordid aspects of its story.

● **The Adventures of Picasso** is billed as "a thousand loving lies" by director Tange Danielsson. Some of these fibs are as offensive as they are affectionate and will ruin the taste of the film for many viewers. In addition to these bursts of boorishness, though, the picture contains some of the funniest and most inventive comedy routines in memory, not to mention some of the most outrageous characterizations in movie history. The story is an absurdly fictitious version of Picasso's career, but that's just the starting point for a film that ridicules every available subject from "La Bohème" to Gertrude Stein, in an international language largely comprising nonsense syllables. Too bad its lapses into boisterous vulgarity will limit the audience and appeal of a frequently engaging farce.

● **The Fiendish Plot of Dr. Fu Manchu** is a minor footnote to the career of Peter Sellers, who plays the villain and also the Scotland Yard man who chases him. It's the kind of picture where someone says "Fu Manchu" and someone else says "Gesundheit." Silly.

short takes

Floyd and Nelson in 'Honeysuckle Rose': a musical question

Paul Mazursky: a plea

New York

Honeysuckle Rose is a movie that asks the musical question, how much country-Western can we stand in a single season? Country songs and themes have cropped up in all kinds of pictures, from "Urban Cowboy" to "Bronco Billy" and "Roadie." And there's more to come. Even Smokey and the Bandit refuse to fade quietly away, with Part II of their misadventures currently racing across the scene.

"Honeysuckle Rose" takes its cue from "Intermezzo," the venerable tale about a famous musician and his infidelities. Only this time the hero is a popular singing star, played by Willie Nelson, a singing star himself. He falls in love with his best friend's guitar-picking daughter, which almost wrecks everyone's lives, not to mention the big concert at the climax of the film.

The cowboy-style characters of "Honeysuckle Rose" are an earthy lot, and their story has moments that are hardly delicate. The picture's main problem is not so much crudity of images and language, though, as crudity of ideas. The resolution of the story bothers me, for example, with its childish suggestion that a little drunken horseplay is all the hero needs to clear his mind and point him back to his proper place in life.

Then too, "Honeysuckle Rose" is a rather dull picture. If you've stored up any movie lore, you'll know how the plot is going to develop, and there won't be a single surprise along the way. It's a stale situation, really, and there's little reason to rehash it yet again.

Still, for many fans the bottom line of the film will be Willie Nelson, who makes a good showing on the wide screen with a charisma that was barely suggested by his bit part in "The Electric Horseman." He's an unlikely movie star for the '80s — long-haired, weatherbeaten, and far from boyish, with a truly lived-in face. Yet he has captured the imagination of a lot of listeners, and now moviegoers are eagerly following his trail. We'll be seeing more of him in the future, for certain.

Another new picture about a romantic triangle is **Willie & Phil**. It comes from Paul Mazursky, whose films include the successful "An Unmarried Women."

The story focuses on two young men who meet at a showing of "Jules and Jim." Like the heroes of that classic, they then fall headlong in love with the same woman and spend the rest of the movie trying to sort out their mightily mixed emotions.

"Willie & Phil" contains a few explicit glimpses of sexual activity, and some of its language is vehemently vulgar. Though it's a comedy, Mazursky is not aiming at gentle entertainment. In its way, it's a strongly cautionary tale — laced with humor and absurdity, but pleading for some way out of the "desperate freedom" that has trapped the main characters.

Shortly after seeing "Willie $ Phil," I asked Mazursky about the themes of the movie, which takes place during the 1970s. "This isn't the age of anxiety," he replied. "It's the age of confusion. This freedom is confusing the kids who engage in it. Since you can supposedly do anything, it all becomes aimless."

Faced with this situation, Mazursky finds that even the '60s look good by comparison. "There was a passion then," he says. "People weren't confused; they were fighting. Passion gives you something to hold on to. But in the '80s, there's not much serious political or religious conviction around, at least among the urban crowd. There's just a lot of openness, and I don't know where it's going. Even today's films are metaphors for this — aimless movies that don't mean anything."

As Mazursky sees it, "People want someone to close things off, and tell them what to do. Willie and Phil would be a lot better off if someone would grab them by the collar and tell them where it's at. But there's no magic solution like that, so they have to go through their experiences of confusion and pain. Maybe it's all a reflection of me and my perceptions. Lots of people around me seem to be drowning in a lack of direction, questioning old values, and not sure about the new values because we replace them so quickly.

"Willie and Phil really like each other, and their friendship is a major part of the movie. But they really are baffled; they can't figure out what to do. Finally the woman makes a decision for them. Women *did* gain a lot of strength from the '70s, since they had a huge cause to fight for.

"So in the end, Willie and Phil do go off and lead ordinary, middle-class lives. And that's tremendously important. I believe deeply in my family — I've been married 27 years to the same woman, I have children, and I don't know where I'd be without them. Willie and Phil have trouble attaining these things, because young people are terribly confused about wanting a family, and the responsibility of having a kid seems stranger and more challenging than it did in the '50s. But in the end, even Willie and Phil manage to leave their exotic romance and go on to normal, everyday lives.

"So the movie becomes a kind of fairy tale for our time. I'm attempting to elevate the ordinariness and middle-classness into something a little larger than life — something universal, even though it's very small."

(Clip out and rubber cement to back of paste-up)

PROJECT EVALUATION CHECK LIST
ASSIGNMENT 14: DAILY TAB-SIZE NEWSPAPER PAGE

This check list is designed to assist you in identifying the specific points upon which this assignment will be evaluated. Your instructor will indicate by the use of a check mark those areas requiring additional attention.

PASTE-UP PLANNING

_____ 14″ X 18″ illustration board
_____ 11½″ X 14½″ paper area (blue pencil)
_____ 63 X 83 pica image area (blue pencil)

PASTE-UP PREPARATION

_____ Elements trimmed smoothly
_____ Elements trimmed to correct dimensions
_____ Elements positioned according to rough layout
_____ Image area width and depth correct
_____ Accurate alignment of elements
_____ Borders in correct point size, square, and applied correctly
_____ Boxes in correct point size, square, and applied correctly; corners join and cut square with no overruns
_____ Uniform application of adhesive and burnished
_____ Protective tissue overlay and cover flap attached

*FINAL EVALUATION*_____

SILHOUETTE HALFTONE

INFORMATION

Although most continuous tone photographs are photographed and printed as rectangular halftones, sometimes the subject looks better if it is printed without a background. The silhouette halftone has an immediate and abrupt transition from the printing to nonprinting areas. The example shown at the right is a rectangular halftone; the same subject matter is treated below as a silhouette halftone.

In preparing art for a silhouette halftone, outline the original continuous tone copy in the desired shape on a tissue overlay, and specify the removal of all halftone from the remaining background area. The stripper does this by opaquing on the halftone negative. This is time-consuming and costly.

Another method available to the artist eliminates having the stripper do the silhouetting. A film overlay (such as red masking film) is prepared by hand cutting a mask into the overlay. The overlay is used as a mask to photographically outline or silhouette the halftone image. The camera operator makes two film negatives—one of the mask and one of the halftone. The film negative of the mask creates a window opening behind which the halftone negative is taped, thus creating a silhouette.

MATERIALS REQUIRED

Paste-up tools
Proportion scale
Rubber cement
Masking tape and transparent tape
Amberlith® or Rubylith® masking film
One 8″ × 10″ continuous tone portrait photograph
 or use repro halftone on p. 345

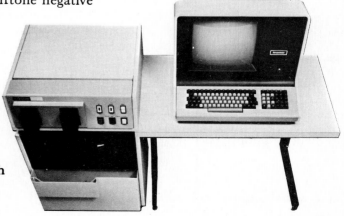

One piece of 11″ × 14″ illustration board
One piece of 11″ × 15″ tissue overlay paper
One piece of 11″ × 16″ cover flap paper

PROCEDURE

1. Fasten the illustration board squarely and smoothly to the table work surface with the 11″ dimension running horizontally.
2. Mount the black and white continuous tone photograph (or repro halftone on p. 345) in the center of the illustration board with rubber cement.
3. Cut a piece of Amberlith® material the size of the photo. Leave at least 1″ extra at the top for taping. Hinge the piece of material (emulsion side up) at the top with transparent tape.
4. Using a sharp X-acto® knife, cut lightly around the portrait edges (subject), and peel off the excess emulsion from the background. A piece of masking tape will be useful for "lifting" the unwanted emulsion off its acetate carrier. To avoid cutting into the photo, place a piece of thick acetate between the masking film and photo while cutting the silhouette.

   Note: The Amberlith® silhouette of the portrait will be photographed by the camera operator to make a negative film mask. The negative will be opaque except for the transparent window of the portrait shape. When the photograph of the portrait itself is screened into a halftone, there are usually some unwanted background areas or dots that appear in the negative. The mask negative will be placed over the halftone negative of the portrait and will block out the background areas, thus leaving the portrait image without a background.

5. Attach a tissue overlay sheet to the illustration board.
6. Mark instructions to the camera operator on the tissue overlay. These include crop size (eliminating unwanted areas) and the percentage of reduction or enlargement. Use a red pencil for this purpose.
7. Mark the crop marks on the tissue overlay for the desired silhouette area of the photograph.
8. Assume that the portrait silhouette will be reduced to 4″ in depth. Use the diagonal line method (see information sheet) and proportional scale to determine the percentage of reduction. Write the percentage of reduction on the tissue overlay in the lower right-hand corner.
9. Note the new depth and width in inches on the tissue overlay along with the percentage. Repeat this procedure for a 120% enlargement.
10. Remember that whether the copy is planned for same size, reduction, or enlargement, the percentage must be written on the tissue overlay.
11. When there are several photographs, they should be lettered in sequence and "keyed" to their positions on the paste-up.
12. Attach a piece of colored text paper (cover flap) to the illustration board.
13. Write your name on the front of the Evaluation Check List sheet, and rubber cement the sheet to the back of the paste-up.
14. Turn in assignment for evaluation.

SCALING ARTWORK BY THE
DIAGONAL LINE METHOD

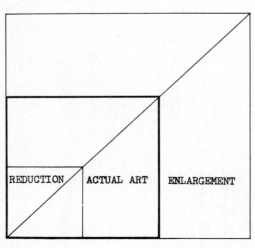

To enlarge or reduce an illustration, draw a vertical line through the artwork. As you scale the artwork, up or down, remember that the proportions do not change.

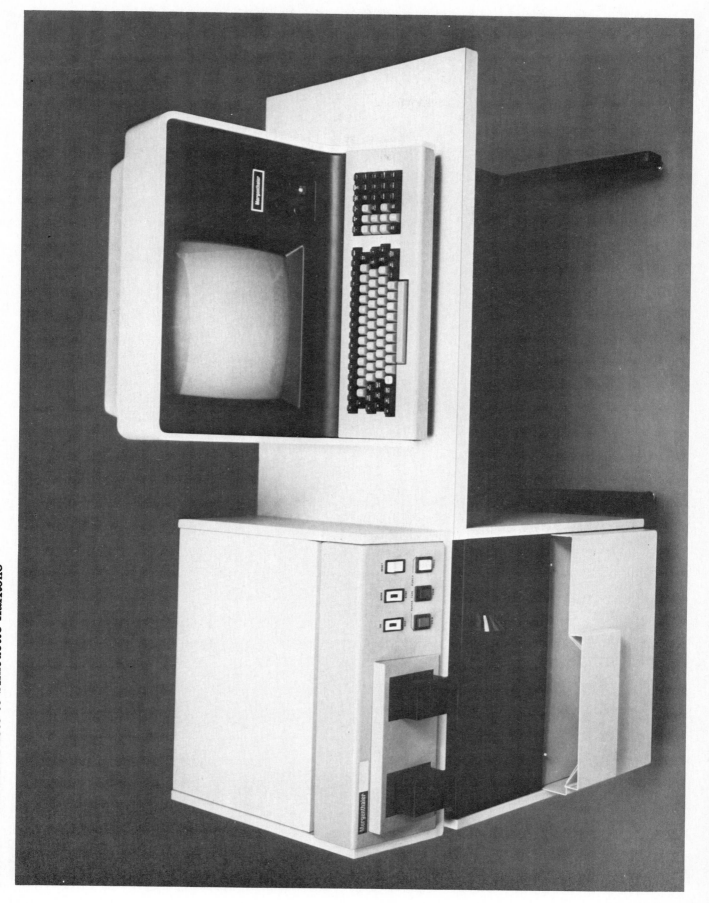

(Clip out and rubber cement to back of paste-up)

Name_____

PROJECT EVALUATION CHECK LIST
ASSIGNMENT 15: SILHOUETTE HALFTONE

This check list is designed to assist you in identifying the specific points upon which this assignment will be evaluated. Your instructor will indicate by the use of a check mark those areas requiring additional attention.

PASTE-UP PLANNING

_____ 11" X 14" illustration board

PASTE-UP PREPARATION

_____ 8" X 10" continuous tone photograph adhered to board
_____ Amberlith® material attached correctly
_____ Silhouette outline cut accurately and smoothly
_____ Crop marks in red on overlay for same-size reproduction
_____ Percentage for reduction noted in red
_____ Percentage for enlargement noted in red
_____ Overall cleanliness of assignment
_____ Protective tissue overlay and cover flap attached

FINAL EVALUATION _____

CATALOG PAGE WITH OVERLAY

INFORMATION

This assignment involves a detailed page of a typical equipment catalog. It includes an overlay consisting of red masking film. The overlay method is used because the best tint screening occurs in the negative stage, and many paste-up artists prefer that the printer assume the responsibility for handling tint areas in the copy. If tint screens are applied directly to the paste-up, they are seldom finer than 85 line; tint contact screens used with an overlay are normally 120 to 133 line. Quality is the primary advantage of using tint contact screens at the negative stage rather than in the paste-up.

MATERIALS REQUIRED

Paste-up tools
Masking tape and transparent tape
Rubber cement and/or waxer
Adhesive border tape
Pressure-sensitive registration marks
Red masking film
Print trimmer and scissors
One piece of 10″ × 13″ heavy acetate
One piece of 11″ × 14″ illustration board
One piece of 11″ × 15″ tissue overlay paper
One piece of 11″ × 16″ cover flap paper

PROCEDURE

1. Fasten the illustration board squarely and smoothly to the table work surface with the 11″ dimension running horizontally.

2. Using a nonreproducing blue pencil or pen, draw a paper size area of 8½″ X 11″.

3. Ink in crop marks with ½″ thin, black lines. Center marks are not needed.

4. Position three register marks just outside the paper area at the left center, right center, and bottom center of the board.

5. Wax the reproduction proof, and place it on a stiff cutting board. Cut around each block of copy and illustration, leaving 1/16″ white space around the edges. Be sure that the edges are clean, sharp, and accurate.

6. Use light-blue pencil lines to indicate copy element positions on the board.

7. Position all elements with light pressure for position check only.

8. Using a T-square and triangle, align the elements in their proper positions on the board. When you are satisfied that the positioning is correct, burnish the elements into place. Use a clean piece of white paper over the copy elements.

9. Place the piece of 10″ X 12″ acetate over the paste-up, and tape it with masking tape at the top and bottom. This will protect the paste-up during the next operations.

10. Cut a piece of 10″ X 13″ red masking material (such as Rubylith®), and place it emulsion side up over the paste-up. Tape with transparent tape at the top to form a hinge.

11. Cut the masking film to overlap the black outline of each camera; allow the film to butt against the boxes created by the 2-point border. Cut slowly and carefully over the illustration outline. Cut through the emulsion layer of the masking film only. The object is to cut an outline around each camera so that the boxed area prints in a second color. Cut the emulsion at least halfway into the black lines so that tight register is achieved. Carefully peel the emulsion away from the areas not wanted.

12. Remove the piece of protective acetate from under the masking film.

13. Position three register marks on the overlay precisely over the three register marks on the board.

14. Apply a color swatch sample near the bottom of the overlay, and label it SECOND COLOR (name and number of color) and indicate screen tint percentage.

15. Attach a piece of colored text paper (cover flap) to the illustration board by taping it with masking tape on the reverse side at the top. Fold over the extra 2″ at the top, and cut back at a 30-degree angle on both sides. Indicate tint screen percentage desired on the bottom of the overlay.

16. Write your name on the front of the Evaluation Check List sheet, and rubber cement the sheet to the back of the paste-up.

17. Turn in assignment for evaluation.

NEW 3N1 CAMERA
A SHEETFILM CAMERA, A ROLLFILM CAMERA, OR A BLOW-BACK CAMERA—ALL IN ONE!

1

SMALL IN PRICE
BIG IN FEATURES
Standard Camera

2

3

3n1 CAMERA PACKAGE
Item #210750

3n1 CAMERA PACKAGE
Item #210751

...is Available at all Branches of

Western/Palmer/Midwestern/Smart

BROWN / APECO®

Price and Specifications Are Subject to Change

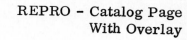

1 A FEATURE-PACKED 20" x 24" SHEETFILM CAMERA

Start with an extraordinary new Brown process camera with a 21" x 25" sheetfilm capacity, 20" x 24" image area, a 30" x 40" copyboard, 4000-watt Spectramatic quartz lighting, electric shutter system, optional motorized lensboard, and a wealth of other features for speed and precision in all color separation and plate-ready negative work.

Choose a 9-foot or 12-foot precision-machined Tri-Track with 14" or 19" lenses respectively for up to 3X enlargements and 4X reductions. New rack-and-counter re-registration gives you direct readouts accurate to 1/1000th of an inch.

One-spot operation! Save time, save steps. Focusing, lights, shutter, vacuum pump, lensboard movements, and electric timer are controlled from darkroom.

As a 20" x 24" sheetfilm camera, the new Brown "3N1" has no peer in price, features, versatility — or adaptability. Read on . . .

2 A HIGH-PRODUCTION ROLLFILM CAMERA

With the addition of a specially engineered cassette unit, the Brown "3N1" becomes a rapid-fire rollfilm camera. It accepts film rolls from 10" to 24" in width. With automatic controls in the gallery, you just dial the length of film you need, from 8 inches to 20 inches, in accurate half-inch increments. One man has complete control of operations without leaving the gallery.

Eliminate waste! You don't use more film than you really need, and there's no need to stock a wide variety of film sizes. It's an ideal system for commercial shops, newspaper and publication printers, and in-plant departments where fast, high-production line-work is the order of the day.

When half-tones and color separations are called for, the hinged cassette swings away and you're immediately back in action for sheetfilm operation.

But hold on, there is still more . . .

3 A "BLOW-BACK" CAMERA, TOO

Fitted with a custom-engineered transaction copyboard and a transilluminator, the Brown "3N1" converts into a blowback camera/enlarger. In addition to handling normal camera work, you can take on those big-size jobs that once were reserved for enlarging specialists.

The 40" x 50" copyboard accepts large engineering drawings and other super-sized artwork. Zoom it down in size to negatives as small as 8½" x 11" for quantity reproductions or convenient storage. Enlarge stored negatives back up to full size anytime — quickly, easily, inexpensively, and with unerring accuracy.

Simply swing the Blow-Back unit out of the way and you're back in business with your full-feature 20" x 24" sheetfilm camera.

The Brown "3N1" has it all — including a sensible price. Dollar-for-dollar, feature-for-feature it's today's finest 20" x 24" sheetfilm, rollfilm, or Blow-Back camera value.

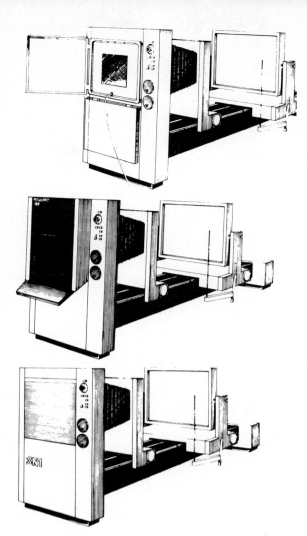

SMALL IN PRICE BIG IN FEATURES

Standard Camera

Track Length:	9' or 12'
Color-corrected lens for 9' track:	14" wide angle
for 12' track:	19" APO
Enlargement/Reduction:	3XE to 4XR
Film Size:	21" x 25"
1 to 1 Image Size:	20" x 24"
Copyboard:	30" x 40"
Transparency Opening:	22" x 28"
Ground Glass — stored in rear case	
4 Adjustable Lamps:	4000 watts
Drive System:	Cable Drive
Maximum Length with 9' Track:	12' 2"
with 12' Track:	15' 2"
Rear Case Width:	47¼"
Rear Case Height:	66"
Optical Center:	48"
Maximum Gallery Width: Lamp Arms extended	124"
Power: specify 50 or 60 Hz	240V. A.C. Single phase 17 Amps.
Net Weight:	1520 lbs.

3 n 1 CAMERA PACKAGE; 12' Track, 19" Lens Item # 210750	$ 5,460.00
3 n 1 CAMERA PACKAGE; 9' Track, 14" Lens Item # 210751	5,510.00
** *Domestic Crating	400.00
** *Export Crating	475.00
3 n 1 ACCESSORIES	
Re-register Device	495.00
Lensboard Movement	300.00
"Blow-Back"	3,000.00
Left Hand Operation (Copyboard and Scales Only)	175.00
Extra lens calibration	160.00

NEW 3N1 CAMERA
A SHEETFILM CAMERA, A ROLLFILM CAMERA, OR A BLOW-BACK CAMERA—ALL IN ONE!
Western/Palmer/Midwestern/Smart

BROWN/APĒCO®

Price and Specifications Are Subject To Change Without Notice.

*Padded van preparation charge is 20% of domestic crating charge.
**Uncrated customer pick-up is 30% of domestic crating charge.

...is Available at all Branches of

(Clip out and rubber cement to back of paste-up)

Name_____

PROJECT EVALUATION CHECK LIST
ASSIGNMENT 16: CATALOG PAGE WITH OVERLAY

This check list is designed to assist you in identifying the specific points upon which this assignment will be evaluated. Your instructor will indicate by the use of a check mark those areas requiring additional attention.

PASTE-UP PLANNING

_____ One 11″ × 14″ illustration board
_____ 8½″ × 11″ paper size area

PASTE-UP PREPARATION

_____ Elements trimmed smoothly
_____ Elements trimmed to correct dimensions
_____ Elements positioned according to rough layout
_____ Accurate alignment of elements
_____ Rubylith® overlay cut accurately and smoothly
_____ Register marks placed on board and overlay (in register)
_____ Uniform application of adhesive and burnished
_____ Crop marks in black ink approximately ½″ long
_____ Ink color and number noted; screen tint percentage desired noted on overlay
_____ Overall cleanliness of paste-up
_____ Protective tissue overlay and cover flap attached

FINAL EVALUATION _____

assignment 17

RULED BUSINESS FORM

INFORMATION

The drawing pen is a useful tool used by the paste-up artist in the preparation of various kinds of forms work. The drawing pen is designed to produce uniform black ink lines ranging from hairline through approximately 4 points in width.

Many business forms are set on phototypesetting equipment and include vertical and horizontal rules. However, some forms are by necessity ruled by hand. The paste-up artist should have the skill to hand rule lines of consistent weight and various widths.

MATERIALS REQUIRED

Paste-up tools including drawing pen
India ink
Print trimmer and scissors
Rubber cement and/or waxer
Masking tape and transparent tape
One piece of 11" X 14" illustration board
One piece of 12" X 14" tissue overlay paper
One piece of 13" X 14" cover flap paper

PROCEDURE

1. Fasten the illustration board squarely and smoothly to the table work surface with the 14" dimension running horizontally.
2. Using a nonreproducing blue pencil or pen, outline a paper area of $8\frac{1}{2}$" X 11" and an image area of $47\frac{1}{2}$ X $62\frac{1}{2}$ picas on the board.
3. Following the layout, rule in the guidelines for all vertical and cross rules, boxes, borders, and type elements in light-blue pencil or pen.
4. The artwork in the upper-left corner of the form bleeds off the top edge $\frac{1}{8}$".

5. Wax the proof, and cut out the necessary elements as needed. Position the elements lightly for spacing purposes.

6. When you are satisfied that all elements are positioned and spaced correctly, check alignment with the T-square once again, and burnish the paste-up elements carefully.

7. Rule in all horizontal and vertical rules according to the thickness indicated on the rough layout. Maintain uniform line weight when using the pen. Clean up all overruns with white opaque.

8. Ink in crop and center marks with thin, black lines approximately $\frac{1}{2}''$ long.

9. Attach a piece of tissue paper along the $14''$ edge of the board by taping it with transparent tape on the reverse side at the top. Fold over the extra $1''$ at the top of the paste-up.

10. Attach a piece of colored text paper (cover flap) to the board by taping it with masking tape on the reverse side at the top. Fold over the extra $2''$ at the top, and cut back at a 30-degree angle on both sides.

11. Write your name on the front of the Evaluation Check List sheet, and rubber cement the sheet to the back of the paste-up.

12. Turn in assignment for evaluation.

VAN DYKE
PRINTING
HOUSE

CLIENT:

SALESMAN:

BINDERY:

SPECIFICATION:

PAPER:

INK:

PLATE DEPARTMENT:

PRESSMAN:

SHIPPING INFORMATION:

SPECIAL INSTRUCTIONS:

358

CLIENT:

PAPER:

PRESSMAN:

SPECIAL INSTRUCTIONS:

SHIPPING INFORMATION:

PLATE DEPARTMENT:

SPECIFICATION:

SALESMAN:

BINDERY:

INK:

*VAN DYKE
PRINTING
HOUSE*

(Clip out and rubber cement to back of paste-up)

PROJECT EVALUATION CHECK LIST
ASSIGNMENT 17: RULED BUSINESS FORM

This check list is designed to assist you in identifying the specific points upon which this assignment will be evaluated. Your instructor will indicate by the use of a check mark those areas requiring additional attention.

PASTE-UP PLANNING

_____ 11″ X 14″ illustration board
_____ 8½″ X 11″ paper area (blue pencil)
_____ 47½ X 62½ pica image area (blue pencil)

PASTE-UP PREPARATION

_____ Elements trimmed smoothly
_____ Elements trimmed to correct dimensions
_____ Elements positioned according to rough layout
_____ Accurate alignment of elements
_____ Ruling uniform and in correct width in black ink
_____ Ruling accuracy at corners (horizontal and vertical terminal points)
_____ Uniform application of adhesive and burnished
_____ Crop and center marks in black ink approximately ½″ long
_____ Protective tissue overlay and cover flap attached

FINAL EVALUATION _____

assignment 18

DIE-CUT FOLDER

INFORMATION

To die cut discs and squares or cut paper and cardboard into unusual shapes, a sharp hollow die is used. It is similar to a cookie cutter in operation. The die is locked into a die-cutting machine and brought down with considerable force through the stack of paper or cardboard.

Single sheets can also be die cut on letterpress equipment. In this case, the die can be nicked on the edge in two or three places so that the cut outs will not fall out as the sheets pass through the press. The cutouts are removed later.

The layout or paste-up artist involved with a die-cut printed piece must give the printer or die maker a precise same-size inked outline of the cutout. Sometimes it is helpful to provide a same-size model of the die-cut piece. A pair of scissors is used to cut the angles, locking tabs, etc.

MATERIALS REQUIRED

Paste-up tools
Print trimmer and scissors
Rubber cement and/or waxer
Masking tape and transparent tape
Adhesive border tape
Two pieces of 14″ × 20″ illustration board
Two pieces of 15″ × 20″ tissue overlay paper
Two pieces of 16″ × 20″ cover flap paper

PROCEDURE

1. Fasten a piece of illustration board squarely and smoothly to the table work surface with the 20″ dimension running horizontally.

2. Using a nonreproducing blue pencil or pen, outline a paper area of $10\frac{1}{2}'' \times 17''$ and an image area of $10\frac{1}{2}'' \times 17''$ on the board.

3. Following the rough layout for the inside panels of the folder, rule in the appropriate guidelines in light-blue pencil or pen for the various type and art elements. Use a compass to form the arcs (in light-blue pencil) at the top of each panel. Note the various pieces of artwork that bleed (from $\frac{1}{8}''$ to $\frac{1}{4}''$) on the inside panels.

4. Wax the proofs, and begin cutting elements as needed.

5. Position the elements (light pressure for position only), and make sure that the elements fit according to the rough layout. Make allowance for the art elements that bleed.

6. When you are satisfied that all elements are positioned and spaced correctly, check alignment with a T-square, and then burnish the elements carefully.

7. Using a roll of adhesive border tape, lay the 6–point rule in the center panel.

8. Rule in crop, center, and fold marks with thin, black lines. Indicate fold lines at the top and bottom just outside the image area. Use black ink to make several dashes approximately $\frac{1}{8}''$ long (see rough layout).

9. Attach a piece of tissue overlay paper to the illustration board by taping it with transparent tape on the reverse side at the top of the paste-up.

10. Attach a piece of colored paper (cover flap) to the illustration board by taping it with masking tape on the reverse side at the top. Fold over the extra $2''$ at the top, and cut back at a 30–degree angle on both sides.

11. Fasten the second piece of illustration board squarely and smoothly to the table work surface with the $20''$ dimension running horizontally.

12. Following the steps described above, proceed with the cover side of the folder. The dimensions for both sides of the folder are the same.

13. When you have finished the second paste-up, attach a tissue overlay and cover flap.

14. Prepare a die-cutting dummy for the printer by cutting a piece of bristol board or index stock to the exact dimensions of the folder. Cut the required arcs with a pair of scissors, and carefully fold the dummy. Mark each panel with a pencil to indicate copy content and page number.

15. Write your name on the front of the Evaluation Check List sheet, and rubber cement the sheet to the back of one paste-up. Place the paste-ups and die-cutting dummy in a Manila envelope to keep the assignment intact.

16. Turn in assignment for evaluation.

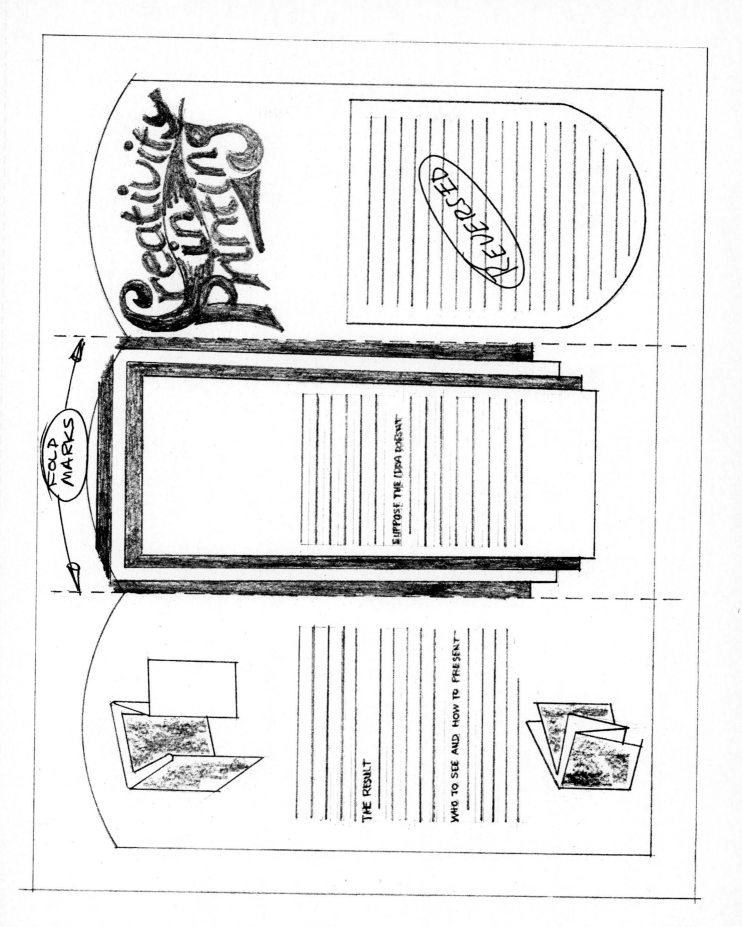

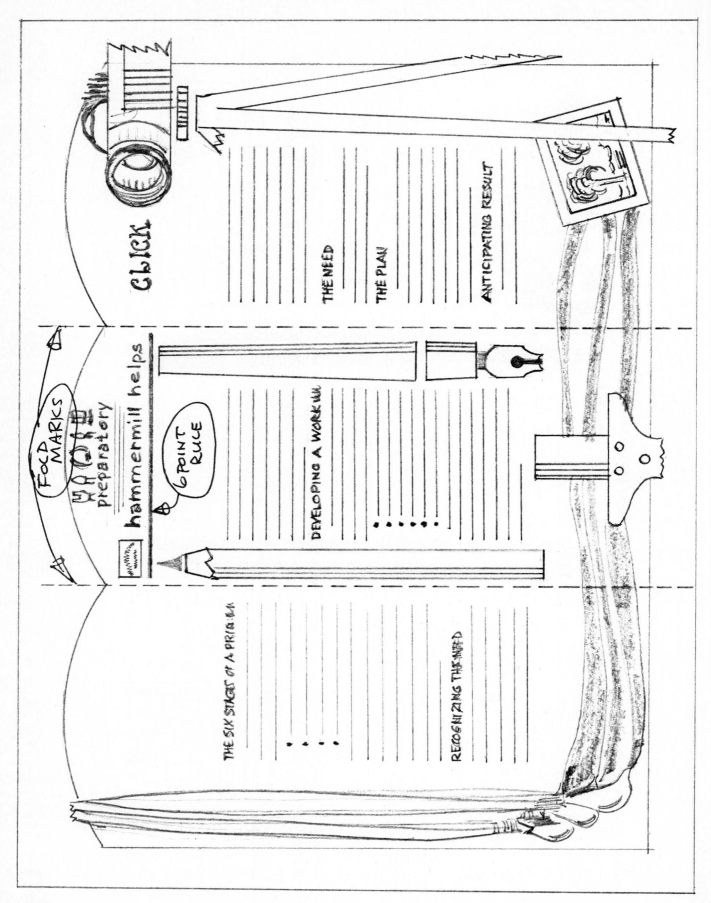

THE SIX STAGES OF A PRINTING PIECE

The Printing Industry of America developed a sales program recently which describes the six stages that every printed job must go through regardless of size, number of colors, or complexity. The first step in creative printing is to recognize these six stages:

1. **Recognition of a need.**
2. **Crystallization of an idea.**
3. **Preparation of contents.**
4. **Visualization.**
5. **Pricing.**
6. **Decision.**

Regardless of its size, a printed piece will not be complete until all of these steps or stages have been accomplished. A creative printer should not only be able to recognize these six stages but should be able to determine what stage the job is at any given time. If the printer participates in any of the first four parts, he is fulfilling, to some degree, the role of a creative printer.

RECOGNIZING THE NEED

The old quotation, "necessity is the mother of invention" concept must certainly be remembered by the creative printer. A need certainly must exist before we can begin the evolvement of the other five steps of a printed job. Normally business procedures and entire industries themselves are created after someone has recognized a specific need and has gone about the task of properly fulfilling that requirement.

Certainly there are situations where an idea is conceived and then research is undertaken to find a need where this idea could serve a purpose of fulfillment. But the proper identification of that need is vital before an idea can be expected to be adopted.

DEVELOPING A WORKABLE PLAN

Regardless of how large or small a print job may be, there must be a plan. Planning starts with analyzing the user's situation and need. The printer should ask himself pertinent questions:

1. Is the user aware of the need; and if so, why has it not been previously satisfied?
2. Can you find a better solution to fill the user's need than the ideas presented to you?
3. Will the user of the print job give consideration to your attempts to creatively meet his need?
4. What objections might you encounter?

5. What better results can a user expect from your suggestions?
6. Are your ideas economically feasible?

The chances are that in order to answer these questions the printer will have to do some research work into the user's business or programs now being used. To present an idea which previously has been discarded or one that is not economically feasible may be a waste of everyone's time.

Once you have determined a favorable answer to the six questions above, you can begin translating your idea into a presentation for the user's consideration. For any substantial program a written presentation that follows a step by step procedure may be in order. Even if you are going to present the idea verbally, you should get it down on paper so you can present the idea completely and logically. A general outline of this plan should follow this form:

THE NEED

This section should contain a statement of the nature of the problem or sales opportunity which you feel you can handle better with your proposal.

THE PLAN

This section should be a complete and full explanation of the plan that you have, along with samples, dummies, etc. It is important at this point to convince the user of your ability to produce the program adequately. This can usually be done by exhibiting high quality jobs previously produced or testimonials about prior work accomplished. At times, a list of equipment contained in your shop may be in order, but remember, you are selling an idea, not a printing press.

ANTICIPATING RESULT

This section should clearly project what you hope to achieve with the presentation of this idea and what result the user may expect if he adopts your program. Bear in mind that people buy benefits not features; and regardless of how difficult it may be for you to swallow, the user is more interested in himself than he is in you. The simple wording of, "Here is what the plan can do for you," is many more times effective than, "Here are the features of my plan."

THE RESULT

This section should contain not only an estimate of the approximate cost but a comparison of the cost in

relation to the anticipated results. A simple statement of cost will not draw this important comparison that can lead to the acceptance of an idea.

WHO TO SEE AND HOW TO PRESENT

Just as important as developing an idea and plan is the reaching of the right person. You should qualify your prospect so that your presentation is made to the executives who have the authority to make the decisions, preferably to the executive who will profit most by your idea. Seldom does a subordinate have the power to decide on a substantial program nor can he be expected to present the program or proposal to top management in as convincing a manner as you could. You may need his cooperation in reaching the right person, but you must tell your story to the decision maker. Caution . . . don't put yourself in the position of having "gone over the head" of a purchasing agent or a department head. Instead, gain the permission to present the idea through him and keep him informed of the progress. In making the actual presentation, you must be aware that anything new and different will almost automatically arouse resistance and skepticism. Because of this, you must move somewhat cautiously toward the decision. If you can display enthusiasm and true interest in the needs of the user, the decision is more apt to be favorable.

SUPPOSE THE IDEA DOESN'T SELL?

Someone said, "Ideas are like children. Our own are the best ones." Because we believe our ideas are "just right" it is sometimes disappointing if the idea does not receive immediate and enthusiastic acceptance. There may be some procrastination for some time in making the decision, or budgetary problems may make a favorable decision impossible at the time. Even more disappointing, the idea may be turned down completely.

If this occurs, one should not become too discouraged. Most executives appreciate a real creative sales effort, and your future work and activity will be more seriously considered and appreciated, because, suddenly, you have become a "creative printer!"

REPRO –
Die-Cut
Folder

hammermill helps

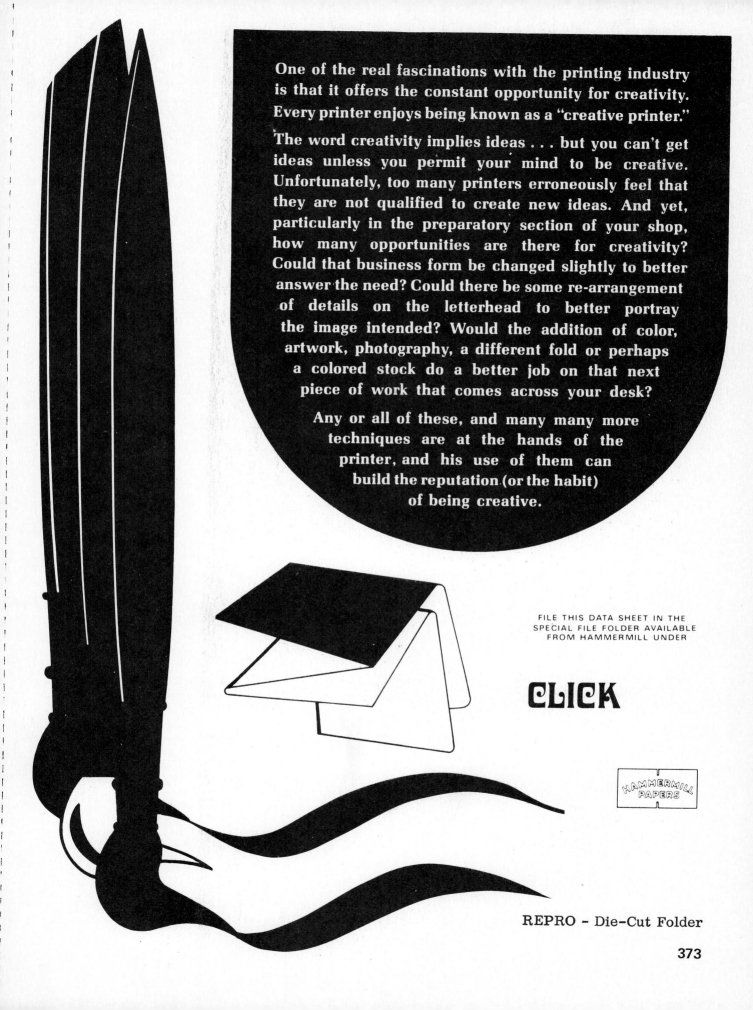

One of the real fascinations with the printing industry is that it offers the constant opportunity for creativity. Every printer enjoys being known as a "creative printer."

The word creativity implies ideas . . . but you can't get ideas unless you permit your mind to be creative. Unfortunately, too many printers erroneously feel that they are not qualified to create new ideas. And yet, particularly in the preparatory section of your shop, how many opportunities are there for creativity? Could that business form be changed slightly to better answer the need? Could there be some re-arrangement of details on the letterhead to better portray the image intended? Would the addition of color, artwork, photography, a different fold or perhaps a colored stock do a better job on that next piece of work that comes across your desk?

Any or all of these, and many many more techniques are at the hands of the printer, and his use of them can build the reputation (or the habit) of being creative.

FILE THIS DATA SHEET IN THE SPECIAL FILE FOLDER AVAILABLE FROM HAMMERMILL UNDER

CLICK

HAMMERMILL PAPERS

REPRO - Die-Cut Folder

373

Name_____

PROJECT EVALUATION CHECK LIST
ASSIGNMENT 18: DIE-CUT FOLDER

This check list is designed to assist you in identifying the specific points upon which this assignment will be evaluated. Your instructor will indicate by the use of a check mark those areas requiring additional attention.

PASTE-UP PLANNING

_____ Two 14" × 20" illustration boards
_____ 10½" × 17" paper size area (blue pencil)
_____ 10½" × 17" image area (blue pencil)

PASTE-UP PREPARATION (inside panels)

_____ Elements trimmed smoothly
_____ Elements trimmed to correct dimensions
_____ Elements positioned according to rough layout
_____ Accurate alignment of rule
_____ Artwork bleeds from ⅛" to ¼"
_____ Accurate alignment of type, artwork, and logo
_____ Uniform application of adhesive and burnished
_____ Crop and center marks in black ink, approximately ½" long; fold marks in black ink, ⅛" dashes
_____ Protective tissue overlay and cover flap attached

PASTE-UP PREPARATION (outside panels)

_____ Elements trimmed smoothly
_____ Elements trimmed to correct dimensions
_____ Elements positioned according to rough layout
_____ Accurate alignment of type and artwork
_____ Uniform application of adhesive and burnished
_____ Crop and center marks in black ink, approximately ½" long; fold marks in black ink, ⅛" dashes
_____ Protective tissue overlay and cover flap attached

FINAL EVALUATION _____

assignment 19

COMBINING PROCESS COLOR INKS

INFORMATION

Transparent or process inks blend together to form a secondary color when they are printed one on top of another. Printing a transparent blue over a transparent yellow ink will produce green. The process color inks include yellow, blue (cyan), red (magenta), and black. Black ink is combined with the other three colors in most cases to achieve detail and greater depth.

It is possible to plan combinations of the process colors to produce a variety of other colors. For example, red and yellow produce orange; red and blue produce violet. A study of the color wheel will suggest other combinations that may be planned into the layout.

It is also possible to achieve any desired percentage of a color by using percentage tint screens singly or in combinations. It must be remembered that when using tint screens in combination, proper screen angles should be maintained to avoid the moiré effect. This is an objectionable pattern that distracts from the artwork and is hard on the eyes.

Because of the time and materials limitations, this assignment calls for the use of solid color overlays. Percentage tint screens will not be used.

MATERIALS REQUIRED

Paste-up tools
Amberlith® masking film
Rubber cement and/or waxer
Pressure-sensitive register marks
Masking tape and transparent tape
Orthochromatic film

Print trimmer and scissors
Orthochromatic film chemistry
3–M Color Key materials
One piece of 11″ × 14″ illustration board
One piece of 11″ × 15″ tissue overlay paper
One piece of 11″ × 16″ cover flap paper
One piece of 10″ × 12″ index paper for mounting Color Key proofs

PROCEDURE

1. Select one of the line drawings provided in this assignment. Make a Xerox copy of the line drawing.
2. Refer to an ink manufacturer's color chart to determine the color combinations you desire to reproduce. Remember, the primary colors are yellow, blue, and red. The line drawing will print in black. You may use the other colors in combination to achieve desired results.
3. Using a pencil on the Xerox copy, indicate the color combinations desired. This will be useful for future reference when actual separation of color begins.
4. Fasten the illustration board squarely and smoothly to the table work surface.
5. Outline a paper area of 8″ × 11″. Ink in all crop marks with ½″ thin, black lines. Center marks are not required.
6. Using rubber cement or wax, adhere the original line drawing in the center of the paper area.
7. The line drawing represents everything that will print in black ink on the press. Attach a piece of Amberlith® that is one inch larger all around than the paper size area. This will be the yellow printer overlay. Outline with the X-acto® knife all areas that are planned for yellow. Be sure to cut the masking material at least halfway into the black lines of the line drawing so that there will be no chance of gaps showing through.
8. Remove all unwanted emulsion with a piece of masking tape. Place a small piece of masking tape in the lower right-hand corner of the overlay, and mark it yellow. Give name and number of ink from ink manufacturer's book.
9. Attach another piece of Amberlith® of the same size for the blue printer overlay. Attach the overlay as shown in the sample layout. Cut the outline needed, remove all excess emulsion, and then mark the overlay blue. Give name and number of ink.
10. Attach a third piece of Amberlith® for the red printer overlay. Cut the outline, and remove unwanted masking film from the acetate base. Mark the overlay red, and give the name and number of ink.
11. Apply three sets of positive register marks at the following locations just outside the paper area: left center, right center, and bottom center. Place one set of register marks directly on the board with the other sets directly over them on the overlays. Use a magnifier if necessary.
12. Cover the paste-up with a piece of colored text (cover flap) paper.

   Your instructor will demonstrate the operation of the process camera and related darkroom procedures.

13. Complete the next phase of this assignment by photographing and processing your four line negatives.
14. Any pin holes in the film negatives should be opaqued after the film is thoroughly dry.

   Your instructor will demonstrate the use of the 3–M Color Key. This is a film material suitable for proofing color jobs. The procedure requires an exposure in the platemaker and one-step development.

15. Complete the final phase of this assignment by preparing 3-M Color Key proofs of your negatives.
16. Using transparent tape along the top edge of each overlay, mount the proofs on a sheet of 10″ × 12″ white index paper. Indicate the paper size area (8″ × 11″) with blue pencil.
17. Write your name on the front of the Evaluation Check List sheet, and rubber cement the sheet to the back of the paste-up. Place the paste-up and proof in a Manila envelope.
18. Turn in assignment for evaluation.

LAYOUT FOR PROCESS INK COLORS

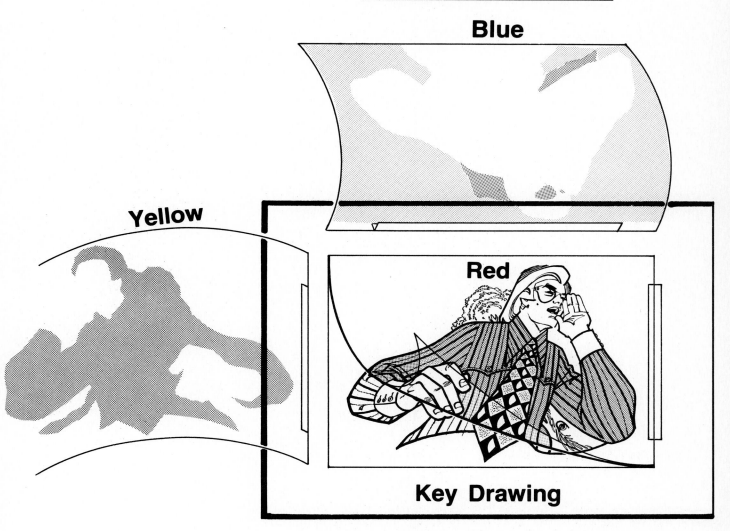

The 'flap' method of preparing color overlays.

Name_____

PROJECT EVALUATION CHECK LIST
ASSIGNMENT 19: COMBINING PROCESS COLOR INKS

This check list is designed to assist you in identifying the specific points upon which this assignment will be evaluated. Your instructor will indicate by the use of a check mark those areas requiring additional attention.

PASTE-UP PLANNING

_____ 11" X 14" illustration board
_____ 8" X 11" paper area
_____ 10" X 12" index paper for Color Key mounting

PASTE-UP PREPARATION

_____ Line drawing trimmed smoothly
_____ Line drawing adhered to illustration board smoothly
_____ Uniform application of adhesive
_____ Yellow printer overlay cut accurately and smoothly
_____ Blue printer overlay cut accurately and smoothly
_____ Red printer overlay cut accurately and smoothly
_____ Register marks applied to board and overlays accurately
_____ Four negatives processed to solid step 4
_____ Color Key film developed correctly
_____ Color Key film mounted in register on index paper
_____ Crop marks included on board in black ink approximately ½" long
_____ Overall cleanliness of assignment
_____ Process color inks noted (name and number) on board and overlays
_____ Cover flap attached

*FINAL EVALUATION*_____

20

RECORD ALBUM JACKET

INFORMATION

The recording industry is one of the largest enterprises in the world today. Graphic arts play an important part in the promotion and packaging of its products. Album covers for 33⅓ rpm records are designed to capture the imagination and interest of the buyer. In most instances, color printing is used to dramatize and create spectacular design results.

This assignment involves the preparation of a four-color record album jacket. In addition, the reverse side of the album is pasted up to include credit lines and manufacturing data.

MATERIALS REQUIRED

Paste-up tools
Print trimmer and scissors
Rubber cement and/or waxer
Masking tape and transparent tape
Amberlith® masking film material
Pressure-sensitive register marks
Two pieces of 15″ × 15″ illustration board
Two pieces of 16″ × 15″ tissue overlay paper
Two pieces of 17″ × 15″ cover flap paper

PROCEDURE

1. Fasten one of the pieces of illustration board squarely and smoothly to the table work surface. The cover side of the record album jacket will be pasted up first.
2. Outline a paper area of 12½″ × 12½″. *Note:* The press sheet will be larger than 12½″ × 12½″ since the job will be printed eight up (front and back)

on a large offset press. The individual jackets will be die cut, trimmed, folded, and glued.

3. Position three register marks on the board just outside the paper size area at the center left, right, and bottom. Adhesive register marks supplied on rolls are suitable for this purpose.

4. The image area should be $12\frac{1}{2}'' \times 12\frac{1}{2}''$. Note that the color bands (green and red) appear to bleed top and bottom. However, since the jacket opening is on the right side, no trim will be taken on the top or bottom of the jacket since these edges will be folded over. Therefore, the color bands run to the edge of the image area only at the top and bottom.

5. Following the layout, rule in the appropriate guidelines in light-blue pencil or pen for the various type elements, artwork, and colored bands. The green and purple bands are 9 picas in width, and the red and blue bands are 11 picas in width. Note the approximate starting and ending points (vertically) for the green, purple, and blue bands. The green band aligns $27\frac{1}{2}$ picas from the left edge of the jacket. The capital "G" is 3 picas from the left edge and 3 picas down from the top edge. The lines that read WITH THE NAKED EYE are positioned approximately 10 picas in from the left edge of the jacket in the vertical position shown on the rough layout.

6. Wax the proofs, and begin cutting elements needed for the cover.

7. Position the elements (light pressure for position only) on the board. This includes the elements that print in black. Follow the rough layout carefully.

8. When you are satisfied that all elements are positioned and spaced correctly, check the alignment with a T-square, and then burnish the elements.

9. Draw all crop and center marks in thin, black lines approximately $\frac{1}{2}''$ long.

10. Obtain four pieces of $12\frac{1}{2}'' \times 14''$ Amberlith® masking film to serve as overlays for the colored bands and solids for the type.

11. Position a piece of masking film (emulsion side up) over the board so that the 14″ dimension runs vertically. Use transparent tape to affix the masking film along the top edge approximately 1″ outside the paper size area. (*Note:* The flap method of overlaying will be used in this assignment. This involves attaching the masking film alternately at top, left, right, bottom, and again at the top for the cover flap. Check the procedure in your textbook.)

12. Using an X-acto® knife, cut the emulsion of the masking film lightly (do not cut through acetate carrier) along the blue guidelines previously drawn on the board. Follow the blue guidelines that represent the green band. Carefully remove the unwanted portion of the masking film; leave only the band that represents green.

13. Affix registration marks to the overlay precisely over the registration marks on the board. Mark the overlay 50% PMS green on a small piece of masking tape. Affix the tape to the overlay in the lower right-hand corner.

14. Attach the second piece of masking film to the board directly over the first overlay. Remember to attach the masking film at the left side this time.

15. Following the same procedure as before, cut the emulsion along the guidelines drawn for the red band. Affix registration marks to align with the previous two sets. Mark the overlay 50% PMS red.

16. Attach the third piece of masking film to the board over the first and second overlays. Remember to attach the masking film at the right side this time.

17. Cut the emulsion along the guidelines drawn for the blue band. Allow the blue to overlap the red band approximately $\frac{1}{32}''$ to avoid any possibility of white space along the edges of the two bands. Mark the overlay 40% PMS blue. *Note:* Since blue and red combine to make the color purple, it will be necessary to use the blue overlay to cut the blue portion of the purple band. Allow the blue to overlap the red and green bands approximately $\frac{1}{32}''$ to achieve tight registration. Mark the overlay 40% blue for purple. Affix registration marks to align with the previous sets.

18. Attach the fourth piece of masking film to the board over the other three overlays. Remember to attach the masking film at the bottom this time.

19. Cut the emulsion along the guidelines drawn for the purple band exactly the same size as the blue cut for the 40% band. On the same overlay, cut

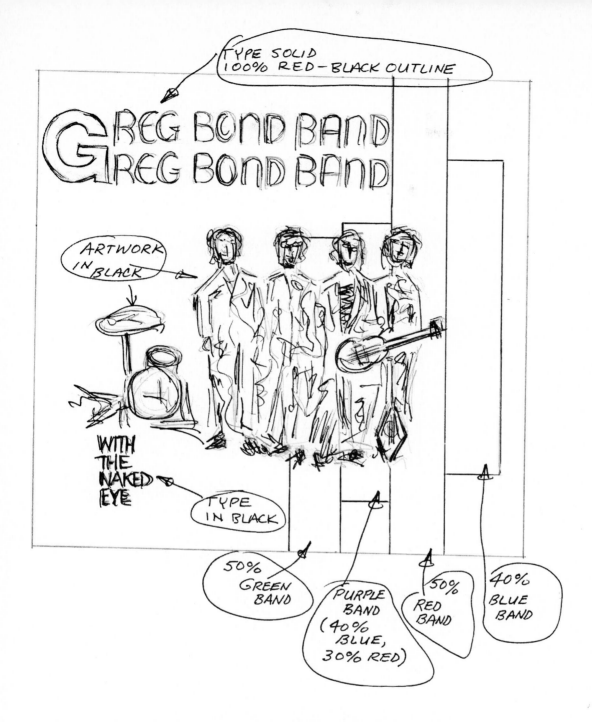

along the black type outline of the lines GREG BOND BAND. This portion of the overlay represents solid red inside the type outlines. Cut the emulsion so that it extends into the black type outline to avoid showing white space. Mark the overlay Type—100% PMS red. Affix registration marks to align with the previous sets.

20. Attach a piece of colored text paper (cover flap) to the illustration board.
21. Fasten the second piece of illustration board squarely and smoothly to the table work surface.
22. Following the rough layout provided, proceed with the reverse side of the jacket.
23. Attach a tissue overlay and cover flap to the illustration board.
24. Write your name on the front of the Evaluation Check List sheet, and rubber cement the sheet to the back of one paste-up.
25. Turn in assignment for evaluation.

Produced By
GREG BOND (SPECIAL THANKS
TO BARBARA SPENCER)
WITH BOB WHITE AND KEN HIRD

Recorded By
GEORGE ANDERSON AND DAN TANNER
AT THE VILLAGE RECORDER
WITH ASSISTANCE AND ADDITIONAL
RECORDING BY TOM SNYDER
SOME TRACKS RECORDED BY
BARBARA SPENCER AT HOME

Mastered By
PHILLIP GREEN AT TOP RECORDS

Art Direction And Design
VIGON NAMAS VIGON

Graphic Arts
PETER NICKOLIN
CAROL OSHIMA

DIGITAL MIX-DOWN EQUIPMENT
FURNISHED BY HIGH FIDELITY, INC.
ASSISTANCE BY DAVE TUCKER

STUDIO CREW: ART BANNER,
ANNE LINDSEY, CYNTHIA PARSONS

THIS ALBUM IS DEDICATED TO
THE OFFICERS AND CREW OF THE
U.S.S. LAKE CHAMPLAIN (CVA-39)

HIGH FIDELITY RECORDS, INC. · HOLLYWOOD, CA · NEW YORK · LONDON · TOKYO · 1981 HIGH FIDELITY RECORDS, INC.

1
Over & Over
The Ledge
Think About Me
Save Me A Place
Sara

2
What Makes You Think You're The One
Storms
That's All For Everyone
Not That Funny
Sisters Of The Moon

3
Angel
That's Enough For Me
Brown Eyes
Never Make Me Cry
I Know I'm Not Wrong

4
Honey Hi
Beautiful Child
Walk A Thin Line
Tusk
Never Forget

REG BOND BAND
REG BOND BAND
REG BOND BAND

G WITH THE NAKED EYE

REPRO –
Record
Album
Jacket

(Clip out and rubber cement to back of paste-up)

Name_____

PROJECT EVALUATION CHECK LIST
ASSIGNMENT 20: RECORD ALBUM JACKET

This check list is designed to assist you in identifying the specific points upon which this assignment will be evaluated. Your instructor will indicate by the use of a check mark those areas requiring additional attention.

PASTE-UP PLANNING

_____ Two 15" X 15" illustration boards
_____ 12½" X 12½" paper size area (blue pencil)
_____ 12½" X 12½" image area

PASTE-UP PREPARATION (cover of jacket)

_____ Line drawing and type elements trimmed smoothly
_____ Line drawing and type elements adhered to illustration board according to rough layout
_____ Uniform application of adhesive and burnished
_____ Green overlay cut smoothly and accurately; ink color noted
_____ Red overlay cut smoothly and accurately; ink color noted
_____ Blue overlay cut smoothly and accurately; ink color noted
_____ Red overlay for 30% band and type solid cut smoothly and accurately; ink color and percentages noted
_____ Register marks applied to board and overlays properly attached
_____ Overlays marked for color and percentages
_____ Crop and center marks in black ink approximately ½" long
_____ Cover flap attached to board

PASTE-UP PREPARATION (back of jacket)

_____ Elements trimmed smoothly
_____ Elements trimmed to correct dimensions
_____ Elements positioned according to rough layout
_____ Accurate alignment of elements
_____ Uniform application of adhesive and burnished
_____ Crop and center marks in black ink approximately ½" long
_____ Protective tissue overlay and cover flap attached

*FINAL EVALUATION*_____

INDEX

Note: Page numbers in italics refer to glossary entries.

Adhesive shading, 87–91
Adhesive transfer letters, 13 *fig.*, 98, 99 *figs.*
Advertisements:
assignments, 237–45, 263–71, 299–305, 307–19, 321–31
typeface styles for, 60, 61
Advertising pieces, paper grade used for, 169
Airbrushing, *196*
Airbrush renderings, 77
Airline flight schedule, assignment, 273–79
Alignment, in paste-ups, 108–10
Announcements, paper grade used for, 169
Antihalation coating, 136, 137
Antique finish, 166
Art preparation, 71–92
cropping, 74–76
enlargements and reductions, 71–74
kinds of orginal copy, 76–78
photomechanical transfer (PMT), 92
special-effects copy, 78–92
Ascenders, 17, 60, *196*
Assignments:
airline flight schedule, 273–79
business reply mail card, 229–35
bus schedule, 247–61
catalog page with overlay, 349–55
combining process color inks, 377–87
daily tab-size newspaper page, 333–41
die-cut folder, 363–75
direct mail advertisement, 263–71
display advertisement, 237–45

letterhead, envelope, and business card, 207–17
newsletter make-up, 291–97
newspaper display advertisement, 299–305, 307–19
Pacific Telephone brochure, 281–89
paste-up orientation, 117–20
point system, 203–5
poster, 219–27
record album jacket, 389–97
ruled business form, 357–61
silhouette halftone, 343–47
supermarket display advertisement, 321–31
Asymmetrical type lines, 22
ATF Typesetter, 38
Author's alterations (AA), *196*
Automated page make-up, 53–56
Automatic Illustrated Documentation System (AIDS), 53–56
Automatic letterspacing, on photo-display units, 40–41

Balance, design principle, 66
Bank checks, paper grade used for, 169
Baronial envelopes, 171
Base material, for paste-ups, 95
Basis weight, 167, 168 *fig.*
Baskerville type, 59 *fig.*
Bellows extension, of process camera, 126
Benday, *196*
Bindery worker, 11
Binding, 177–80
loose-leaf, 178
mechanical, 177–78
padding, 180
perfect, 180
sewn case-bound, 179
sewn soft-cover, 179
wire-stitching, 178
Black letter, *196*

Black pigments, 192
Blanket, *196*
Blanks, 170
Bleed, 97, *196*
Blueline, *196*
Body, of printing ink, 190
Body, of typeface, 17, 18, 19
Body type, *196*
Boeing Aircraft, 263
Boldface, 68, *196*
Bond papers, 168 *fig.*, 169, *196*
Book covers, hot stamping, 188
Book jackets, paper grade used for, 169
Booklet covers, paper grade used for, 169
Booklets:
paper finish used for, 166
folding, 181–84
Book papers, 168 *fig.*, 169, *196*
Books:
cutting and trimming, 180–81
creep allowance, 156–58
envelopes for, 171
offset printing process, 144, 147
paper finishes used for, 166
paper grain used for, 167
pocket-sized, binding, 180
typeface style used for, 60
Borders, 97, 99, 100 *fig.*, 101 *fig.*, 102 *figs.*
Brayer, 26
Bristol board, 95, 168 *fig.*, 169
Broadside, *196*
Brochures, 93, *196*
assignments, 247–61, 273–79, 281–89
Brownprint, *196*
Burnishing:
after alignment, 108
of transfer letters, 98, 99 *fig.*

Business cards:
assignment, 207–17
typeface styles used for, 60
Business forms:
assignments, 229–35, 357–61
offset printing, 148
paper grade used for, 169
paste-up, 93
Business papers, 169
Business reply mail card, assignment, 229–35
Bus schedule, assignment, 247–61

Camera-ready copy. *See also* Paste-up.
defined, 67, *196*
with phototypesetting, 32
Candy wrappers, paper grade used for, 169
Capital letters:
letterspacing, 20
mortising, 20
term for, 14
Caps and small caps, *196*
Caption, *196*
Case-bound binding, 179, *196*
Caslon old face style, 58 *fig.*
Castor, 30
Catalog page:
assignment, 349–55
offset printing, 148
paper finish used for, 166
paper grain used for, 167
Cathode ray tube (CRT) devices, 39, 53–56
Centered type lines, 22
Certificates:
hot stamping, 188
typeface for, 61
Characters:
defined, 14
formation on CRT devices, 39, 53
in hot-type composition, 24
in linotype matrices, 29

Characters (*cont.*)
in monotype matrices, 30
on punched paper tape, 46–47
on Selectric Composer, 34
spacing. *See* Letterspacing.
on text phototypesetting photo unit, 49
on typewriters, 32
Characters per pica, *196*
Chinese white, *196*
Cleanliness, of paste-ups, 110
Clean tape, 51
Clip-art images, 13 *fig.*
Clipping machine, 161, 162 *fig.*
Coated papers, 166, *196*
Cold type:
defined, 12–13, 14, *196*
mortising, 20
preparation, 16
Cold-type composition, 32–56
photocomposition, 36–56
strike-on method, 32–36
Cold-type paste-ups, proof-reading, 27–28
Collating, 186, *196*
Color:
flat color paste-up, 112–13
gravure printing, 151
offset lithography, 144–47
Pantone Matching System, 112–13
in printing ink, 192
register, 113–115
solid-color paste-up, 115–16
specifying, 112
Color preprint inserts, 151
Color separation:
versus flat color printing, 112
type of film used, 135
Combination copy, 78
Commercial announcements, 61
Commercial register, 113
Composing machine, *196*
Composing stick, 24, 25 *fig.*, 31
Composition, *196*
cold-type, 32–56
hot-type, 24–31
Comprehensive layout, 67, 69 *fig.*, 196
Comp Set 500, 38 *fig.*
Compugraphic CG 7200, 44–45
Compugraphic Corporation, 62
Computer-assisted correction, 51–52
Computerized typesetting, 38–56, *196*
Computers:
with CRT systems, 53
on text phototypesetting systems, 48–49
Condensed type, *196*
Contact printing, 41, 129
Contact screen, 131–33, *196*
Continuous tone, *196*
Continuous tone copy, 76 *fig.*, 78
automated page make-up, 55
combined with line copy, 78, 92
darkroom operations, 130–34
keying, 110–11
preparation for paste-up, 99, 102, 105
special-effects conversions, 78, 81–82 *figs.*

Contrast, design element, 66, 67 *fig.*
Copy, 63, *196. See also* Continuous tone copy; Line copy.
Copyboard, of process camera, 124, 125 *fig.*, 127
Copy elements:
attaching to paste-up, 106–8
preparation for paste-up, 99–105
transfers, 97–99, 100–102 *figs.*
Copyfitting, *196*
Copy preparation, 63–71
design, 63–66
layout planning, 67–68
markup, 68–71
Corrections:
on punched paper tape, 46–47
with text phototypesetting systems, 51–52
Counting keyboard, 47
Cover papers, 168 *fig.*, 169
Crop marks, on paste-up board, 95–97
Cropping, 74–76, *196*
Cursive type styles, 61
Cuts, 25
Cutting, 180–81

Dandy roll, 167
Darkroom, 135
Darkroom cameras, 122. *See also* Process cameras.
Darkroom operations, 128–34
contact printing, 129
continuous tone copy, 130–34
film processing procedures, 136–37
line copy, 128–29
Dead form, 28
Dead matter, 28
Debarker, 161, 162 *fig.*
Deckled edges, 167
Decorative type, 61–62
Descender, 17, 60, *196*
Design principles, 63–66, 67 *figs.*
Developer, 136–37
Diagonal line methods, 72
Diagrams, 76
Diaphragm, of process camera, 124
Die-cut folder, assignment, 363–75
Die-cutting, 188, *196*
Differential spacing, *197*
Direct entry keyboards, 46, 47, 48
Digester, 161, 163 *figs.*
Diplomas, typeface for, 61
Direct mail advertisement, assignment, 263–71
Dirty proof, *197*
Discretionary hyphenation, 48–49
Display advertisements, assignments, 237–45, 299–305, 307–19, 321–31
Display lines:
composed on photodisplay units, 40
specifications for, 68, 71
typeface styles for, 60, 61–62
Display type, 18, *197*
Distribution, 28, 31
Doctor blade, 150, 152
Drawing table, 95
Drawings:
continuous tone, 77
cropping, 74–76

enlargement and reduction, 71–74
in pen and ink, 76
Drilling, 184, 185 *figs.*, 197
Dropout halftone, *197*
Dummy, 68, *197*
Duotones, 81–83, 134, *197*
Duplicating forms, 169

Eggshell finish, 166
Elements, of design, 63–66
Elements, on Selectric Composer, 33
Em, *197*
Em quad, 19, 23
En, *197*
Enamel paper, *197*
Enlargements, 71–74
focusing controls, 127
with Photomechanical Transfer, 92
En quad, 19
Envelopes, 171–72
assignment, 207–17
Estimates, of printing paper, 172
Etched printing. *See* Gravure printing.
Exception dictionary, 48

Face, of type, 17, 31, *197*
Family, of type, 14, *197*
Felt side, 167, *197*
File cards, paper grade used for, 169
Film. *See also* Photographic film.
platemaking from, 8–9
stripping, 6–7
Filmotype machine, 43
Film positive, 129
Film processing, 136–37
Film processors, 137
Film positive screen tints, 86–87
Filmstrip fonts, 42, 44
Film structure, 136
Finishing, 180–88
collating, 186
cutting and trimming, 180–81
die-cutting, 188
drilling, 184
folding, 181–84
gathering, 184
hot stamping, 188
jogging, 186
perforating, 187
punching, 184
scoring, 186
Finish size guidelines, 95
Fixing bath, 137
Flat, *197*
Flat-bed cylinder rotary press, 140, 141 *fig.*
Flat-color paste-up, 112–13
Floppy discs, 52
Flush left, *197*
Flush right, *197*
Focusing controls, 127
Folders:
assignment, 363–75
paper finish used for, 166
Folding, 181–84
Folios, 68, *197*
Font, 14, *197. See also* Type font.
Food wrappers, printing process, 151
Foot margin, *197*
Foot of the job, *197*
Ford Motor Company, 263
Form. *See* Type form.
Formal balance, 66
Format, *197*

Fotosetter, 36–37
Fourdinier papermaking machine, 164–65
French fold, 183
F-stop, 126

Gallery cameras, 122. *See also* Process cameras.
Galley:
defined, 24–25
from linotype machine, 28
making up, 25
proofing, 26
tieing up, 26
Galley proofs, 26, 27 *fig.*, 197
Ganging, *197*
Gathering, 184, 186 *figs.*, 197
Glass (halftone) screen, 131
Glossary, 196–99
Goldenrod material, 7, 8
Grades, of printing paper, 168–70
Grain, of paper, 167, *197*
Graphic arts:
business's need for, 1–2
scope of, 1
Graphic arts specialists:
employers, 1
job descriptions, 3–11
Gravure printing, 150–52, *197*
imposition, 155
ink characteristics, 191
paperboard printing, 170
principles, 150
printing characteristics, 151
types of presses, 151–52
uses, 151
Gray screens, 133
Gripper bite, *197*
Ground glass, of process camera, 126, 127 *fig.*
Gutenberg, Johann, 24, 138

Hairline, *197*
Hairline register, 113, 116
Halftones, *197*
art preparation, 77
block method of paste-up, 104, 110
keying, 110
kinds, 133
outline method of paste-up, 102–4, 110
principles, 130
print method of paste-up, 104–5
rescreening, 105
suitable paper finishes, 166
two-color (duotones), 134
type of film used, 135
Halftone screens:
contact, 78, 81–82 *figs.*, 131–33
darkroom operations, 131–33
duotone, 134
glass, 131
for special effects, 134
Halftone tint, *197*
Hand-cut images, 13 *fig.*
Hand-lettered images, 13 *fig.*
Hand-set type, 24–28, 31
Handwriting, typefaces like, 61
Harmony, design element, 66
Headings, letterspacing, 20
Highlights, *197*
Holding dimension, 72, 73 *fig.*
Horizontal center guidelines, 95
Horizontal process camera, 122–23
Hot metal images, 13 *fig. See also* Hot type.

Hot stamping, 188, 189 *figs.*
Hot type:
    defined, 12, 14
    distribution, 28
    mortising, 20
    tieing up, 26
Hot type composition, 24–31
    hand set, 24–28
    machine set, 28–31
Hyphenation, 48–49. *See also*
    Justify.
Hyphenless typesetting, 49

IBM, 263
IBM Electronic "Selectric"
    Composer, 34, 35 *fig.*
IBM Magnetic Card Selectric
    Composer, 35
IBM Selectric Composer, 33–34
Idiot tape, 48
Illustration board, 95
Illustration Scanner, 55
Illustrations, 99
Image area guidelines, 95, 97
Image assembly, classifica-
    tions, 13 *fig.*
Image master, 49
Imposition, 155–60, *197*
Index bristol papers, 169
Indirect entry keyboards, 46–
    47
Informal balance, 66
Information International,
    Incorporated, 53
Intaglio, 150. *See also* Gravure
    printing.
Intertype, 36–37
Italics, 68, *197.*

Jogging, 186, 187 *fig., 197*
Justified tape, 47
Justify, justification, 21, *197*
    by computer unit, 48–49
    with counting keyboard, 47
    with Electronic "Selectric"
        Composer, 34
    with hand-set hot type, 24
    on Magnetic Card Selectric
        Composer, 35
    with Selectric Composer, 34
    in strike-on composition,
        32–33
    on Varityper, 36
Justowriter, 38

Kern, 23, *197*
Key, keying, 110, *197*
Keyboard:
    on Compugraphic CG 7200,
        44
    of linotype machine, 28
    of monotype machine, 30
    on photodisplay units, 40,
        41 *fig.*
    on second-generation
        phototypesetters, 38, 39
        fig.
    on text phototypesetting
        system, 45, 46–48, 51
Keylines, keylining, 115, *197*
Key plate, *197*
Killing, 28
Kodak Photomechanical
    Transfer (PMT), 105
Kraft envelopes, 171

Label papers, 169–70
Latent image, 136
Layout, *197*
    comprehensive, 67, 69 *fig.*
    making up with hand-set
        hot type, 25
    photocomposition, 53
    rough, 67, 68 *fig.*

Layout artists, 3, 63
Layout planning, 67–68
Leaders, *197*
Leads, leading, 20–21, 28, 197
    with hand-set hot type, 24
    specifying in markup, 68
Ledger sheets, paper grade
    used for, 169
Legend, *197*
Length, of printing ink, 191
Lens, 124–26
Lensboard, 124–26, 127
Letterheads:
    assignment, 207–17
    hot stamping, 188
    paste-up, 93
    typeface styles for, 60
Letterpress, 138–42, *197*
    flat-bed cylinder press, 140,
        141 *fig.*
    imposition, 155, 156 *fig.*
    ink characteristics, 191
    makeready process, 139
    paperboard printing, 170
    paper grades used with, 169
    perforating, 187
    platen press, 140, 141 *fig.*
    principles, 138, 140 *fig.*
    printing characteristics, 139
    rotary press, 142
    spoilage schedule, 173
    uses, 139–40
Letterspacing:
    with adhesive transfer let-
        ters, 98
    on Filmtype machine, 43
    functions and guidelines, 20
    instead of hyphenation, 48,
        49
    on photodisplay units, 40–
        41
    on Photo Typositor, 44
    selective (kerning), 23
    on Varityper Headliner, 42
Ligature, *197*
Light face, *197*
Light table, 7, 95
Line conversions, 78
Line copy, 76, *197*
    automated page make-up, 55
    combined with continuous
        tone, 78, 92
    darkroom operations, 128–29
    reversals, 91
    type of film used with, 135
Line gauge, *197*
Line spacing, *197*
Linotype machine, 28, 29, 37
Logic, for end-of-line deci-
    sions, 48
Logotype, *197*
Long inks, 191
Loose-leaf binding, 178
Lowercase letters, 14
    features of, 17
    avoiding letterspacing, 20
    specifying in markup, 68
Ludlow machine, 28, 31

Machine finish paper, 166
Machine-set type, 28–31
Magazine, of linotype ma-
    chine, 28
Magazines:
    binding, 180
    cutting and trimming, 180–
        81
    envelopes for, 171
    letterpress printing, 138
    paper grain used for, 167
    paper finish used for, 166
    paste-up for, 93
    printing processes, 144, 147
    typeface style used for, 60

Magenta screen, 133
Magnetic discs, 49, 50 *fig.*, 52
Magnetic diskette, 52–53
Magnetic tape:
    with CRT systems, 53
    with indirect-entry text
        phototypesetting system,
        46, 47
    for photocomposition, 39
Mail order catalogs:
    binding, 180
    gravure printing, 151
Makeready, 139
Make-up, *197*
Manila envelopes, 171
Manual letterspacing, 40–41
Margins, *197*
Markup, 68–71, *197*
Masking film, 84, 85 *fig.*
    with halftone block method,
        104
    for paste-up of solids, 116
Matrix:
    in early phototypesetter, 37
    in linotype composition, 28
    in Ludlow composition, 31
    in monotype composition,
        30
Measure, *197*
Mechanical, 67, 69 *fig.*, *197.*
    See also Paste-up.
Mechanical binding, 177–78
Memo pads, 180
Menus, paper grade used for,
    169
Middletones, *197*
Milling, of printing inks, 192–
    94
Mimeograph forms, 169
Mixing, of printing inks, 192,
    193 *figs.*
Modern typefaces, 59–60
Moiré, 105, *197*
Money orders, paper grade
    used for, 169
Monophoto, 37
Monotype machine, 28, 30,
    37
Mortising, 20, *198*
Multicolor printing:
    by offset lithography, 144–
        47
    on screen press, 153

Negative, *198*
Newsletter make-up, assign-
    ment, 291–97
Newspaper display advertise-
    ment, assignments, 299–
    305, 307–19
Newspaper headlines, type-
    face styles for, 60
Newspaper page, assignment,
    333–41
Newspapers:
    color preprint inserts, 151
    letterpress printing, 138
    offset printing, 144, 147
    paste-up, 93
    Sunday magazines, 151
    typeface style used for, 60
Newsprint, 170
Noncounting keyboard, 48
Nonpareil, *198*
Nonregister, 113
Notebooks, padding, 180

Offset duplicator press, 144
Offset lithography, 142–48,
    198
    imposition, 155
    kind of type used for, 14
    paper characteristics re-
        quired, 166

paper grades used for, 169,
    170
paste-up for, 93
with perforation, 187
with phototypesetting, 32
principles, 142, 143 *fig.*
printing characteristics, 139
printing ink characteristics,
    191
screen rulings, 88
sheet-fed presses, 144–47
spoilage schedule, 173
steps in, 2 *fig.*
type of film used, 135
web-fed presses, 147–48
Offset printing plates:
    installing on press plate
        cylinder, 10 *fig.*
    making, 8 *figs.*, 9 *fig.*
    with screen tint, 87
Oldstyle Roman, 58–60, *198*
Opacity, of printing papers,
    168
Optical center, 65, *198*
Optical character recognition
    (OCR) systems, 52–53
Ornaments, 97, 99
Orthochromatic film, 135
Outdoor advertising:
    paper grade used for, 170
    screen printing, 153
Oval halftone, 133
Overlay method, 114, 115
Overprinting, *198*

Pacific Telephone brochure,
    assignment, 281–89
Packaging:
    paper grade used for, 170
    printing process used for,
        138
    of printing inks, 194
Padding, 180
Page make-up, automated,
    53–56
Page Makeup System, 56
Page numbers, in dummy, 68
Pagesetter, 56, 57 *fig.*
Pagination, *198*
Pamphlets:
    cutting and trimming, 180–
        81
    envelopes for, 171
Panchromatic film, 135
Pantone Matching System
    (PMS), 112–13
Paperboard, 170
Paper cutters, 180–81
Paper cutting, 174, 175–76
    figs.
Paper finishes, 166
Paper grades, 168–70
Papers. *See* Newspapers; Print-
    ing papers.
Paper stock, 164
Paragraph indentation, 68
Parallel fold, *198*
Paste-up, 4, 93–120, *198*
    attaching copy elements,
        97, 106–8
    base material, 95
    checking alignment, 108–10
    check list, 111
    color register, 113–15
    drawing in guidelines, 95–97
    final assembly, 110–11
    flat-color, 112
    importance of cleanliness,
        110
    orientation assignment, 117–
        20
    overlay method, 114–15
    photographing, 5–6

Paste-up (cont.)
preparation of illustrations, 99–105
of solids, 115–16
terms, 67
tools for, 94
transfer elements, 97–99, 100–102 figs.
Paste-up artist, 4
Paste-up board, 4, 95
Perfect binding, 180, 198
Perfecting presses:
with letterpress printing, 142
with offset lithography, 144, 145 fig., 146 fig.
Perforating, 187, 198
Personal invitation, typeface style for, 61
Photocomposition, 36–56
on CRT system, 53–56
first-, second-, and third-generation phototypesetters, 36–39
output unit, 49–50
for paste-up, 97
with photodisplay units, 40–45
principle, 36, 37 fig.
with text phototypesetting systems, 45–56
Photodisplay units, 40–45
Compugraphic CG 7200, 44–45
Filmotype machine, 43
operating principles, 40–42
Photo Typositor, 44
Strip Printer, 42
Varityper Headliner, 42–43
Photoengravings, 25
Photographic film, 135–37
processing, 136–37
structure, 136
types, 135
Photographs. See also Continuous tone copy.
cropping, 74–76
enlargement and reduction, 71–74, 92
image classification, 13 fig.
preparing for paste-up, 99–105
Photo-offset lithography. See Offset lithography.
Photomechanical transfer (PMT), 92
Photoprint, 99
Photosensitive chemicals, 9
Phototypesetters:
computerized, 39
first-generation models, 36–38
letterspacing capabilities, 23
second-generation machines, 38–39
vs. strike-on composition, 32
text typesetting systems, 45–46
third-generation systems, 39
Phototypesetting operator, 4
Photo Typositor, 44
Photo unit, of text type-setting system, 49–50
Pica, 16, 23, 198
Pigments, in printing inks, 192
Plastic binding, 178, 184, 198
Platemaker, 8–9
Platen press, 140, 141 fig., 170
Poetic type line, 22
Point-of-purchase displays, paper grade used for, 170
Points:

assignment, 203–5
defined, 198
in leading, 20–21
in letterspacing, 20
and quad size, 19
and slug sizes, 21
and unit system, 23
Positive, 198
Postcards, paper grade used for, 169
Posterization, 83
Posters:
assignment, 219–27
outdoor, 153
paper grade used for, 169
Press operator, 9–10
Printed circuits, 152
Printers, use in duotones, 81
Printing bristol papers, 169
Printing impositions, 155–60
Printing inks, 190–94
additives, 192
drying characteristics, 191 fig., 192
milling, 192–94
mixing, 192
packaging, 194, 195 fig.
pigments, 192
vehicles, 190–91
Printing papers, 161–75
basis weights, 167, 168 fig.
coated, 166
common formulas, 174 fig.
cutting, 174, 175–76 figs.
with deckled edges, 167
envelopes, 171–72
estimating, 172
finishes, 166
grades, 168–70
grain, 167
manufacture, 161–65
opacity, 168
selection hints, 176
spoilage allowance, 173
watermarks, 167
wire and felt sides, 167
Printing plate
first step in preparing, 5
installation, 9–10
platemaker, 8–9
Printing processes, 138–53
gravure, 150–52
letterpress, 138–42
offset lithography, 142–48
screen process, 152–53
Process cameras:
horizontal, 122–23
parts of, 124–27
vertical, 123–24
Process camera operator, 5–6
Process color inks, assignment, 377–87
Process photography, paste-up for, 93–120. See also Paste-up.
Process printing, 198
Processor, of text photo-typesetting system, 50
Production form, 72, 73 fig.
Programs:
folding, 181–84
paper grade used for, 169
paper grain used for, 167
paper finish used for, 166
Progressive proofs, 198
Projection-printing principle, 41
Proof, 26, 198
on Magnetic Card Selectric Composer, 35
revised, 28
Proofing, 26
Proof press, 26
Proofreading, 27–28, 110, 198

Proofreaders' marks, 27
Proportion, design principle, 65
Proportional scale, 74, 75 fig.
Publication Printers:
automated page make-up, 54
use of floppy discs, 52
Punched paper tape, 39, 46–47, 48
Punching, 184

Quad, 19, 198

Ragged copy, 22, 198
Ream, 167, 198
Record album jackets:
assignment, 389–97
paper grade used for, 169
Reductions, 71–74
focusing controls, 127
with Photomechanical Transfer, 92
Register, 113–15, 198
Register marks, 114–15, 198
Relief printing. See Letterpress.
Reports, envelopes for, 171
Reproduction proof, 97
Rescreening, 105
Reversal line copy, 91
Rhythm, design element, 66, 67 fig.
Right-angle fold, 198
Ring binding, 178, 184
Roman, 198
Roman oldstyle type, 58–60
Rotary letterpress, 142
Rotogravure, 198. See also Gravure.
Rough layout, 67, 68 fig., 70 fig.
Round halftone, 133
Rubber cement, 108, 110
Rub-off transfer letters, 98
Runaround, 198
Running head, 198

Saddle stitch, 178, 198
Safety papers, paper grade used for, 169
Sans serif, 60, 198
Scoring, 186, 187 fig.
Screened print method, 104–5
Screenlines, 134 fig.
Screen process printing, 152–53, 198
ink drying characteristics, 191 fig.
for paperboard printing, 170
presses, 153, 154 figs.
principles, 152
printing characteristics, 153
uses, 152–53
Screen tints, 84–91
adhesive shading method, 87–91
film positive method, 86–87
principles, 84–86
Script type, 61
Self-cover, 198
Senefelder, Alois, 142, 143 fig.
Series, of type, 14
Serif, 17, 198
in Roman oldstyle, 58, 59 fig.
square, 60
in text letter type, 61
Setoff. See Offset lithography.
Set width, 17–18, 23
Sewn bindings, 179
Shadow, 198
Sheet-fed presses:
gravure, 151

letterpress, 142
offset lithography, 144–47
screen printing, 153
Sheetwise job, 158
Short inks, 191
Side stitch, 198
Side-wire stitching, 178
Signatures, 155, 198
collating, 186
folding, 181–84
gathering, 184
Silhouette, 198
assignment, 343–47
Silk screen. See Screen process printing.
Sized and supercalendered (S&SC) paper, 166
Slugs, 21, 28
with hand-set hot type, 24
in linotype composition, 28, 29
in Ludlow composition, 31
Small caps, 198
Soft cover binding, 179
Solid matter, 20, 198
on letterpress, 139
in paste-ups, 115–16
Spacebands, 29
Spaces, 19, 24, 32
Spacing:
horizontal, 19–20
versus hyphenation, 48, 49
letterspacing, 20
on linotype machine, 29
on photodisplay units, 40–41
on Selectric Composer, 34
specifying in markup, 68
vertical (leading), 20–21
wordspacing, 19–20
Special-effects copy, 78–92
duotones, 81–83
line conversions, 78
masking film, 84
posterization, 83
screen tints, 84–91
surprinting, 91–92
Special-effects screens, 134
Spiral binding, 178, 184, 198
Spoilage allowance, 173
Square halftone, 133
Square sans serif type, 60
Stationery:
assignment, 207–17
paper grade used for, 169
typeface style for, 60
Stencils, 152
Step-and-repeat machine, 8 fig.
Stop bath, 137
Strike-on composition, 32–36
on Electronic "Selectric" Composer, 34
on Magnetic Card Selectric Composer, 35
on Selectric Composer, 33–34
on standard typewriter, 32–33
on Varityper, 36
Strike-on images, 13 fig.
Stripper, 6–7, 155
Strip Printer, 42
Style, of type lines, 22. See also Type styles.
Subheads, 68, 71
Sunday newspaper supplements, 151
Supermarket display advertisement, assignment, 321–31
Surprinting, 91–92
Swatchbook, 113

Tablets, 180
Tack, of printing ink, 191

Telephone directories, binding, 180
Text Editing and Composition System, 54
Textletter type, 61
Text phototypesetting systems, 45–56
  computer unit, 48–49
  with CRT systems, 53–56
  keyboard unit, 46–48
  making correction, 51–52
  with OCR systems, 52–53
  photo unit, 49–50
Text-size types, 18
Thumbnail sketches, 67, 68 *fig.*
Ticket stubs, perforation, 187
Timetables, 30
Titles, letterspacing, 20
Tools, for paste-up, 94
Transfer lettering, 97, 98
Transit advertising, paper grade used for, 170
Transitional typefaces, 59
Transportation schedules, assignments, 247–61, 273–79
Triangle, *198*
Trim, trimming, 180–81, *198*
  machines for, 174, 175–76 *figs.*
  planning for, 156, 160
Trim allowance, 156, 157 *fig.*, 160 *fig.*
Trimmed size, *198*
T-square, 94, *198*
Type:
  dimension measured, 18
  distribution of, 28
  features of, 17–18

hand-set, 24–28
  sizes available, 18. *See also* Type sizes.
  two kinds, 14–16
  units of measurement, 16
Type case, 24, 25 *fig.*, 28
Typeface, 17, 31
Type family, 14, 15 *fig.*
Type font, 14
  on Compugraphic CG 7200, 44
  with Electronic "Selectric" Composer, 34
  on Filmotype machine, 43
  in monotype matrix, 30
  with photodisplay units, 40, 41
  on Photo Typositor, 44
  on Selectric Composer, 33
  on text phototypesetting photo unit, 49
  on Varityper, 36
Type form, 26, 28
Type lines:
  arrangement, 21–22
  specifying width in markup, 68
  vertical spacing, 20–21
Typemaster, 42
Type series, 14
Typesetting:
  arranging type lines, 21–22
  defined, 12
  horizontal spacing, 19–20
  two types, 12–13
  unit system, 23
  vertical spacing, 20–21
Type sizes:
  on Compugraphic CG 7200, 45

on Filmotype machine, 43
on linotype magazines, 28
measurement of, 16–18
  with photodisplay units, 41
  and quad size, 19
  specifying in markup, 68
  with Strip Printer, 42
  unit system, 23
  with Varityper Headliner, 42
Type styles:
  classifications, 58–62
  on Compugraphic CG 7200, 44
  on Photo Typositor, 44
  specifying in markup, 68
Typewritten copy:
  composition, 32–36
  markup, 70 *fig.*, 71
Typographic specimens, 62
Typography, 13, *198*

Unit system, 23
Unity, design principle, 66, 67 *fig.*
Unjustified type lines, 22
Uppercase letters, 14, 68

Vacuum back, of process camera, 126–27
VariTyper, 36
VariTyper Headliner, 42–43
Veloxes, 93, 104–5, *198*
Vehicles, for printing ink, 190
Vertical center guideline, 95
Vertical process camera, 123–24

Vignette, *198*
Visual display terminals (VDTs), 51–52

Wash drawings, 130
Washing bath, 137
Watermark, 167, *199*
Waxing, 106–8
Web-fed presses, 142, 147–48
Web offset, *199*
Wedding bristol papers, 169
Widow, *199*
White pigments, 192
Wire side, 167, *199*
Wire stitching, 178
With the grain, *199*
Wordspacing, 19–20
  with adhesive transfer letters, 98
  in lieu of hyphenation, 48, 49
  on photodisplay units, 41
Work-and-turn jobs, 158, 159, *199*
Working edge, 95
Wrong font, *199*

X-acto knife:
  with adhesive shading, 89
  cutting borders with, 99, 101 *fig.*
  with masking films, 84, 116
  for mortising, 20
  for paste-up attachments, 106, 107 *fig.*, 108